BLACK LAND

Black Land

IMPERIAL ETHIOPIANISM AND AFRICAN AMERICA

Nadia Nurhussein

PRINCETON UNIVERSITY PRESS
PRINCETON & OXFORD

Published by Princeton University Press
41 William Street, Princeton, New Jersey 08540
6 Oxford Street, Woodstock, Oxfordshire OX20 1TR

press.princeton.edu

Library of Congress Control Number: 2019941480
First paperback printing, 2022
Paperback ISBN 978-0-691-23462-5
Cloth ISBN 978-0-691-19096-9

British Library Cataloging-in-Publication Data is available

Editorial: Anne Savarese, Lauren Bucca, and Jenny Tan
Production Editorial: Karen Carter
Cover Design: Layla Mac Rory
Production: Merli Guerra
Publicity: Alyssa Sanford and Keira Andrews

This book has been composed in Miller

For my father

And what is more, these leaders cannot be put into air-tight racial or national compartments—they belong to humanity. They belong to posterity. Like stones thrown into the world-lake, their ripples extend to the whole perimeter.

—DAVID A. TALBOT, "EMPEROR HAILE SELASSIE MOVES AHEAD"

CONTENTS

ILLUSTRATIONS

ACKNOWLEDGMENTS

THERE ARE INNUMERABLE people who supported me throughout the writing of this book. To my colleagues at Johns Hopkins University and at the University of Massachusetts–Boston, I owe immense thanks, especially Christopher Nealon, Jeanne-Marie Jackson, Eric Sundquist, Douglas Mao, Jared Hickman, Hollis Robbins, Lester Spence, Katrina McDonald, Jessica Marie Johnson, Sari Edelstein, Holly Jackson, Eve Sorum, Cheryl Nixon, Matt Brown, Betsy Klimasmith, Cecily Parks, and Aaron Lecklider. I have been overwhelmingly lucky to find myself included in such generous communities, surrounded by such brilliant minds. I have been lucky, too, to have the opportunity to discuss ideas with exceptional students at both institutions.

I thank the Beinecke Rare Book and Manuscript Library at Yale University for the award of an A. Bartlett Giamatti Fellowship to conduct research there, which was responsible for generating a good deal of the work presented here. I am grateful, too, to the receptive audience who attended the talk I gave during my tenure there. Of course, much of this book has been presented at conferences and symposia over the course of the last decade, and it has improved as a result of feedback from those audiences. A landmark conference in Addis Ababa sponsored by *Callaloo* in 2010 introduced me to GerShun Avilez, Salamishah Tillet, Dagmawi Woubshet, and others whose comments gave clarity to this project in its infancy. Thank you to Joseph Rezek, Theo Davis, and Harvard's Mahindra Seminar in American Literature and Culture; the probing questions and comments I received from this audience on a chapter draft—particularly from Sandy Alexandre in her role as respondent—were instrumental in shaping the project as a whole. In addition, I have benefited enormously from both formal and informal discussions at conferences, over email, over coffee, and elsewhere with Susanna Ashton, Russ Castronovo, Ed Folsom, Susan Gilman, John Gruesser, Daniel Hack, Jeannette Jones, Adam McKible, Cherene Sherrard-Johnson, and Lisa Siraganian. Conversations with Christian Crouch, Jean-Christophe Cloutier, and Karl Jacoby were especially generative.

I am enormously indebted to the curators and librarians at the various libraries, museums, and archives where I conducted research for this book. Thank you to Nancy Kuhl, Elizabeth Frengel, and the rest of the staff at the Beinecke Library and at Manuscripts and Archives at Yale University; Skyla S. Hearn at the DuSable Museum of African American History; Peter Harrington and Holly Snyder at the John Hay Library at Brown University; and the librarians at the Houghton Library at Harvard University, Syracuse University Library, and the New York Public Library. Thank you to the wonderful librarians at Johns Hopkins University, especially Gabrielle Dean, Donald Juedes, and Heidi Herr, and the staff of the interlibrary loan office. I am also grateful for the help I received from Lael J. Ensor-Bennett and Ann Woodward, curators of the Visual Resources Collection at Johns Hopkins University, regarding the book's many illustrations.

At Princeton University Press, Anne Savarese and Thalia Leaf have been an absolute joy to work with, and I am glad for the opportunity to thank them here for ushering this book into the world, as well as to thank the anonymous reviewers selected by the press for their invaluable feedback. I thank also Brian Halley at the University of Massachusetts Press, who offered to talk with me about my project early in the writing process, which was a tremendous help.

An earlier version of chapter 2 appeared as an article in *Callaloo* 33, no. 1 (2010): 278–89; a part of chapter 6 was published as an essay in *A Companion to the Harlem Renaissance*, edited by Cherene Sherrard-Johnson (New York: Wiley-Blackwell, 2015), 423–39. I thank Johns Hopkins University Press and Wiley-Blackwell, respectively, for allowing the reprinting of those pieces here. Thank you to the Morgan Library and Museum, the Beinecke Library and the Manuscripts and Archives Division at Yale University, and the British Museum for permission to reproduce the images included in this book.

While engaged in a project that resonates with me so intimately, it is unsurprising that talking with those closest to me has yielded some of the critical insights that have contributed most greatly to my thinking. Thank you to my sister Siham and my brother Safy, whom I appreciate more than I can say. My extended family, too, has been wonderfully supportive throughout the writing of not only this book but the previous one, the publishing of which prompted my New Jersey aunts and uncles—Getachew, Shewaye, Kadra, and Elham—to close the family restaurant for a night in order to throw me an incredible party. I am grateful always for the intellectual and emotional support provided by the brilliant Asali Solomon, going back to our childhood days at the University of California at Berkeley, and by her equally brilliant husband, Andrew Friedman. Nicholas Nace has read numerous drafts of numerous parts of this book, and I could not have written this book without his help. Thank you to Dr. Bereket Selassie, who has, since my childhood, been a stunning model of scholarship. My father, fellow writer, to whom this book is dedicated and without whose love and encouragement I could not have written it, has been my greatest champion throughout my life. Who else would have bought me a cake depicting the cover of my first book for the aforementioned New Jersey party? I write for him and for the memory of my mother.

Finally, my immeasurable love and gratitude go to Chris Witt, my awesome partner in life and my tireless supporter in all things, including this.

BLACK LAND

Introduction

Princes shall come out of Egypt; Ethiopia shall soon stretch out her hands unto God.

—PSALMS 68:31, KING JAMES BIBLE

THREE YEARS AFTER the bloody Chicago Race Riot of 1919, during which postwar racial tensions erupted into violence that resulted in dozens of deaths and hundreds of injuries, the Chicago Commission on Race Relations published *The Negro in Chicago: A Study of Race Relations and a Race Riot*. In a chapter section called "The 'Abyssinian' Affair," the commission recounted the story of the Star Order of Ethiopia, "a small group of Negroes styling themselves 'Abyssinians'" who, on 20 June 1920, publicly and ceremonially burned two American flags. According to the Chicago Commission, the flag burning "intended to symbolize the feeling of the 'Abyssinian' followers that it was time to forswear allegiance to the American government and consider themselves under allegiance to the Abyssinian government."[1] The debacle resulted in the shooting and injuring of several people and the killing of two.

The quotation marks framing "Abyssinians" and the derisive tone used throughout the publication ironize and mock the sense of identification this group of Chicago African Americans felt with Ethiopia, then commonly known as Abyssinia, a remote country in East Africa that represented for them an alternative imperial force to which they could pledge citizenship and loyalty following a period when U.S. imperialism was in its ascent. As the Chicago Commission put it, the Abyssinian group was one of many that appealed to "the dark-skinned races" of the world and "sought to weld them all together into a great nation."[2] Furthermore, the long imperial history of Abyssinia seemed to encourage African American identification specifically with a regal line. Members of the group went by the honorifics "The Great Abyssinian" and "The Prince" and sold a package for one dollar to interested parties that included a picture of Ras Tafari, who would later become Emperor Haile Selassie.

The black press was generally critical of the group, not only for the violence that erupted during their parade (for which Grover Cleveland Redding and Oscar McGavick, the leaders of the "Abyssinian Affair," were eventually executed) but for their emigrationist ideology. The *Chicago Defender*, for example, said of the United States, "This is our home, our country, our flag."[3] Others even went so far as to pathologize the desire to repatriate. Regarding Redding, one article reported that "the extravagance of his claims in promotion of a home-going expedition to Chicago colored folks to 'their Abyssinian fatherland' was cited as evidence that he might not have been mentally responsible for the disturbances that followed."[4] Another article—an Associated Negro Press piece published throughout the country—called Redding "a fanatic who has virtually lost his mind brooding over the question of the race going over the seas to redeem Africa from the 'oppression of the white race.'"[5] A St. Louis newspaper said of McGavick that he was "crazed with the 'Back to Africa' disease."[6] A black police officer, who had been wounded during the scene, said that the Abyssinians "had been parading through the sts. all the afternoon and acting like 'nuts' to my way of thinking."[7] But Ethiopianism, at this historical moment, was a strangely attractive product marketed by and to African Americans. Redding, according to the Chicago Commission, fabricated an ancestral claim to Abyssinia "as a means for exploiting credulous Negroes," selling them Abyssinian pamphlets and other materials, such as the aforementioned Selassie portrait and the "propaganda" flyer reproduced here.[8] Followers were encouraged to sign a pledge of allegiance, volunteering to "return" to Ethiopia and serve the nation in diverse fields such as electrical engineering and poultry raising.[9]

The most evocative among the components of the Star Order of Ethiopia's propaganda packet was an Abyssinian flag. A nation's flag, of course, is very symbolically freighted: from the time we are children, we pledge allegiance to it; Olympic athletes drape their bodies with it; we wave them, or fly them half-staff, in times of national tragedy. Rather than an anarchic rejection of nationality, then, the Star Order's desecration of the American flag was in actuality only half of the act, the full act being the exchange of that flag for the Abyssinian one carried by Redding during the parade. In other words, the metaphorical flag burning/flag raising was understood by the group to be akin to the burning of a phoenix giving rise to the "true"

THE LION OF JUDAH

TREATY

BETWEEN THE

KING OF ETHIOPIA

AND THE

UNITED STATES

His Majesty Menelik II., King of Kings of Ethiopia

TO REGULATE

COMMERCIAL RELATIONS

BETWEEN THE TWO COUNTRIES

Signed at Addis-Ababa, December 27, 1903.
Ratification advised by the Senate, March 12, 1904.
Ratified by the President, March 17, 1904.
King of Ethiopia notified of Ratification, August 2, 1904.
Proclaimed, September 30, 1904.

BY THE PRESIDENT OF THE UNITED STATES OF AMERICA

A PROCLAMATION

WHEREAS a treaty of commerce between the United States of America and His Majesty Menelik II., King of Kings of Ethiopia, was concluded on the twenty-seventh day of December, one thousand nine hundred and three, the original of which treaty, being in the Amharic and French languages, is word for word as folllows:

FIGURE 0.1. Flyer (originally captioned "Propaganda Literature Used by 'Abyssinians' in Recruiting Followers"), in *The Negro in Chicago: A Study of Race Relations and a Race Riot* by the Chicago Commission on Race Relations (Chicago: University of Chicago Press, 1922), facing p. 60.

pan-African nationality under the Ethiopian flag. It is also worth noting that, in 1919, an Abyssinian delegation arrived in New York on the first ocean liner to ever fly the Abyssinian flag in the United States, and this was followed by another flag raising at the Capitol. The visual symbolism of this recognition—coincidentally at the same time that black people were being attacked and murdered not only in Chicago but throughout the country during the Red Summer, the sanguinary name James Weldon Johnson gave to the horrific racial violence that broke out across the United States—cannot be overstated. Despite the *Chicago Defender*'s insistence that the American flag "is our flag," here was an alternative to a national identity that could feel like a betrayal and a lie. To include the Abyssinian flag in the Star Order's parade and "propaganda packet" facilitated the surrendering of one citizenship for another. What looked like a broad turn toward black internationalism looks now more like an attempt to recover a specific black nation.

But what does it mean to claim Abyssinianness, or Ethiopianness, as Redding and his followers did? The Star Order of Ethiopia's pledge contained the following potentially incendiary language: "This is to certify that I have signed my name as an Ethiopian in America in sympathy with our motherland Ethiopia. I henceforth denounce the name of Negro which was given me by another race."[10] From this perspective, "Ethiopian," a term debased through its use in blackface minstrelsy, could still be rescued, as it gestured toward a so-called noble history. "Negro," on the other hand, could not be emptied of its negative implications so easily and the group encouraged the performative jettisoning of it. To quote Cedric J. Robinson, "Ethiopia" was "a term signifying historicity and racial dignity in ways the term 'Negro' could not match."[11] A 1921 prospectus cited by the Chicago Commission also addresses the issue of the connotative value of terms of identification:

> Ancient history knows no "Negro," but ancient history does know Ethiopia and Ethiopians. Change a family's name and in a generation you cannot tell whether its foreparents were rogues or saints. It is the same with a race. . . . Take away our birthright, our ancient honorable name, "Ethiopian" and you have stopped the very fountain of our inspiration. If we are "Negroes" we are by the same dictionary also, "Niggers." The moment we realize, however, that we are "Ethiopians," we can see the beams from the lamps of Ethiopian culture lighting a pathway down the shadowy ages, and the fires of ambition are rekindled in our

> hearts, because we know that we came from the builders of temples and founders of civilization.[12]

Along with the biblical signification, the civilizationist argument upon which this prospectus rests—that identifying as an "Ethiopian" will allow us to "see the beams from the lamps of Ethiopian culture lighting a pathway down the shadowy ages," and that "we came from the builders of temples and founders of civilization," which is a requisite indicator of value—was the primary argument advanced for identification and sympathy with Ethiopia. A perspective promoted by W. E. B. Du Bois, described by Fikru Negash Gebrekidan as "an Ethiocentric view of history" supported by recent scholarship, traces its roots to Herodotus and Diodorus Siculus in order to argue that ancient Egypt's civilization owed its development to ancient Ethiopia, with culture flowing along a "south-north axis."[13] Because most civilizationist arguments assumed the view that black cultures were uncivilized, the antiquity of Ethiopian culture provided African Americans with a well-documented example of originary blackness that exploded the logic of racist accounts of civilization.

The literal allegiance expressed by the Star Order of Ethiopia was perhaps the logical next step after the metaphorical—and uncontroversial—allegiance to a country that had long held a unique symbolic significance for African America. Ideologies of Ethiopianism were cultivated around Psalms 68:31, the epigraph cited at the beginning of the chapter, based upon the premise that a time would come when the black race would rise as prophesied and Africa, once Christianized and thus developed, was expected to take its rightful place in the world. "Ethiopia" has been associated historically with a number of civilizations whose ancient declines and anticipated restorations suit the parameters of the prophecy: the Kingdom of Kush in Nubia (present-day Sudan), the Aksumite empire (present-day northern Ethiopia), and the Land of Punt (probably present-day Eritrea and Ethiopia), among others. None of these corresponds exactly to the geographic boundaries of modern-day Ethiopia. But the vagueness around the name "Ethiopia" is in fact an essential aspect of its power and signification. Ethiopia was practically a place of myth. From the Greek for "burnt-faced ones," the Ethiopians were said to live in a far-off place where, according to Homer, they dined with the gods.

Whether invoked as a temporally distant primal nation, as an abstract nation of the black race or synecdoche for Africa in general, or as an imaginary locus of biblical or antique nostalgia, the figure of Ethiopia resonates throughout the African American literary tradition. Phillis Wheatley, in "To the University of Cambridge, in New-England," refers to herself as an "Ethiop," as does William J. Wilson, using the term as a nom de plume for contributions to *Frederick Douglass' Paper*, the *Weekly Anglo-African*, and the *Anglo-African Magazine*; Frances Ellen Watkins Harper and Paul Laurence Dunbar wrote poems titled "Ethiopia" and "Ode to Ethiopia," respectively. However, as these examples illustrate, references to Ethiopia as an abstraction, as a metaphoric nationalizing of racial union, were far more common than references to Ethiopia as a contemporary nation. Composed mainly of abstract racial invocations that emerged as variations on the familiar Bible verse cited above, this "Ethiopian" literary tradition, as Wilson Jeremiah Moses calls it, constituted an important strand of African American writing prior to the Harlem Renaissance.[14]

Black Land: Imperial Ethiopianism and African America explores the varied African American literary and cultural views of Ethiopia as they developed from inchoate ideologies of Ethiopianism that saw the empire as largely mythic and fantastic into ideologies increasingly grounded in knowledge both historical and contemporary, and more explicitly engaged with the politics of imperial Abyssinia in particular. Ethiopianism as a concept, even before a term existed for it, signified in a number of ways from at least the eighteenth century onward, and one of the goals of this book is to bring forward and consider its various forms as they gained visibility by the end of the nineteenth century: in particular, martial Ethiopianism, documentary Ethiopianism, and spectacular Ethiopianism. Although the malleability of Ethiopia's signification for African America made it especially well-suited as a model of black nationhood and a source of spiritual citizenship, invariably the concept of its long-standing imperial identity was central to this signification. Put another way, this book follows the development within African America of imperial Ethiopianism, the larger rubric under which the above variations may be subsumed. Whether assuming a military attitude, or adopting an archaeological perspective, or expressing a fascination with pageantry, each of these variations on Ethiopianism begins and extends from a commitment to the imperial.

Although it was not until the 1931 constitution that the country of Abyssinia officially took the name "Ethiopia," the correspondence between the two names goes back much further. "Ethiopia" was conflated with "Abyssinia" in the fourteenth-century *Kebra Nagast* ("Glory of Kings"), which

Mohammed Hassen Ali and Seyoum Hameso aptly term "an Abyssinian politico-religious epic."[15] The *Kebra Nagast* gave textual authority to a then newly articulated mythology of Abyssinia's long imperial history, legitimizing a "Solomonic" dynasty that claimed to reach back three thousand years earlier to the union of King Solomon and the supposedly Ethiopian Queen of Sheba.[16] An extremely important and enduring religious text, the *Kebra Nagast* nevertheless served immediate political ends—allowing a challenger to the throne to overthrow the non-Solomonic Zagwe dynasty—while articulating a coherent national myth for Abyssinia. This medieval-era mythology of the Solomonic Dynasty was resurrected by Abyssinia's emperors in the late nineteenth century. Having emerged from a period known as the "Age of Princes" in the seventeenth and eighteenth centuries, during which political power was decentralized among a number of provinces, Abyssinia now had a strong imperial center and was recognized by the world as an ancient empire that had been strengthened and restored. By the turn of the twentieth century, its borders—established in concert with European colonial powers—extended to British East Africa and French, British, and Italian Somaliland in the east and south; and Eritrea and Sudan in the north and west, respectively.[17] "Abyssinia," stated *Harper's* magazine in 1868, "if we are not critical as to boundary lines, is the ancient Ethiopia."[18]

In the modern era, as the only African nation (with the unique exception of Liberia) to remain independent during the Scramble for Africa—the European dividing of the continent formalized by the 1884 Berlin Conference—Abyssinia symbolized black resistance to oppression and became the spiritual center of an imagined Black Empire. "The pan-African construction of Ethiopian identity," as Teshale Tibebu writes, "made Ethiopia the concentrated expression of Africa."[19] What few, again, have examined is that the allure of Abyssinia lies precisely in its identification as the black *imperial* archetype, as it was the only strong territorial black empire in Africa at a time when pan-African movements were generally working to develop abstract international networks—consider, for example, the First Pan-African Conference, held in London in 1900. In other words, this emphasis on locus and hierarchical African primacy distinguishes this brand of Ethiopianism from earlier ones (on the one hand) and from most egalitarian diasporic pan-Africanisms (on the other). Through performative declarations of citizenship like the one by the Star Order of Ethiopia, the attempt to affiliate African Americans and Abyssinians depended upon the centralization of a transnational black empire *under one crown*. In their defense of Ethiopia against Fascist Italy's attacks in the 1930s, many black people around the world behaved, to quote George Padmore, "as though they were the subjects of the emperor."[20] Working as a centripetal gravitational force, imperial Ethiopianism seeks to draw African Americans home.

With this in mind, I take up a question Etsuko Taketani asks in her book *The Black Pacific Narrative* mainly in relation to black America's admiration for imperial Japan: "What were the grounds of the appeal that empire—as opposed to democracy—held for American blacks in the prewar period?"[21] But the scope of this question, when we consider the model of imperial Abyssinia, can be extended profitably beyond the years around World War II and reconsidered as one of particular intraracial consequence. It was in 1920 that the Star Order of Ethiopia's Redding, who claimed the official title of "Prince of Abyssinia and royal envoy extraordinary and minister plenipotentiary of the empress of Abyssinia to the United States," led his parade in Chicago while wearing colorful robes and riding a white horse. Newspaper articles mockingly referred to him as an "Abyssinian King." His self-representation reflects the Orientalist fascination with actual Abyssinian kings—especially Emperors Tewodros, Menelik, and Selassie—evidenced in numerous newspaper and magazine pieces from the period.

But this attraction to the splendor of "fantastic raiment," as one article described Redding's attire, cannot be reduced simply to Orientalism.[22] When viewed contemporaneously, an association with imperial Ethiopia had immediate, practical, and quotidian racial ramifications within the United States. On 9 August 1920, President Woodrow Wilson officially proclaimed the renewal of the 1904 commerce treaty between Abyssinia and the United States described in the Star Order of Ethiopia's "propaganda" flyer.[23] Article I of this treaty, which included an allowance for Abyssinians conducting business to "be able freely to travel" within the United States, had significant implications for Jim Crow. This point was not missed by the Abyssinian group in Chicago, notes the commission. Confusion surrounding the issue of whether foreign blacks were subject to the restrictions of Jim Crow and where they fit into U.S. racial schemata meant that the members of a 1919 Abyssinian delegation were welcomed at the Waldorf Astoria on the one hand while, on the other, a dinner organized at the National Democratic Club by the Persian consul general was suddenly canceled when the race of the guests was found out. In addition, one of the members of the same delegation, upon his return to the United States in 1922, was not permitted to stay at certain hotels and theaters.[24] The public presence of foreign blackness in the form of

Abyssinian dignitaries who may, in some cases, be permitted to transcend Jim Crow laws had the potential to disrupt the rigidity, clarity, and supposed absoluteness of the racial structure of the United States in a manner that sidesteps the issue of percentages of whiteness and blackness altogether. Unlike Homer Plessy,[25] the Abyssinian dignitaries did not have "white" skin. Furthermore, it is an ironic coincidence of history that the *Plessy v. Ferguson* decision was reached during the same year (1896) that the Abyssinian military defeated Italy during the Battle of Adwa, a defeat by a comparatively underdeveloped and under-armed force that was so embarrassing for the Italians that it became an important factor in the decision to invade the country a generation later. Viewed as a challenge to theories of white supremacy, the Abyssinian victory at the Battle of Adwa could provide evidence for racial equality that was easily transferable to the American milieu.

Because of the challenge Ethiopian historicity and sovereignty presented to racist civilizationist approaches, and perhaps because of the widespread belief that Abyssinians did not in fact consider themselves black, many scientists, philosophers, and historians struggled contortively to find a distinction between the innate racial qualities of Abyssinians and other black people. As Immanuel Kant wrote a century earlier: "The Abyssinians are of Arabic descent, [they] are witty, [physically] well-shaped, but dun-coloured, with woolen hair, upright, not quarrelsome. There are some white moors among them; yet the Kaffirs who dwell in these places [of the Abyssinians] are not only ugly, but also as misshapen and malicious as the other Negroes."[26] This was a typical Enlightenment view. According to Lorenz Auf der Maur, "The zenith of admiration for the 'noble Abyssinian' may be said to be reached with Edward Gibbon, who pits the noble, oriental 'Abyssinian' against the savage 'Ethiopian' (or sub-Saharan African), like many of his contemporaries."[27] For Kant, Gibbon, and others, giving up the notion that Abyssinians were black was apparently more bearable than giving up the notions upon which white supremacy rested.

However, Kant's racist remark does point toward the well-known multiplicity of black ethnicities in Ethiopia. What is typically understood as "Ethiopian," both within and without the country, is more properly that which is associated with the term "Abyssinian": a narrowly defined ethnic and religious identity emerging from the provinces of the geographically central highlands. As John Markakis points out in *Ethiopia: The Last Two Frontiers*, historians have "focused narrowly on the Abyssinian core"—mainly the Christian Amhara (and sometimes Tigray) elite—at the expense of the peripheral ethnic and religious groups.[28] Because the nineteenth-century Ethiopian empire saw itself "as the restoration of the *status quo ante*, the legitimate recovery of territories that Ethiopia had allegedly lost in times past," it required the restored Ethiopian nationality to be unified and coherent. Faced with such a heterogeneous, multilingual population, however, the "true" Ethiopian identity perceived itself to be under threat and its boundaries became even more entrenched and pronounced and even less inclusive. It is this Ethiopian empire—not the ancient, storied one but one yoked together through conquest and built upon hierarchies—with which African American sympathies ended up aligning in the late nineteenth and early twentieth centuries.

Ethiopia, in the context of African American studies, is not usually included in conversations about imperialism except as a subject of it—in other words, not as an example of imperium itself. This neglect can be traced to, as Taketani puts it, "the view that imperialism in the twentieth century is a practice of, and has its roots in, Western civilization."[29] Recent scholarship in the field of Ethiopian studies, on the other hand, especially in its attention to the Oromo people of Ethiopia, has presented a view of Ethiopian imperialism that revises the historical record.[30] For example, Markakis goes so far as to claim that Ethiopia was "not a victim but a participant in the 'scramble,'" and the title of "empire" is "not a misnomer, since Ethiopia's rulers governed their new possessions more or less the same way and for similar ends as other imperial powers were doing."[31] Even as long ago as 1935, Ethiopia was debated as a case study in an article by Robert Gale Woolbert that appeared in the journal *Foreign Affairs*. Despite its poverty, relative lack of industrialization and modernization, and general underdevelopment, Woolbert argues, if "one attribute of an empire is that it holds alien peoples in subjection," then we must consider Ethiopia an empire, because "there can be no question that a single people rules over various subject peoples."[32] In other words, the example of Ethiopia is, ironically, a critical *failure* of black solidarity, where both the "alien peoples" and the oppressors are black. Moreover, Woolbert argues in another article that "though Ethiopia is an empire she is not a nation," lacking any "such thing as an Ethiopian national sentiment," and therefore Mussolini "frankly proposes to supplant Ethiopian imperialism . . . with Italian imperialism." Woolbert doubts "whether even a successful war waged against a common foe would do much toward knitting the empire together spiritually."[33]

The problem is: if, in the late nineteenth and early twentieth centuries, the example of Ethiopia as a model of black empire is valuable for multiple reasons—as an illustration of the problematic civilizationist argument, as proof of the absurdity of Jim Crow and white supremacy, as a specific locus to which black solidarity movements can tether themselves—then one is faced with the dilemma that, simply put, black people oppress black people there. Like the ethnic conflicts still fracturing twenty-first-century Africa, the tensions of imperial Ethiopia fly in the face of Edward Wilmot Blyden's concept of a unified "African personality." In his argument for Liberian emigration, Blyden argued that because "the aborigines are not a race alien from the colonists," success was inevitable: "When alien and hostile races have come together, . . . one has had to succumb to the other; but when different peoples of the same family have been brought together, there has invariably been a fusion." This certainly was not the case in Liberia, and although Ethiopia, too, brings together "different peoples of the same family," it has always been plagued by interethnic and religious tensions.

This means that by the 1930s—when Ethiopia was threatened by Italy's efforts to colonize it—many African American writers viewed Ethiopia, an imperial state that had doubled in size during Emperor Menelik's reign, through an ill-fitting anti-imperialist lens. In fact, Menelik's "campaign of expansion" was exactly coincident with the Battle of Adwa, which was, from the Ethiopian perspective, an anti-imperialist conflict. Prompted in part by a desire for resources, as deforestation and soil erosion had destroyed much of Abyssinia, Menelik looked to the rich lands of the south.[34] During the expansion, he subsumed the "entire plateau . . . with the occupation of the Oromo state of Jimma in 1897," and the lowlands were seized immediately after that.[35] In subjugating the Oromo, the Ethiopian elites promoted the idea that they had "an historic mission 'to civilize the barbarians' "—which, as Mohammed Hassen points out, "has been the common cry of colonizers"—and, in doing so, depicted the Oromo "as a people without a history" and "as 'the enemies of the Amhara.' "[36] Years later, Emperor Selassie, too, was known for his efforts to consolidate and strengthen the Ethiopian empire while strengthening his own absolute power. In fact, he allegedly said, using rhetoric that sounds unabashedly imperialist, "I am Emperor not only of Ethiopia but of all Africans, and chief of all Negroes, even those under foreign domination," effectively declaring African Americans (along with other black peoples around the world) subjects of a transnational Ethiopian empire.[37] His last phrase—"even those under foreign domination"—is the boldest part of this announcement, claiming a sovereignty that trumps any other existing sovereignty. His drive for imperialist expansion does not stop with East Africa. He is, in a sense, like Grover

Cleveland Redding and the Chicago Abyssinians, burning the American flag on behalf of all African Americans. But the first efforts to consolidate the Ethiopian empire in the modern period can be traced back to Emperor Tewodros, who reigned from 1855 to 1868. The British and American press's intense fixation upon Tewodros's imperial drive emerged with the start of the Anglo-Abyssinian War in 1867, a war sparked by Tewodros's imprisonment of a British legation in the country. After failed diplomatic efforts, the United Kingdom resorted to military action to rescue the British hostages. The war concluded with the 1868 Fall of Magdala, which resulted in the emperor's suicide.

The 1867–68 Anglo-Abyssinian War joins, in this book, the two most important moments in Italo-Ethiopian military history—the aforementioned 1896 defeat of the Italian armed forces at Adwa and the Italian occupation of Ethiopia in the 1930s—which were largely responsible for rendering a contemporary Ethiopia visible in the eyes of many African Americans. It literally put Ethiopia on the map. Cartographic representations in newspapers and magazines gave a newborn segment of American citizenry (as 1868 also marked the passing of the Fourteenth Amendment in the United States) a bound and delineated geographic space onto which to project an abstract black nationhood. In addition, the Anglo-Abyssinian War in a sense revolved around questions of boundaries—who belongs in the empire and who doesn't, who is free to travel and who is bound and fettered—which reinforced the reterritorialization of Ethiopianism in this moment. Moreover, the press promoted the "Christian island bound by a ring of Islam" characterization of the Ethiopian empire, regardless of its inaccuracy, underscoring the boundaries of the empire as ideological and giving Western readers a reason to sympathize with a nation perpetually under threat.

Even the center of this island, however, was uncertain. As late as 1900, an article in *Pearson's Magazine* titled "A Capital That Moves" notes that Addis Ababa is "an unique capital in that it arose almost in a single night, and is destined to disappear as speedily."[38] The author refers here to the common practice of deforestation rendering Abyssinian capitals uninhabitable after a short while, but in describing the capital city essentially as a shifting target, he gestures toward a more generalized aspect of the image of Ethiopia in the West. An expansive Abyssinia was compelled to fix its borders. In 1891, Menelik, uneasy with colonial encroachment, "defined in a well-publicized circular to European rulers what he considered to be the legitimate boundaries of the country."[39] When we consider the carving of Africa, Ethiopia becomes reconfigured as negative space: that which is not colonial Africa. To quote Major R. E. Cheesman, whose article in the inaugural issue of *Geographical Magazine* was cited liberally in a 1935 article titled "No Longer the Dark Continent . . . Except in Spots," published in the travel magazine *"So You're Going" News*:

> When the African littoral lands were occupied by the European powers the boundaries between them and Abyssinia were laid down by treaty and were delimited by such vague definitions as a certain parallel of latitude or a certain number of miles from the coast, with very few references to topographical features on the ground. The reason was that the country was totally unexplored and unmapped and such detail as was shown on the blank spaces that formed the map of the area was either very far from its true position or did not exist. It follows that the nomads whose grazing grounds had been cut through by a line made by foreigners had no means of knowing exactly where the line ran, nor any intention of keeping to it if they had. . . .
>
> This unsatisfactory and explosive state of affairs has been going on spasmodically from the time the first treaties were made, in some cases about thirty years ago. It would, indeed, be extremely difficult for a Boundary Commission to operate on some sections of the frontier.[40]

As the article's title suggests, Ethiopia was in some sense believed to be the darkest spot of the "dark continent," inscrutable to Europeans and, as the multiple rounds of delegates who went missing during the Anglo-Abyssinian War demonstrate, a place from whose bourn no traveler returns. Leaving aside the issue of border disputes between the Ethiopian government and the governments of various European powers, the nomads cited by Cheesman who transgressively ignore boundaries between colonial and noncolonial land imperil the colonial project itself. Ironically, as Ethiopia gained attention as a defined locus or target, it started to seem to the West more and more like a strange imperial Bermuda Triangle, pulling everything and everyone into its wake.

This centripetal force, however, can help us to understand the irony behind the celebration of Ethiopian imperialism and monarchism. As a model, the nation provides a way to imagine a network of black peoples, led by a black emperor. In describing the structure of the Ethiopian empire, Markakis writes that it "resembles a wheel with spokes but without a connecting rim," because "there is no direct interaction among peripheral elites and regions, who interact only with and through the centre."[41] We can see how this model might appeal to a leader such as Marcus Garvey. As Yogita Goyal writes:

> his pan-Africanism, if we can call it that, was not just a loosely defined vision of solidarity among all African-descended peoples. Instead, he envisioned an African empire that would both mimic and rival European imperialism. To do so, Garvey derived inspiration from a variety of sources, including the British empire, Zionism, the "supergovernment" of the Pope and the Catholic Church, and even the example of European colonization of Africa.[42]

Goyal, however, overlooks one of the most obvious contemporaneous sources for Garvey's vision: it mimics Abyssinian imperialism. Regardless of Garvey's later disdain for Selassie—he argues that "the American Negro should, through his own agency, establish contact with the Abyssinian Negroes" and that "no one should allow himself to be deceived into believing that much more can be accomplished through Haile Selassie himself"[43]—he did not lose faith in the imperial model, as long as the leader at its center was heroic and worthy of centralized power.

This version of Black Empire depends not upon an abstract and diffuse network of universal black collectivity but upon specific and bilateral axes of black solidarity. *Black Land* considers the model of the proposed relation between Ethiopians and African Americans that attempted to affiliate the two peoples by pointing to a center (the "Hot Spot of *the World*," as the caption to a map printed in a 1935 issue of the *Baltimore Afro-American* read) and locating Addis Ababa as metropole, a predictable symbolic choice but an unlikely literal choice. Furthermore, because the assumption of Ethiopian citizenship by some African Americans was seen as nothing more than the recovery of a lost cultural identity and the rejection of a false one, a sense of *nostos* buttresses the centralization of a transnational black empire under one crown, as the centripetal diasporic force imagined to be drawing African Americans home operates most effectively with a strongly defined center. This is the paradox of this particular brand of black transnationalism and diasporic nostalgia: it built itself around the example of Ethiopia while also holding democratic ideals.

Coincident with an explosion in periodical development, Abyssinia was increasingly the focus of news coverage. The military conflicts in the country in the late nineteenth century were well known to newspaper and magazine readers in the United States and Great Britain. As Benedict

Anderson points out in *Imagined Communities*, even when there are no stories in the newspaper about a nation (his example is Mali) for months, "the novelistic format of the newspaper assures [readers] that somewhere out there the 'character' Mali moves along quietly, awaiting its next reappearance in the plot."[44] *Black Land* follows the narrative of the "character" Ethiopia during moments when news of the nation dominated the "plot" and argues that African American Ethiopianism evolved in response to the emergence of the nation in the late nineteenth century as an adversarial presence in current world events. But African nations' roles as newspaper characters, passing in and out of sight as world events dictate, are complicated by the continent's seeming timelessness, a feature out of step with the seriality of the newspaper's construction and format, as Kenneth W. Warren writes:

> The series of rivers in [Langston Hughes's] "The Negro Speaks of Rivers," however, is really one continuing flow of water. Though it, too, assures us of Africa's continued existence, it does so only in terms of an endless extension of an "original bond." One never imagines that Mali ceases to exist; Africa is always there. Upon reencountering Mali, however, the voyager in Hughes's poetic vision also asserts that "time" has not meant anything to it or, for that matter, to any African geography. The Nile in "The Negro Speaks of Rivers" is the Nile of the pyramids. There is nothing new in Africa.[45]

This misconception—that there was nothing new in Africa—was of course belied by the dramatic happenings regularly chronicled by the press, to which Du Bois gestures in the closing phrase of his 1915 *The Negro*, "Semper novi quid ex Africa!" (a quotation from Pliny: "Something new always comes out of Africa"). And yet Ethiopia, unlike Haiti and Liberia—the other frequently cited examples of black independent nations to which African Americans looked with pride—was associated with its age even in this up-to-the-moment reportage; it was not a black nation of the future but one of the inert and static past. To quote Edward Gibbon's enduring assessment in *The History of the Decline and Fall of the Roman Empire*, the Ethiopians were supposed to have "slept near a thousand years, forgetful of the world, by whom they were forgotten."[46] As a result, as Aric Putnam argues through a reading of J. A. Rogers's pamphlet *The Real Facts about Ethiopia*, the country could be employed readily "as a metaphor for a new, international context in which black community can be performed," as it was experienced as "a time and not a place."[47] Ethiopia's participation in modern world events seemed oxymoronic, but this simultaneous modernity and antiquity allowed African Americans to find in it both a history and a currency.

The literary and journalistic texts discussed here demonstrate how views of Ethiopia's relationship with African America engendered new concepts of Black Empire. This book's first chapter attempts to uncover the beginnings of a more grounded Ethiopianism in its treatment of nineteenth-century lyric verse by Walt Whitman, Paul Laurence Dunbar, and others written on the topic of Ethiopia, when abstract Ethiopianism was a prominent ideology in African America. In this chapter, I argue that the old woman of Whitman's "Ethiopia Saluting the Colors," wearing a turban of red, yellow, and green, stands in for an Ethiopian military force. As Ed Folsom has pointed out, Abyssinia's emperor Tewodros gained international notoriety during the Anglo-Abyssinian War in 1867. Folsom shows how Tewodros and Lincoln were compared by the press but does not mention that Abyssinia under Tewodros was also, strangely, compared to the Confederacy. Here I address the politics of Whitman's poem, particularly in the poem's "recognition" of the flag, in light of the press's treatment of the Anglo-Abyssinian conflict.

Dunbar's interpretation of the Ethiopian flag's symbolic value, in "Ode to Ethiopia" and "Frederick Douglass," positions him uncomfortably alongside Whitman, a poet he found distasteful. His poems present an "Ethiopia" invigorated with nationalism and, unexpectedly, with militarism. Finally, this chapter also addresses two poems about Tewodros by women: "Magdala," which appeared in the 1875 book *Songs of the Year and Other Poems* by "Charlton" (nom de plume of an American woman by the name of Charlotte Pendleton), and "The Death of King Theodore," in E. Davidson's 1874 *The Death of King Theodore and Other Poems*. Charlton's and Davidson's poems are striking in their glorification of the Abyssinian king, in stark contrast to depictions of him in the British media, including racist caricatures in *Punch*.

My second chapter reads Pauline E. Hopkins's *Of One Blood; or, The Hidden Self* in the context of the African American periodical in which it was serialized, the *Colored American Magazine* (edited by Hopkins). Published only a few years after the surprising Italian defeat at Adwa, the novel contributed to the magazine's project of what I call "documentary Ethiopianism" as expressed in histories and biographies but also preserved the fantastic conception of Ethiopia that helped create Ethiopianism in the first place. Several critics have commented upon the generic fluidity in Hopkins's work, and I argue that the confusion produced in these hybrid genres—specifically in imaginative histories and historical fictions—resulted in some conflicting messages about Ethiopia and its symbolic value. *Of One Blood* is exemplary in this respect, as a fictional text that introduces the mysticism that the historical and ethnographic texts of the *Colored American Magazine* avoid while still participating in documentary Ethiopianism by sending its characters to Ethiopia.

In my reading of this novel, I look to the character of Mira, a ghost whose writing serves as a plot device to reveal answers to Reuel, the novel's protagonist. Through Mira's interpretive (not creative) "writing," she points with a ghostly finger and takes the form of Ethiopic writing itself—a fantastic incarnation of documentary Ethiopianism. Finally, through identifying and explicating a neglected quotation in the novel as a poem by Sarah Piatt, I discuss how *Of One Blood* activates what I call the Regalization Fantasy, a fantasy intrinsic to imperial Ethiopianist ideology. As a result of the fantasy's paradoxical inclusivity and exclusivity, the imperial model of Ethiopianism seen in *Of One Blood* contains the irritant that leads to its own dismantling by midcentury.

The book's middle chapters follow the development of a strand of Ethiopianism that integrated spectacle into its presentation. Chapter 3 introduces three incidents of Ethiopianist aristocratic impersonation or imposture: that of Isaac Brown, a Jamaican man who successfully passed himself off as Menelik's nephew at the turn of the century; that of Joseph Emanuel Blayechettai, who in the 1920s claimed to be the kidnapped son of a king of Tigre, an Abyssinian province; and that of Virginia Woolf, whose participation in the Dreadnought hoax in 1910, during which she dressed as an Abyssinian prince, was notorious. These impersonations are dramatic illustrations of what I term "spectacular Ethiopianism," a variant especially prevalent in the first two decades of the twentieth century. Interestingly, these performances of spectacular Ethiopianism were preceded in the nineteenth century by the reciprocal costuming of Prince Alemayehu, the son of Emperor Tewodros orphaned by the Anglo-Abyssinian War, and his guardian, the eccentric English explorer Captain Tristram Speedy; the mirror images and narratives of Alemayehu and Speedy appear to have informed these early twentieth-century impressions.

Rather than simulate nobility, two Americans sought to construct spectacular Ethiopian empires of their own. In chapter 4, I examine the case of Harry Foster Dean, whose *The Pedro Gorino: The Adventures of a Negro Sea-Captain in Africa and on the Seven Seas in His Attempts to Found an Ethiopian Empire* recounts the tale of his ambition to build a black empire in Africa, an effort that led one of the major British participants in the Scramble for Africa to call him "the most dangerous 'negro' in the world."[48] I also address the unofficial diplomatic role of William Henry Ellis, a flashy African American millionaire and the first American to visit with Emperor Menelik in 1903. (Ellis was not the only African American to visit Abyssinia prior to the Second Italo-Abyssinian War; in 1922, for instance, A'Lelia Walker, daughter of the famed Madame C. J. Walker and host of a Harlem Renaissance salon, visited Empress Zauditu.) Ellis did his best to curry favor with Menelik but was rumored to be planning to oust the emperor in order to take his seat on the throne.

The fifth chapter begins with a scene from George White's 1936 *Scandals*, reprised in the 1937 film *You Can't Have Everything*, that featured the dance team Sam, Ted, and Ray (also known as Tip, Tap, and Toe) as Haile Selassie and two of his army's soldiers. Many reviews considered this scene the best one of White's Broadway musical revue, and a photograph from this scene was even included in the cover story of the 6 January 1936 issue of *Time* magazine, a profile of Haile Selassie declaring him the magazine's "Man of the Year." With hints of so-called "Ethiopian minstrelsy," the image of Selassie in the public eye was an odd amalgam of ancient solemnity and slick modernity—a turn toward the familiar in the articulation of spectacular Ethiopianism. As with Menelik and Tewodros before him, literary and journalistic accounts of Selassie depicted a leader who evinced an attraction to technology and modernization that was undermined by an Ethiopian culture and landscape deemed somehow averse to modern life. This chapter also addresses two theatrical representations of Ethiopia: Arthur Arent's censored 1936 Federal Theater Project *Ethiopia*, which was generically categorized as a "living newspaper," and an important turn-of-the-century libretto, *Abyssinia*, starring blackface performers Bert Williams and George Walker. In this context of theatricality and minstrelsy, I explore how caricature was used to depict various Ethiopian political figures—sometimes positively and sometimes negatively—as what I term "Savage Statesmen."

The last three chapters of this book examine the challenges to imperial Ethiopianism that began to surface during the Italo-Ethiopian War, despite the pervasiveness of pro-Ethiopian writing that characterizes this period. In my sixth chapter, I address the explosion of verse dealing with the "Ethiopian Crisis," or the Second Italo-Abyssinian War, such as J. Harvey L. Baxter's *Sonnets for the Ethiopians* and Melvin Tolson's "The Bard of Addis Ababa." Returning to traditional tropes of nineteenth-century Ethiopianism even in the face of modern warfare, Baxter calls upon the nation's resources of antiquity to produce a counteroffensive against the ancient Roman Empire that Mussolini looked upon with such nostalgia.

In addition, I look to occasional verse by lesser lights and unknown bards such as Rufus Gibson and Jay N. Hill and by important figures such as Marcus Garvey. The tenor of Garvey's elegies written in honor of fallen Ethiopian war heroes Ras Nasibu of Ogaden and Ras Desta presents a fascinating contrast to his expressed disdain for Selassie. I consider these poems alongside another poem dedicated to Ras Nasibu written by Baroness Maria Atzel and printed in the *New Times and Ethiopia News*, a newspaper published by Sylvia Pankhurst, an English suffragist, anti-Fascist, and prominent defender of Ethiopia. The agitprop role of the *New Times and Ethiopia News* has not yet been fully examined, and this chapter discusses its global importance. The newspaper reprinted Langston Hughes's "Letter from Spain," where it was placed in dialogue with newspaper accounts of Askari soldiers serving in the Italian armed forces in Ethiopia.

In my seventh chapter, I consider two of George S. Schuyler's novellas published serially in the African American newspaper the *Pittsburgh Courier—The Ethiopian Murder Mystery: A Story of Love and International Intrigue* and *Revolt in Ethiopia: A Tale of Black Insurrection against Italian Imperialism*, both written in response to the Second Italo-Abyssinian War. These novellas interact and engage with the newspaper's propagandistic reportage of the war in provocative ways: Schuyler's fiction mimicked the articles formally, encouraging in the newspaper's readers a fluid reading practice transcending the fictional/nonfictional divide. Whereas Hopkins's amalgamations of fictional and nonfictional Ethiopianist writing in the *Colored American Magazine*, only a few years after the Battle of Adwa, proved somewhat unmanageable, Schuyler in the 1930s was able to assume his readers' intimate familiarity with the contemporary nation and therefore actively manipulate the newspaper's generic features. In its articles—including those written by Schuyler—the *Courier* tended to build upon an already existing sympathetic support for Ethiopia through the royal family, particularly through the figure of Selassie. However, in his melodramatic Ethiopian stories, Schuyler exploits the public's fascination with monarchy only to expose, in the end, the ironies behind that misguided sympathy.

During the Second Italo-Abyssinian War, Harlem's solidarity with Ethiopia was at its height, with volunteers offering to fight in the Ethiopian military and organizing riots, parades, and boycotts for the cause. Just after the war, Claude McKay wrote *Amiable with Big Teeth: A Novel of the Love Affair between the Communists and the Poor Black Sheep of Harlem*, the subject of my eighth chapter, hidden in the Rare Books and Manuscripts archives at Columbia University until its discovery by

Jean-Christophe Cloutier and published for the first time in 2017. McKay's novel hinges upon the question of what it means to be an "authentic" Ethiopian imperial representative: for example, one of the novel's characters, Alamaya, admits cagily that a signed letter from the emperor establishing his bona fides "was authentic but not genuine"; later, as part of a scheme to raise funds for the Ethiopian cause, Alamaya and his secret communist colleague "invent" an Ethiopian princess by costuming a local Harlem woman.[49] In fact, it is Professor Koazhy, a costumed figure modeled after Marcus Garvey, and not the meek visiting Ethiopian prince Alamaya, who proves to be the "authentic" Ethiopian prince for the crowds watching the parade that opens the novel.

By the 1960s, as we see in Hughes's dedicatory poem to Selassie, with which this book concludes, the existence of a centralized Ethiopian empire would actually challenge the viability of an imagined extra-imperial network of black internationalism. Unlike the Chicago Abyssinians, who saw a "pathway" pulling directly from African America toward ancient Ethiopia, lit by cultural lamps that could ignite their own "fires of ambition," Hughes and others in the second half of the century would recognize the deficiency of this centripetal model. "Ethiopia the Shadowy," as W. E. B. Du Bois called it, would again fall into the shadows, no longer holding its once central position as and promise for a national metaphor of black solidarity.[50]

CHAPTER ONE

Recognizing the Ethiopian Flag

"Abyssinia! Abyssinia!" I hear some reader exclaim; "and where and of what special importance is Abyssinia to me, that I should turn from topics of immediate interest nearer home to give it even a passing thought? And yet,—now that you mention it,—was not that the name of the country concerning whose barbarous habits a mendacious old Scotchman, named Bruce, told our grandfathers such marvellous legends? And have I not lately seen in my morning newspaper, every week or two, a scanty telegram headed Abyssinia? Is not Abyssinia a wild, out-of-the-way place, somewhere in Asia, or Africa, or some other uncivilized part of the world, where irascible John Bull, peering about to find a new opening for commerce, has managed to get at loggerheads with a savage potentate called King Theodore?"

—G. REYNOLDS, "ABYSSINIA AND KING THEODORE"

IN 1867, ETHIOPIA'S emperor Tewodros—also known as Theodore and Theodorus—was making international news for imprisoning a group of British dignitaries, an act that led to England's military intervention in the country and, ultimately, to the emperor's suicide using a pistol given to him by Queen Victoria. "Magdala," an 1875 poem by "Charlton" (nom de plume of American poet Charlotte Pendleton), was one of many cultural responses to what became known as the Anglo-Abyssinian War:

> . . . in a hapless year, there came a band
> Of white faced strangers prying through the land,
> Then Theodorus, wrathful that they thus

Unbidden came, bade all his trusty men
Bind them with chains, and from this deed there sprung
Foul desolation over all the land.[1]

How did this ill-fated international incident capture the imagination of Charlton and other writers in the United States and Britain? The 1896 defeat of the Italian armed forces at Adwa and the Italian occupation of the country in the 1930s are well-known moments in Ethiopian military history when the country served as a model of opposition to imperialism, but the 1867–68 Anglo-Abyssinian War, an earlier moment during which Ethiopia entered the American field of vision as an oppositional force, has been largely neglected. Although Tewodros held Britain in "a special, almost affectionate regard," even taking vengeance upon a nephew who had murdered the British consul to Abyssinia and an Englishman named to Tewodros's court, Anglo-Abyssinian relations began to sour when Tewodros perceived Britain to be "conspiring with his avowed enemy, the 'Turks'"; ironically, according to Bahru Zewde, "the nation he had hoped would be his most reliable ally turned out to be his most bitter enemy."[2]

The narrative crafted around the war exaggerates its importance in the defeat of Tewodros. As Zewde writes, "The fate of Tewodros was already sealed before the British started their journey to the interior" due to internecine tensions and domestic antagonists who were collaborating with the British.[3] In any case, numerous books about Ethiopia were published in London in the aftermath of the skirmish in order to shape the British reader's understanding of it, such as Richard Chandler's *Abyssinia: Mythical and Historical* (originally published in *St. James Magazine*) and Henry Dufton's *Narrative of a Journey through Abyssinia in 1862–3, with an Appendix on "The Abyssinian Captives Question."* Many of these books circulated in the United States as well. For instance, the 1874 publication of the Boston Athenaeum's catalog lists nineteen new acquisitions about Abyssinia (including one reprint) published between 1867 and 1870. In 1868, the New York–based *Putnam's* worried that "ere long we shall have a flood of Abyssinia literature upon us."[4]

The context of the 1867–68 Anglo-Abyssinian War, and the publications printed in its aftermath, can help us read contemporaneous literary engagements with Ethiopia profitably. At a time when the influence of the British Empire was unrivaled, and when the United States were reuniting as a single nation once again under a single flag, the flag conveyed national identity, coherence, and strength. As such, literature about Ethiopia frequently raised the flag in revealing ways. Not coincidentally, it was under Tewodros that modern Ethiopia as a nation-state was beginning to centralize under one authority, and the flag, as a symbol of that nation, was transitioning from a military to a national significance. Rather than a collection of warring provinces, Ethiopia was presenting itself to the world as a nation.

Walt Whitman's Ethiopia

Whitman had evidently researched Africa thoroughly years before writing "Ethiopia Saluting the Colors." In a note written a decade prior to the poem, he had called Ethiopia "a country doubtless of hot-breathed airs and exhalations cities, ignorance, altogether unenlightened and unexplored" and Abyssinians "a large fine formed race, . . . black, athletic, fine heads."[5] In "Salut au Monde!" (first published as "Poem of Salutation" in the 1856 *Leaves of Grass*), he writes, "I see the high-lands of Abyssinia, / I see flocks of goats feeding, I see the fig-tree, tamarind, date, / I see fields of teff-wheat, I see the places of verdure and gold," ostentatiously displaying his knowledge of a grain unique to Ethiopia.[6] Therefore, although most readings of "Ethiopia Saluting the Colors" (written in 1867 and first published in the 1871 *Leaves of Grass*) understand "Ethiopia" as a generalization intended to signal something like abstract blackness, it is clear that the poem depends, as Ed Folsom has demonstrated, upon Whitman's specific knowledge about Ethiopia. As such, it is perhaps the best-known American poem touching, however indirectly, on the subject of Ethiopia.

Folsom calls this poem "one of [Whitman's] strangest," adding that it "has generally been met with embarrassed silence."[7] Critically speaking, this may be true, but calling this reception "silent" becomes an ironic assessment in light of the fact that the well-known black British composer Samuel Coleridge-Taylor had set the poem to music in 1902, followed in 1915 by the composition of another black composer, Harry T. Burleigh, known as "the American Coleridge-Taylor." Furthermore, Ivy G. Wilson claims a "spectral presence of Whitman in African American literary production," giving the illustrative example of James Weldon Johnson, who credits Whitman with transforming his poetic work upon his reading *Leaves of Grass* around 1900.[8] It has, in fact, been argued frequently that "probably no white American poet has had a greater impact upon black American literature than Walt Whitman," and, strange or no, "Ethiopia Saluting the Colors" became the centerpiece of the Whitmanian canon for many African American readers in the late nineteenth and early twentieth centuries.[9] Consequently, it is worth considering how the poem might have signified for African America.

In the poem, a Union soldier participating in Sherman's march passes and wonders about a "blear, hardly human" elderly black woman.[10] Of the old woman, Folsom claims, "In Whitman's hands, she is the sought-after, postwar, emblematic black for white America: puzzling in her origins, submissive in her courtesy, insistent in her salute, a person with shared and perhaps divided loyalties to her African past and to her American future, she experiences now a dual possession."[11] But what if we did not think of her salute and curtsy as "submissive"? Reading the central action of this poem as that of a black woman straightforwardly saluting an American flag leaves us, as Betsy Erkkila writes, with an "incongruent image."[12] Aside from her abstract "African past" and her "American future," there is the issue of her concrete "Ethiopian present," a present that Folsom addresses in his discussion of the Anglo-Abyssinian War. As British explorer Sir Samuel White Baker said in 1868, "There are countries of small repute that only rise from their obscurity when certain unexpected events call them before the world: thus Abyssinia was simply known to exist, but commanded no attention, until the detention of British subjects by its king forced that wild country before the eyes of Europe."[13] In other words, Ethiopia at that moment was, through the emperor's actions, associated not with submission but confrontation. The idea of lowering embedded in the etymology of "submit" is in direct opposition to the "*rising* from obscurity" Baker mentions. Interestingly, Whitman's old woman, as she is "blear," is also "rising from obscurity." One of the many questions the soldier asks the woman, or thinks of asking her, is, "Why, rising by the roadside here, do you the colors greet?" In asking why, he means not simply "what is your motivation in greeting the colors?" but "what do you intend to perform through this action? What does your elevation mean?"

Although Folsom addresses the Anglo-Abyssinian War as an important context informing the composition of the poem, I think examining the media coverage of the incident more deeply sheds light on what is arguably the poem's central image—the flag. It is not only the central image but a mirror image, as the Union soldier's flag is reflected back to him as the colors of the Ethiopian flag in the woman's turban. As William B. Ness writes, she is "wagging the colors of a defiant contemporary nation . . . in the face of the American colors."[14] As I will discuss in this chapter, the press's treatment of the Anglo-Abyssinian conflict and U.S. congressional and popular solidarity with Britain hinged upon the propriety of "recognizing" the Ethiopian flag.

Grouped with the cluster "Bathed in War's Perfume," "Ethiopia Saluting the Colors" is, as Luke Mancuso writes, explicitly presented by Whitman as a "flag" poem. When reading these as a cluster, one of the things that becomes obvious is that Whitman almost always approaches his beloved flag through apostrophe (as he is generally wont to do). For example, he exclaims in "Bathed in War's Perfume," "O to hear you call the sailors and the soldiers!" He reminisces in "Delicate Cluster," "How I heard you flap and rustle, cloth defiant!" He chants in "Song of the Banner at Daybreak," "Banner so broad, advancing out of the night, I sing you haughty and resolute." He demands in "Thick-Sprinkled Bunting," "Walk Supreme to the heavens, mighty symbol." And in "Lo! Victress on the Peaks!" the title says it all. In addition to addressing the flag, the flag sometimes addresses him, as in "Song of the Banner at Daybreak." Moreover, in this poem—the poem that Ness says "appears to be the grouping's *raison d'être*"—a child tells his father that he in fact wants to be the flag.[15]

All three of these elements—a speaker addressing a flag, a flag addressing a speaker, and the anthropomorphic incarnation of the flag—culminate in "Ethiopia Saluting the Colors," a poem that, though it is in the center of the cluster, appears not to have much in common with these other flag poems unless we understand the old woman to actually *be* a flag. As Ness writes, "Whitman tries to animate his flags by having them leap, flap, talk, and perform other lifelike tricks," but in "Ethiopia Saluting the Colors," he appears to go even further, transmuting a flag into a human being.[16] How should we understand this equation, however? Which is the tenor and which the vehicle? Is he elevating a flag to the status of living being or reducing a living being to the status of a flag? What critics such as Mancuso and Folsom say about the old woman's objectification—that "she presents herself to Sherman's Yankee soldier as a 'hardly human' object" and that "her voice is all *object* instead of subject"[17]—is certainly true. My aim is not to challenge the current view that Whitman's postbellum views of black subjectivity and participation in the reunited nation are complex, problematic, and often racist. But if, as Mancuso continues, "the soldier-persona of the poem cannot even personalize the black 'other' except through a competing national moniker" and, by calling her Ethiopia, he "strips her of any representation within the boundaries of American civil liberties," I think this indirection provides us with the opportunity to examine her representation *without* those boundaries.[18]

My reading here depends upon how we interpret the Ethiopian flag in the context of the poem. It is not simply a competing nationalistic alternative to Old Glory, and I believe that readings of the turban as such do not go far enough. In his discussion of the American flag, Ness draws our attention to the importance of the distinction between banners and pennants as they appear in Whitman's poetry: he writes, "the pennant is clearly identified with war and the national call to arms, whereas the banner is an expansive symbol for the country at large and all that it contains."[19] If we think of the old woman as a flag, she is then, I argue, a pennant and not a banner. In other words, like the Union army's "guidons moving by" in Sherman's march, the colors of the Ethiopian flag worn by the woman had, in 1867, a military rather than national significance.

Evidently, although red, yellow, and green flags were in use as military pennants in Ethiopia, there was in 1867, when Whitman was writing, no single Ethiopian national flag per se. Red, yellow, and green pennants had long been taken into war by Ethiopian armies. At least as early as the eighteenth century, James Bruce observed in his famous travelogue that "the standards of the infantry have their flags painted two colours cross ways, yellow, white, red, or green."[20] Scholar of Ethiopian history Stanislaw Chojnacki writes that the Ethiopian flag "was considered as a distinguishing sign or even a mere decoration of the military units" and cites an example given in Henry Salt's early nineteenth-century narrative: "the soldiers wore round their heads bandlets of yellow, green, or red satin, 'streaming loosely as they rode.' "[21] In other words, they wear headgear very similar to the old woman's.

Military pennants are not necessarily symbols of an abstraction for which soldiers fight so much as visual markers urging them on. The flag had no stable meaning in and of itself. A writer in the *Atlantic Monthly* even remarked in 1868 that "what his flag is to the soldier, religion is to the Abyssinian," indicating his sense that the idea of a flag as an object of devotion was a foreign one. According to Chojnacki, the idea of a national flag "had to be imported" and thus "the mystical meaning of a flag as a national emblem was added much later."[22] He mentions a formative incident:

> An Italian expedition arrived in the kingdom of Šawā in 1877. King Menilek . . . was always keen to learn and therefore inspected the equipment brought by the foreigners. "When the box with our flag fell in his hands," describes Cecchi, "Menelik asked . . . the reason why Europeans have such a respect for that object. Having got the explanation, he wished to be shown how we pay respect to it and this we did at once. When we sat down again he expressed his satisfaction in seeing

> how we, being far from our King and not seeing him, still have such a respect for his flag.[23]

This incident presumably influenced Menelik (who was not yet emperor but ruler of an Ethiopian province) to begin using the three colors in an official imperial capacity later. When Captain M. S. Wellby visited Menelik at the turn of the century, he found that "over the entrance of the palace floated a flag of three pennants of the Abyssinian colours—red, green, and yellow. Sometimes they are hung in one order, sometimes in another, but whether any special meaning is connected with the change I cannot say."[24] Chojnacki dates the "true birth of the national flag" to October 1897, when Menelik "ordered three red, green and yellow pennons to be sewn together and incorporated into one piece for display during the 1898 Franco-Ethiopian expedition to the White Nile."[25] This is thirty years after Whitman wrote "Ethiopia Saluting the Colors."

However, the story is more complex and circuitous than even this chronology would suggest. Red, yellow, and green may not have been officially translated from military pennant to national banner by the time Whitman wrote his poem—and the question of why there was resistance to this translation is itself worth investigating—but there were previous abortive attempts to pin down a national (or at least imperial) banner prior to the establishment of the current tricolor. Emperor Yohannes, Tewodros's successor and Menelik's predecessor who reigned from 1872 to 1889, used a standard for "display . . . on state occasions" that consisted of a yellow band between two bands of red, rather than the lasting combination of red, yellow, and green subsequently established by Menelik.[26] In addition, years before Wellby's visit to Menelik, Yohannes greeted a British visitor with the question, "Do you know my consul in London? My flag waves there." Yohannes followed this question with another, "Will you see the standard of Ethiopia?" Majestically and ceremoniously the heavy flag was unfurled for the foreign guest:

> The national banner was a gorgeous production of silk, a tricolour, the coloured divisions running laterally. The highest portion was crimson, the centre white, and the lowest amethyst blue. The whole was surrounded by a rich gold fringe. On the white ground was a gilt and painted representation of the lion of Judah, with a defiant tail, and a crucifix in his right paw. The staff was blue, jointed, and mounted in brass, and surmounted by a large brass gilt cross. The king seemed very proud of his national emblem, and at his desire Ras Alulu, aided by Mahderal, shook out its folds and struggled about the apartment under its weight.[27]

Although it is described by the visitor as a "national banner," the colors described in fact point to Yohannes's personal imperial flag.[28] In flaunting the heft of the flag (as well as the spectacle of it), the emperor and his court gesture toward the concrete visual significance and immediacy of the military pennants. Yet the Ethiopian flag is at this moment on its way to abstraction, as Yohannes's question about the flag's presence in London suggests. That the flag can exist now at a distance in a foreign land as well as in its immediate splendor in the imperial court expands its signification beyond the concrete. Incidentally, the physical nature of the flag is crucial to Whitman's depictions of it, as he wishes us not only to observe the differences between pennants and banners but to experience the tactile life of the flag—to *see* and *feel* the flag. As Ness writes, "Whitman's flags often have an intense physicality about them, as though he wants to emphasize that they are made of cloth. . . . As so often happens in his poetry, Whitman appears to be emphasizing physicality only to deemphasize it. The constant reminders that the flag is literally only strips of cloth sewn together heighten our awareness of the flag's symbolic identity."[29] Yohannes's and Whitman's flags share this "intense physicality."

Despite the fact that the flag's colors, even in the 1870s or 1880s, were variable and unstable, the combination of red, yellow, and green has had a cultural significance in Ethiopia stretching back to antiquity. Chojnacki, for instance, cites an 1847–48 source written by "French travellers Ferret and Galinier, who recorded . . . that 'red, green and yellow are the main colours of manuscript illuminations'" in Ethiopia.[30] So, Menelik's modern national tricolor had not taken hold by the time Whitman wrote "Ethiopia Saluting the Colors," but the colors red, yellow, and green were closely linked to Ethiopia's cultural heritage, especially when it came to warfare.

The scene in Whitman's poem is therefore of an "Ethiopian" woman wearing the colors often carried into Ethiopian battle as the soldiers of another battle carry their flags past her. As a result, the poem becomes even more martial than has been supposed, giving it even more resonance when Whitman places it in *Drum-Taps*. In contrast to Mancuso's argument that "the black woman reaches out in a gesture of inclusion, interracial comradeship, and political citizenship in a newly interracial democracy," I argue that there is an undertone of military aggression in the woman's greeting, as she rises by the roadside to "greet" the colors.[31] As Ness points out, "The expected form of Ethiopia's salute would be for her to lower her colors respectfully in deference to the American flags," but "in rising from the roadside, Ethiopia is raising rather than lowering her colors in response to the appearance of the U.S. flags."[32] This is indeed a strange moment of one-upmanship, so in light of Ness's claim that "by using the term 'greet,' which is one possible meaning of the word 'salute,' Whitman seems to be emphasizing that Ethiopia's response to the American flag resembles a polite salutation rather than a formal act of submission and allegiance," I'd like to raise a third possibility: that it is a ritualized act or performance of antagonism.[33] In addition to being synonymous with "salute," "greet" may be used to describe the encounter between two military forces.[34]

If this is the case, it then becomes difficult to reconcile this reading with her salute and especially her curtsy. To be sure, there *is* a tension in the poem between a submissive Ethiopia on the one hand and a defiant one on the other; it is as if Whitman, faced with the prospect of a belligerent black nation, could not decide what the nature of the interaction between the soldier and the woman should be. If we look at one of the variants of the poem, we see that in the fourth stanza he considered replacing "Her high-borne turban'd head she wags" with either "With towering form and gestures quaint" or "With hands outstretch'd and muttering lips."[35] While "hands outstretch'd" could be seen as a submissive gesture if we think of her hands outstretched to the soldier, we are meant to hear the familiar biblical reference behind it ("Ethiopia shall soon stretch out her hands unto God") that inspired Ethiopianist ideology and provided textual support for the belief that a black nation would "rise from obscurity." These variant lines introduce further contradictions in contrasting the strength of a "towering form" with the frailty of "gestures quaint." Whitman even goes so far as to write the line, "She bends and bows obeisant" before crossing it out. "Muttering lips" is an interesting potentiality, suggesting that the awkward eloquence of the italicized stanza might be a fantastic monologue imagined by the soldier, since apparently the real language of "Ethiopia" is an unintelligible babble to him. Not only has she seen "strange" things, but she herself is strange, that is, foreign. If we accept that the words in italics aren't actually voiced, then there is no indication that she even speaks English, despite having lived in the United States for a hundred years.[36] She is unassimilably alien.

Instead of the hopeful reunion expected of the encounter between enslaved person and liberating army, their flags divide them. The likelihood of a rivalry between the American flag and the Ethiopian flag materializes most strongly when we read this poem alongside "Thick Sprinkled Bunting," another in the "Bathed in War's Perfume" cluster. The "highest

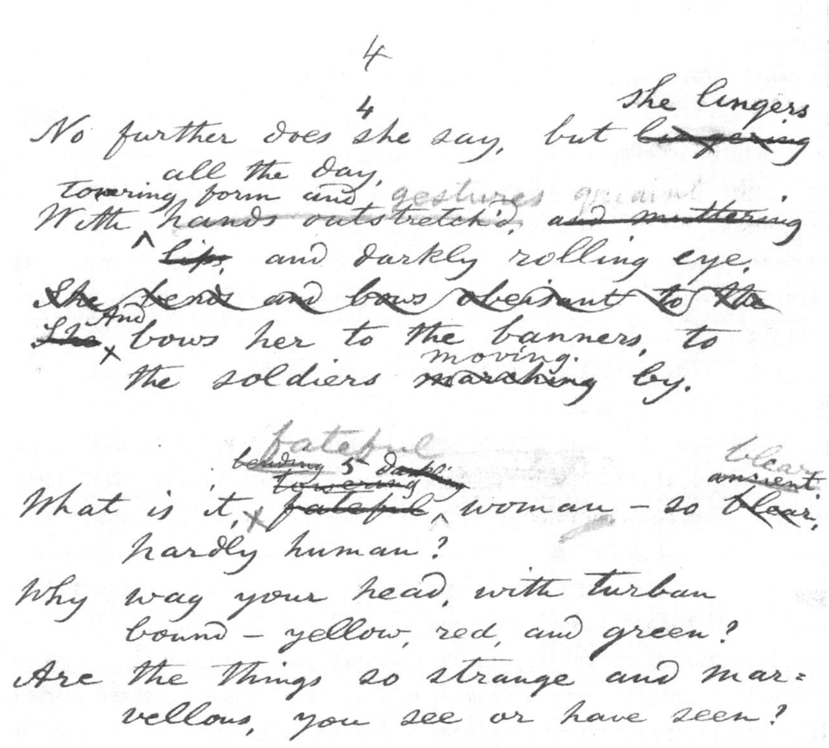
4

No further does she say, but she lingers all the day,
With towering form and outstretch'd, and darkly rolling eye,
And bows her to the banners, to the soldiers moving by.

What is it, fateful woman—so ancient,
hardly human?
Why wag your head, with turban
bound—yellow, red, and green?
Are the things so strange and mar=
vellous, you see or have seen?

FIGURE 1.1. Walt Whitman, variant of "Ethiopia Saluting the Colors," Morgan Library and Museum.

borne" flag here resonates intertextually with the "high borne" turban "Ethiopia" wears on her head, and suddenly the flag she stands for starts to seem pompous, overweening, and even threatening. The American flag—"flag of man"—is bound to best the Ethiopian flag—one of the world's "flags of kings." Whitman beckons to his flag: "run up above them all." Ness points out that "Whitman later reinforces the uplifted status of Ethiopia's flag when he refers to it as her 'high-borne' (literally meaning carried high) turban," but it is worth noting that the lifting of the American flag above flags of foreign kingdoms challenges the Ethiopian flag's attempt to ascend to the level of the Union flag: "Why, rising by the roadside here, do you the colors greet?"—again, not just "Why do you greet these colors?" but "Why do you *rise* to greet these colors?"[37] So, while critics have argued that the woman "presents herself to Sherman's Yankee soldier as a 'hardly human' object," I would argue that the poem's speaker sees her as not less than human but more than human,[38] inscrutable as an abstract martial principle equivalent but opposed to the one he marches under.

Belligerency and Senator Chandler's Analogy

During the Anglo-Abyssinian War, the Ethiopians' apparent belligerence was a popular topic of discussion. An article published in the London-based *Chambers's Journal of Popular Literature, Science, and Art*, titled "How They Fight in Abyssinia," claims that "an Abyssinian is never so pleasantly employed as when he is sharpening [his spear] or brightening up [his shield]." Lengthy and detailed descriptions of various weapons used in the country are accompanied by presumably useful instructions for defeating its warriors. The journalist cites Mansfield Parkyns, who lived in the country during the 1840s and "had many a friendly bout" with Ethiopians: "A European who knows anything of the use of a sword, can without difficulty master the best Abyssinian. . . . A slight feint will open his guard, and then you have him at your mercy."[39] Of these belligerent Abyssinians, according to the journalist, the most belligerent was their emperor, upon whom he bestows the epithet of "Theodore the Truculent."

Although Folsom writes that Tewodros was compared to Lincoln for his achievements within his country, Abyssinia's actions on the world stage were also widely compared to those of the Confederate rebellion in the United States. The parallel, then, would align Whitman's old woman, ironically, with the Confederacy. (This could be another explanation for Whitman's ambivalence in representing the woman's defiance, as evidenced in the poem's drafts.) But, as Folsom reminds us, "Ethiopia Saluting the Colors" is "not a Civil War poem" but a Reconstruction one; therefore, Ethiopia's actions were being compared to a Confederacy that no longer existed, that was no longer a threat. Its past menace was resurrected in Ethiopia's actions.

On 29 November 1867, Senator Zachariah Chandler of Michigan presented an unusual resolution designed to emphasize the parallel between current-day Abyssinia and the Confederacy of the past: a Proclamation of Neutrality regarding the Anglo-Abyssinian War, "granting to the flag of each belligerent the same rights, privileges, and immunities both upon land and water."[40] Recognition of a nation's flag on water is a consequential issue: if the flag of any given nation were not recognized, its actions could be deemed piratical rather than belligerent, and Chandler believed that England's recognition of the sovereignty of the Confederate flag as a belligerent nation contributed to huge losses for the Union. Because Great Britain pursued a course of neutrality in the American Civil War, treating the Confederacy essentially as they treated the United States, Chandler proposed the same in the conflict between Great Britain and Abyssinia and hoped that "if the King of Abyssinia enlisted seamen here, . . . perfect neutrality would be observed."[41] He argued that "when Great Britain by that Proclamation called the rebel flag into existence, it committed an act of hostility against this Government" and that "if we should pass this resolution we recognize a flag that has been recognized on land for thousands of years"—referring here to the presumed age of the nation rather than the formalization of a state flag delineated earlier in this chapter—"and we create a maritime Power on the ocean that did not exist before."[42] So, concludes Chandler, "if this is not good statesmanship, then it is because Great Britain has set us a bad example; the statesmanship is hers, not ours. . . . I am in favour of giving Great Britain a dose of her own medicine, and not a homœopathic one either."[43] Calling it no more than a "Resolution of reciprocity," he argued:

> the contest between Great Britain and Abyssinia, and the contest between the Government of the United States and the rebels, have several points of similarity. . . . Pass this Resolution, Sir, and you put the Abyssinian flag upon the ocean as Great Britain put the rebel flag upon the ocean. They do not need that their flag should be recognized on land. It is already a recognized flag, and has been, as I said before, for thousands of years.[44]

This response to the war with Ethiopia would mean aligning the United States with a black nation, but it also presented itself as a suitable opportunity to repay England for its treachery during the Civil War. That it was Ethiopia was merely a providential accident. As the British *Saturday Review* put it, "The hope of full revenge is to be gratified by the despatch of innumerable cruisers to plunder English commerce, under the flag of any nation which may be engaged in a war with England."[45] And, as a *New York Times* article noted, in looking for retaliatory opportunities to express an anti-British sentiment, Chandler allowed for a strange solidarity between the United States and Ethiopia, as "the 'recognition' of Abyssinia would justify Theodore in subsidizing the piratical craft of American adventurers, who, without ever going within 5,000 miles of Theodore's domain, would prey upon British commerce. And surely they might fly the Abyssinian flag with as much propriety as the *Alabama* did the Confederate."[46] In fact, the parallel between Ethiopia and the Confederacy, according to Chandler, was so appropriate that the previous British resolution of neutrality needed no rewriting other than the substitution of the terms of its formula.

Chandler's view was contrarian; only one other senator supported his controversial resolution, and a vote was not even taken.[47] The response in the U.S. press, however, was varied. Although Chandler's somewhat tongue-in-cheek potential alliance between the United States and Ethiopia may have emerged out of serendipity, some Americans in fact were in awe of Tewodros's defiance, in particular *because* he challenged Britain. Corresponding to Chandler's view that "it is the duty of Congress to promptly recognize King Theodorus as a maritime belligerent," the New York–based periodical *Wilkes's Spirit of the Times*, for example, claimed that the senator's resolution "has widely met with the approbation of the press; it precisely suits the temper of the country, and it has been objected to only by those whose sympathies justified England's interposition in behalf of the Confederates."[48] A series of articles about the Anglo-Abyssinian War in the magazine expressed skepticism about the demonization of Tewodros found in the British press. One claims that "as the English journalists who write upon this matter, are actuated by precisely the same impulses as governed them when speaking of the American rebellion, we need not feel surprised when they assure us, that the Abyssinian government is without justification for its conduct, and that King Theodorus, is such a monster of wickedness as the world has seldom seen."[49] *Wilkes's Spirit of the Times* repeatedly challenged the British view of Tewodros as "the half-drunken, illiterate, and brutal savage which England, for her own purposes, represents him to be," calling these representations "monstrous falsehoods, that have teemed in the English press, about his injustice and barbarity."[50] Finally, at the conclusion of the war, *Wilkes's Spirit of the Times* criticized England for plundering Magdala—"a piece of unrelieved barbarism"—and cited a flattering anecdote about Tewodros by "a reliable observer (Dufton) [that] contradicts, in itself, the numerous barbarous stories with which the English journals stimulated the British mind to justify this formidable expedition."[51] Cautioning American readers, the magazine's editors took it upon themselves to correct a media perspective that they believed to be nothing more than pro-English propaganda.

Other periodicals, on the other hand, found that the incident in Abyssinia proved a greater solidarity between the United States and England. A British monthly claimed that "nothing is more confirmatory of the position we have taken with reference to the improved feeling towards England in the United States, than the late discussion in the American congress on the propriety of recognizing the Abyssinian flag."[52] The British public in general was gratified by Chandler's failure to recruit people to his side. Critical views compared the Chandler debacle to an "undignified burlesque," a "parody," and a "joke." A June 1868 *Galaxy* editorial asserted that "spiteful propositions like that to 'recognize Abyssinia' are born of ignoble minds."[53] Regarding Tewodros, the *Brooklyn Daily Eagle* joked on 2 January 1868:

> After being recognized as a belligerent by Senator Chandler, he refused to be a belligerent. He has refused us the opportunity of retaliating the Alabama depredations on our commerce, and disappointed the bold Fenians who were ready to swarm the seas with privateers sailing under the Abyssinian flag to annihilate British commerce, wipe out the British fleet and ultimately rescue Ireland. All these hopes have been blighted.

Similarly, a *New York Times* article from 11 December 1867 titled "The Abyssinian Gammon in the Senate" offers a sense of the tenor of this conversation. Chandler was mocked relentlessly:

> And now, when he is able again to rise up in the Senate of the United States . . . , and in the wild frenzy of his soul exclaim, as he exclaimed on Monday, "Let the Abyssinians light up old ocean with the burning ships of Great Britain!" he seems to reach the very climax of that wild joy which warriors feel when they are confronted by foemen worthy of their steel, and when they are sustained and backed up by an Abyssinian bruiser who lives upon raw flesh, and sleeps on a couch beside which that of his great ancestor, King Solomon, was virtuous.

Occasionally, even articles celebrating Tewodros, such as the aforementioned *Brooklyn Daily Eagle* article published on 2 January 1868, mocked the emperor for his ready surrender:

> We feel disgusted because we had staked a good deal of faith in Theodorus. He had defied England, he had bearded the British lion—at a safe distance, to be sure—but to defy England, under any circumstances, is no safe business for small potentates. The friends of the African were encouraged; here was a genuine, unadultered [*sic*] darkey, imperial as Caesar, with back bone enough to defy one of the great nations of the earth. We heard stories of his wisdom and valor, of his moderation and justice, and above all, of his fierceness of character. Now, he has backed down without a fight.

Another article expressed frustration that such undeserved hope had been placed in Tewodros in the first place, as if Americans had been fooled into believing in him. Now we can see that "the illusion has been dispelled; Theodorus was a humbug."[54]

This degree of disappointment illustrates that, prior to his defeat, the press in the United States and England—regardless of perspective—understood Tewodros to be a serious threat and one worthy of in-depth examination. A writer in *Every Saturday* refers to him as "the bad boy of Abyssinia" and warns his readers that "there is no Eastern enemy with whom we have ever grappled so dangerous as Theodore of Abyssinia."[55] Two weeks earlier in the same magazine, a profile of Tewodros calls him an "interesting psychological curiosity," who, in his unpredictable and volatile behavior, "unites in himself the most opposite and conflicting qualities"; he is an "Eastern Charlemagne," a "Christian Mahomet," and one who is "more than tinctured with madness."[56] H. A. Burette, in *London Society*, claimed that Tewodros earned "the epithets of 'Abyssinian wild beast,' 'Ethiopian Beelzebub,' &c." by Reverend Henry Aaron Stern, one of the prisoners.[57] The most common descriptors referred to his alleged cruelty and his imperious ambition. Regarding the latter, an 1868 *Atlantic Monthly* article remarked that "for the first time in many years Abyssinia owned a single master" and that Tewodros's imperial designs included the desire "to push out the bounds of the country on every side . . . [,] restoring to Ethiopia its original territory."[58] The so-called "Mad King Theodore" was hungry for expansion.

Given this context, the old woman in Whitman's poem begins to look like not only a rebel military force—that is, a threat to union profound enough to fracture the nation again—but also an imperial force that threatens another imperial power. The Union soldier's recognition of the rebellious Ethiopian flag through the figure of the old woman is an action very much in line with Chandler's diatribes on the Senate floor. Despite the fact that the Union soldier interprets the rising of the Ethiopian flag as an enigmatic threat, he ultimately *does* recognize it (in both senses of the word) and is compelled to respect its sovereignty. The figure of the old woman, therefore, is a tangled bramble of a symbol. She expresses, as critics have pointed out, Whitman's vexed position regarding African American participation and inclusion in the United States; she stands for a rebel force reminiscent of the Confederacy, and she also, paradoxically, stands for an admirable defiance against a nation toward whom there was still some lingering resentment in the United States regarding its role in aiding the Confederacy. "Ethiopia Saluting the Colors," a poem that has often been dismissed due to its conventional meter and rhyme scheme, is therefore a complex amalgam of political views, written during a historical moment when a black nation was suddenly "rising from obscurity."

The Anglo-Abyssinian War and the Domestic Sphere

The Rising Ethiopian was the subject, too, of William Wells Brown's 1873 history *The Rising Son; or, The Antecedents and Advancement of the Colored Race*, in which he devotes chapters to various peoples of the black world, including "The Abyssinians." Curiously, Brown spends nearly the entire chapter on "The Abyssinians" memorializing Tewodros, whom he calls "on the whole, the greatest ruler Abyssinia has ever had," one who fell only after he "fought bravely for his crown, but in vain."[59] Brown's view of Tewodros had the potential to be widely influential, but even relatively obscure Victorian writing about Ethiopia would not have escaped the attention of many African American readers, writers, and editors who, as Daniel Hack and others have pointed out, were "immersed in the transatlantic literary culture of the day."[60] Black readers in the United States would have been exposed to various sorts of American and British writing about the Anglo-Abyssinian War—including the "labored efforts of the English press . . . to defame Theodorus," to quote the aforementioned magazine *Wilkes's Spirit of the Times*[61]—and therefore the masculinist discourse of war should not lead us to neglect the literary and cultural activity by little-known women and even children in the United States and Britain on the subject. These treatments of war tend not to evoke war through the flag as abstract patriotic symbol; instead they depict the war as a battle between an abstraction (Britain) and a personality (Tewodros) caricatured as either savage or romantic, depending upon the source. Like the poem "Magdala" cited at the start of this chapter, which appeared in the 1875 book *Songs of the Year and Other Poems* by "Charlton," another poem titled "The Death of King Theodore," published in the Scottish poet E. Davidson's 1874 *The Death of King Theodore and Other Poems*, presents a sympathetic view of Tewodros from the perspective of a woman writer. These direct literary treatments of war are reminiscent of the indirect participation in imperialism that Amy Kaplan finds in Catharine Beecher's work, in which "the language of empire suffused the rhetoric of domesticity."[62] Both Charlton and Davidson are drawn to Tewodros's domestic narrative of invasion by an alien military, seen in reverse. In fact, what is most striking about both of these poetic treatments of the war is that, in opposition to the versions of Tewodros found in British media coverage of the war, Tewodros is glorified by these poets as a romantic and powerful figure wronged by intrusive Western forces. Tewodros was a figure whose personality, as Richard Pankhurst writes, "evoked no little contemporary admiration," but there was by far a greater degree of "popular anger against the Emperor in Britain," and, according to the *New York Times* foreign correspondent, there had not ever been "so serious an affair . . . entered upon by England with more absolute unanimity on the part of all organs of public opinion."[63] Charlton's and Davidson's favorable portraits run counter to the supposed consensus.

English caricatures and other popular depictions—perhaps unsurprisingly—especially attempted to deflate the image of a threatening black monarch. On the eve of the British expedition to rescue the prisoners, *Punch* published a blackface-inspired caricature by John Tenniel that was lambasted by John Camden Hotten, editor of *Abyssinia and Its People*, as a portrait derived of "ignorance," displaying Tewodros as "a kind of music-hall Jim Crow."[64] It was accompanied, when republished later in *Mr. Punch's Victorian Era*, by a note describing Tewodros as the "half-savage monarch of Abyssinia." Brittania, his adversary, is clearly much stronger and larger than he. In response to her power, his knees are buckled in intimidation, and he looks to be resignedly offering her the keys to the prison cell, his scimitar no match for her trident. As opposed to her clenched and determined jaw, his mouth gapes open weakly in fearful surprise. "The Abyssinian Question," the title of the caricature, is articulated in the caption: she asks, "NOW, THEN, KING THEODORE? HOW ABOUT THOSE PRISONERS?" The caricature argues plainly that he is overpowered and has no choice but to answer "The Abyssinian Question" in the affirmative.

A nearly identical depiction of Tewodros, this time skulking away in a corner, appears in the background of another *Punch* cartoon by Tenniel, published in a different issue later the same year. *Mr. Punch's Victorian Era* retrospectively provides context in the following note:

> Nov. 19. Parliament was opened by Commission, being called together at this unusual time in order to sanction the expedition which it had become necessary to despatch for the relief of the captives in Abyssinia. £2,000,000 was required at once for the purpose, Abyssinia being 160 miles from the Red Sea. The control of the Expedition was entrusted to Sir Robert Napier, a distinguished General of Engineers, then commanding the forces at Bombay, with Sir Charles Stavely as second in command. The advance brigade of the Expedition had left Bombay on the 7th October. It was thought it might ultimately cost four millions or even more. The Income Tax would have to be raised. There was much talk of a missing letter alleged to have been sent to the Queen by King

FIGURE 1.2. John Tenniel, "The Abyssinian Question," *Punch; or, The London Charivari*, 10 August 1867, 57. George Peabody Library, Sheridan Libraries, Johns Hopkins University.

FIGURE 1.3. John Tenniel, "Tuck in Yer Twopenny!" *Punch; or, The London Charivari*, 14 December 1867, 243. George Peabody Library, Sheridan Libraries, Johns Hopkins University.

> Theodore. Mr. Bernal Osborne said the postage of that letter would cost £5,000,000. Of course the House granted the Government what it required, and on 7th Dec. adjourned till Feb. 13.[65]

Here, Benjamin Disraeli, or "Dizzy," says to John (presumably John Bull, epithet for the stereotypical Briton), as he leapfrogs him, " 'NOW, THEN, JOHN, I'M COMING OVER YER AGAIN: TUCK IN YER TWOPENNY!' " In a hat upended on the ground is a tied piece of paper with the word "Abyssinia" on it; clutched in John's hand is one that says "Income Taxes." Presumably, the popular opinion against Tewodros was only compounded by the public's knowledge of just how many of the average Briton's tax dollars were going toward rescuing the prisoners, all because of the emperor's hair-trigger sense of outrage regarding an unanswered letter, as they saw it.

On 28 August 1867, a poetic equivalent of these caricatures was published in *Judy; or, The London Serio-Comic Journal*, under the title "A Model Monarch," to be sung to the tune of "Have you seen her lately?":

> Men we sent out to THEODORE,
> How to behave we taught 'em;
> He took their presents—to get more
> He locked up those who brought 'em.
> How to chastise this wicked man,
> As we were just then thinking,
> His subjects to rebel began,
> And chained him up like winking.
> Oh, THEODORE a monarch is
> Who seems to lie innately;
> Was e'er such conduct known as his
> In Abyssinia lately?
>
> His lips are thick, his eyes like sloes,
> His toe-nails long and taper,
> His wool is curly, so's his nose,
> He's dressed in rags and paper.
> 'Tis said he has two hundred wives
> (A black girl costs a shilling),
> If they offend he takes their lives,
> For he's good at lady-killing.
> Oh, THEODORE a monarch is
> Who seems to lie innately;
> Was e'er such conduct known as his
> In Abyssinia lately?

Contrast, on the other hand, *La Lune*, a French periodical that did not have as much at stake and little social or cultural need to ridicule Tewodros. André Gill's caricature for *La Lune* depicts the two sovereigns—the Lion of Judah and the Lion of England—as equals embroiled in mano-a-mano fisticuffs. If anything, Tewodros, with one of Gill's trademark oversized heads, assumes a position of power over England. The difference between the *La Lune* caricature and those in *Punch* gives a sense of the climate in Britain on the topic of Abyssinia; anti-Abyssinian propaganda such as the caricatures in *Punch* encouraged the British public to view Tewodros as a villain or a buffoon, and sometimes both.

Even in British periodicals that avoided humor or caricature—such as the *Illustrated London News*, which used realistic, detailed visual depictions in its coverage of the Anglo-Abyssinian War—Britain's conduct is presented as noble and Tewodros's as savage. The *Illustrated London News* participated in the glorification of England through its articles and images just as much as *Punch* did in running Tenniel's figure of Brittania. As one article argued, "Our object was in every sense a righteous one—to deliver from the hands of a semi-barbarous potentate those of our countrymen whom he had snatched from their peaceful or benevolent pursuits and laden with fetters; and above all to assert and vindicate the inviolability of the Queen's representative while engaged on her behalf in a peaceful mission to obtain their release."[66] Despite the magazine's dignified and respectful engravings of ordinary and religious Ethiopians by William Simpson and other artists and soldiers, Tewodros himself was almost without exception described as savage.

Children in Britain were certainly aware of—and unwitting participants in—this popular characterization. In a 1900 *Strand Magazine* article titled "War-Pictures in '*Punch*,' 1841–1899," J. Holt Schooling reviews, among other caricatures, Tenniel's "The Abyssinian Question." He writes, "The amusing cartoon . . . reminds me of one of the first toys I can remember to have possessed—one of those little painted plaster figures of King Theodore of Abyssinia, which were sold here in 1866."[67] We might think of these Theodore dolls in the broader context of black dolls sold to white children in the nineteenth century. As Robin Bernstein writes, "In the second half of the nineteenth century, literature, nonfiction, theater, and material culture—the dolls themselves—coordinated with each other to script violent and degrading play with dolls,"[68] and, although her analysis is concerned with the use and abuse of black dolls in the United States, it is easy to see how British children might have welcomed the opportunity to join their culture's popular racially tinged hostility directed toward the Ethiopian ruler. Through dolls and songs, English children could participate

Troisième année. — Nº 9[illegible] 10 CENTIMES 22 Décembre 1867

RÉDACTEUR EN CHEF
F. POLO

ABONNEMENTS
PARIS
Un an............ 5 fr.
Six mois........ 3 »
Trois mois...... 1 50

BUREAUX, 5, CITÉ BERGÈRE

LA LUNE

DIRECTEUR-GÉRANT
F. POLO

ABONNEMENTS
DÉPARTEMENTS
Un an............ 6 fr.
Six mois........ 3 50
Trois mois...... 2

BUREAUX, 5, CITÉ BERGÈRE

THÉODOROS, ROI D'ABYSSINIE — par GILL

LE LION D'ABYSSINIE ET LE LION BRITANNIQUE
Ou rugira bien qui rugira le dernier!!!
Drame en plusieurs actes, précédé d'un prologue : A QUAND LA NOCE? musique d'Amstrong.

FIGURE 1.4. André Gill, "Théodoros, Roi d'Abyssinie," *La Lune*, 22 December 1867, 1.

in the cultural disciplining of Tewodros. Another instance is shared by George Sturt in a memoir titled *A Small Boy in the Sixties* (1927). He cites a childhood song about Tewodros with the lines, "Oh the King of Abyssinia, / Oh the very wicked King!" The prevalence of materials about Tewodros geared toward children is indicated by an 1868 *Galaxy* review of a children's book. The reviewer cites the book's author: "'It all at once struck me,' he says, 'that the British public had no work about boys. . . . We have books . . . about gorillas, elephants, and Emperors of Abyssinia.'"[69] Tewodros's inclusion in this list makes no secret of his perceived savagery.

In stark contrast to representations in the British press and the popular culture of toys and songs, Charlton begins her respectful tribute in "Magdala" with the lines "I sing the fall of Abyssinia / The fate of Theodorus, King of kings!" calling him "heaven born, begotten of the gods."[70] Despite his godliness, he leads an army destined to fail, due to an imbalance of military technologies: "vain are bosoms bared to meet the foe, / 'Gainst cunning engines, belching smoke and fire: / And vain are spears against a foe that stands / Beyond the winged arrows utmost flight." The military scene is introduced by Charlton's descriptions of the pennants carried by the imposing British army:

> through the plains the glistening banners flashed
> And scarlet trappings glimmered in the sun,
> And the loud trumpet woke the faint alarm
> Of distant echoes in the purple hills.
> Before the troubled eyes of dusky tribes
> They passed, a vision of white warriors,
> With gleaming sabres, and with nodding plumes,
> And all laid siege to sunny Magdala.

Unlike Whitman's "Ethiopia Saluting the Colors," there is no face-off between two representative flags in Charlton's poem. Sympathetic to Tewodros, the poem emphasizes Britain's ruthless dominance.

Despite Tewodros's supposed viciousness—"cruel anger gleaming in his eyes / Crouched like a panther ready for the spring"—Charlton instructs her reader to feel sympathy for the king and his people. She demands that we "weep for the fall of Abyssinia." In describing the emperor's defeat, she writes, "Like some lone pine that shudders to its fall / And shakes the earth with dying majesty / Across the path of those that spoiled the land / The mighty monarch, Theodorus, fell." A judgment against the British, who have, in Charlton's view, wrongly "spoiled the land" in their attempt to retrieve the hostages, "Magdala" paints Tewodros as a victim of European aggression and a natural part of the African landscape that has been "despoiled." With the felling of this tree, the earth "shakes"; the event resonates internationally.

With a reference to "Queen of Sheba's sacred dust" and the alleged unbroken line of rule represented by the Ethiopian emperor, Charlton mourns more than the loss of a man; she mourns the weakening of a long-lived dynasty and of Ethiopian sovereignty. In a manner that anticipates Hughes's "The Negro Speaks of Rivers," "Magdala" links Africa's ancient ancestry to the ageless Nile, "whose slimy ebb / And fertile flooding of slow refluent waters, / Recorded time before the years were numbered." Abyssinia, as she puts it, is the "Mother of lands in the dawn of days" who now "sits uncrowned upon the stricken hills," as if the nation itself has been deposed. The idea of the loss of the sovereign, and the loss of order that is presumed to follow, is devastating. Charlton ends the poem with a question that expresses her concern about the interruption to this ancient royal line—"Where is the pomp of all her pageants now, / And where her sons who ne'er should cease to reign!"—but punctuates it with an emphatic exclamation point rather than a question mark. There is no question about her position. Although Charlton titles her book *Songs of the Year and Other Poems*, her correspondence with Daniel Coit Gilman, then president of the newly established Johns Hopkins University, suggests the weight she gives to "Magdala." She offers to "send [him] post haste the volume containing 'Magdala'" in a letter of 12 May 1885.[71] The poem was also selected for an 1883 anthology edited by Henry A. Ford, A. M., with an outlandishly sweeping organizing principle: *Poems of History, by the Most Famous Poets of All Ages, Relating to Most Notable Nations, Eras, Events, and Characters of the Past, from the Time of Adam to the Year 1883*.

Like Charlton's "Magdala," Davidson's "The Death of King Theodore," subtitled "Who Fell while the British Troops Were Storming Magdala," celebrates Tewodros as a hero, even going so far as to assume his voice:

> Surrender! nay, that shall not be!
>   Back my defiance bear;
> Unyielding will I rather seek
>   The refuge of despair.
>
> The royal lion ne'er shall crouch
>   To lick his victor's hand,
> Or bend his neck to foreign power
>   Within his native land.

Alas! my country, 'twas for thee
My hand first drew the sword,
My hope, my aim, to rescue thee
From every foreign lord.

'Twas not to live in regal pomp
That I the diadem wore,
I sought to bring thy glory back,
Thy greatness to restore.[72]

A British woman, Davidson expresses a point of view even more surprising than that of Charlton, who, as an American, had no national investment. Rather than see the conflict through British eyes, Davidson deliberately reverses her position in order to view the situation from the Abyssinian perspective, scorning "foreign [i.e., British] power / Within his native [i.e., Abyssinian] land." The reversal is not obvious at first glance, as Davidson's assertion that "the royal lion ne'er shall crouch / To lick his victor's hand" can refer to either Britain or Abyssinia. It is only in the fourth stanza that we know for certain which perspective the poem takes, as the speaker, addressing his country, seeks "to bring thy glory back, / Thy greatness to restore." Britain could hardly be said to be lacking in glory or greatness at the end of the nineteenth century, but the prospect of restored glory is constitutive of Ethiopianism. The past glory of Ethiopia reaches back to "ere the British lion's growl was heard."

Davidson's portrait of Tewodros focuses on his "defiance" and "unyielding" spirit, which are presented as admirable qualities. Rather than savage or cruel, she describes him as gentle and sympathetic in his dealings with the hostages. He offers willingly to return them, saying that he has no intention of hurting the Europeans. In fact, he points to the treatment and survival of the hostages as evidence of the distance between the truth and the media portrayal of him: "Had I been what they deem'd, they had not / Have met them alive and free." Compared to those subject to the cruelty of European dungeons, he argues, Tewodros's captives experience relatively mild treatment. Closing the poem with an unabashedly elegiac tone, Davidson's voice returns toward the end. Mournfully she writes, "Rest, sable prince," praising his "aims and aspirations" as "noble" and proclaiming his right to rule.

In a preface to her book, of which her tribute to Tewodros was the title poem, Davidson tones down the effusiveness of her praise. The note claims that "the Authoress felt the death of the Abyssinian king very keenly, and wrote the verses on the spur of the moment," as if to apologetically explain away her impetuousness as a variety of Wordsworthian spontaneous overflow of powerful feelings. Soon after sending the poem to a newspaper, "she would fain have withdrawn it when the report arose that Theodore was such a cruel monster." However, after "a close examination," she determined "that, in her opinion, he had done nothing worse than the English did in India, when they shot rebel Sepoys from the cannon's mouth." Painted as a victim of internecine tensions, Davidson's version of Tewodros admirably and selflessly "labored anxiously and wisely for the welfare of his country" against "rebellious subjects" and Europeans who aligned themselves with them. The prefatory note effectively asserts her original view even more strongly, as she privileges her "close examination" over the "report" found in the press.

Paul Laurence Dunbar's "Blazoned" Flag

Unlike Davidson's and Charlton's topical poems, Paul Laurence Dunbar's "Ode to Ethiopia," composed nearly two decades later, can be read more generally as an homage to Abyssinian might. First published in 1893 as a proem of sorts to his first book *Oak and Ivy*, and written a generation after "Ethiopia Saluting the Colors" by a poet who strongly disapproved of Whitman's style, "Ode to Ethiopia" nonetheless shares with Whitman's poem a veiled desire to honor Ethiopian strength through recognition of the flag's sovereignty and the ascension of imperial culture. Dunbar's poem has (for good reason) been understood as a religiously inflected and abstract song of racial pride and uplift, but the poem also, when approached through an Abyssinian lens, reveals a historically informed imperial vision of Ethiopia.

Dunbar opens with an apostrophe—"O Mother Race!"—that offers the poem as a "pledge of faith" and "tribute."[73] This pledge would appear to counter the pledge of allegiance to the flag of the United States, which had been written a year prior to Dunbar's publication of "Ode to Ethiopia," as loyalty to the "Race," as nation, trumps loyalty to one's nominal country. It is illuminating to read this poem through Dunbar's "The Colored Soldiers," a tribute to the patriotism of the heroic black Union soldiers who fought during the Civil War only to find themselves unwelcomed by their fellow white soldiers. In the two poems, Dunbar draws a direct parallel between the blood spilled during slavery and the blood spilled during war: of the soldiers in "The Colored Soldiers," he writes, "their blood has cleansed completely / Every blot of Slavery's shame";[74] in "Ode to Ethiopia," Dunbar argues that African Americans were similarly sanctified by the experience of slavery, baptized and anointed by their own holy blood and sweat. The difference is that the soldiers fight for a nation of which they cannot be a part. When "the flag was drooping low," the black soldiers "rallied to the standard / To uphold it by their might" before "dust [could] pollute your banner." This is not their flag; Dunbar makes this clear by addressing the poem to white Americans and calling the American flag "your banner." On the other hand, the banner of "Ode to Ethiopia" is in no danger of drooping. In fact, it seems to defy gravity as it ascends "high 'mid the clouds of Fame's bright sky," and "truth" allows it to climb even further.

Despite the apparent rejection of American patriotism in "Ode to Ethiopia," the Race appears at first to be defined along national lines, limited to those of African descent who have suffered under slavery only "in this fair land" and who now "stand / Beside their fairer neighbour." Dunbar celebrates these members of the African American Race as Ethiopia's "swarthy children." This lament for those forced into the involuntary labor of slavery lies at the heart of the poet's tribute, but the tribute later is transfigured into a celebration of voluntary labor, especially the work of the artisan. Like the Race in general, Dunbar raises the specter of "the past" only to "forg[e]t" it. African Americans now "sit in honest labour"—honest because free from the immorality of slave labor but honest also because more virtuous than work too far removed from manual labor—and "The forests flee before their stroke, / Their hammers ring, their forges smoke." This picture of the post-emancipation United States, as two harmonious racial nations, is a rose-colored one; Dunbar describes the United States as a "fair land" in order to praise its physical (and ideological) greatness, but "fair" also hints at his expectation that equality and justice will be realized. Followed two lines later by a mention of the African American's "fairer neighbour," Dunbar imagines an optimistic future of integrated cross-racial unity, with the primary sense of "fairer" (to mean lighter-skinned) now joined by the suggestion that today's white American has become more honorable than his slaveholding father.

The recognition of advances made in gaining institutional power, expressed in Dunbar's exaltation of those "voices [that] sound through senate halls / In majesty and power" (here referring to Mississippi senators Hiram Rhodes Revels and Blanche Bruce, who served during Reconstruction), again points toward a vision of the Race that is exclusively African American. However, the poem repeatedly evokes motifs and language associated with the ancient biblical version of Ethiopia, and even gestures occasionally to elements of contemporary Ethiopian imperial power. The black nationalism that Abyssinia represented at the turn of the century joins African American nationalism to provide a concrete alternative to American nationalism—the new "glory" of Dunbar's Ethiopia as opposed to "Old Glory." Primary among these elements is the poem's salute to the Race's "continuous rise," which not only refers to a variety of racial uplift specifically African American but also borrows the international language of the Ethiopianist movement in order to describe the ascension of the Race, rising as the elderly woman in Whitman's "Ethiopia Saluting the Colors" does. In addition, Dunbar concludes the poem with the following lines:

> Our ears shall list thy story
> From bards who from thy root shall spring,
> And proudly tune their lyres to sing
> Of Ethiopia's glory.

Dunbar is, of course, one of these bards, and his ode is one of these songs. In the midst of the poem's language of newness and birth ("from thy root shall spring," "the fruitful seed of better times was growing. . . . Its blossoms now are blowing," etc.) lies a competing strain alluding to an ancient nation, beginning with the title's evocation of Ethiopia itself. Lyre-strumming bards, needless to say, are not of the modern world but introduced as a self-consciously anachronistic affectation, one borrowed later by Melvin Tolson for "The Bard of Addis Ababa." The historic men of the Race (there is no mention of women, other than Ethiopia herself) sing "hymns" but they are also the subjects of the bards' song, a national epic.

Given the fiery imagery Dunbar uses here—the name of the Race "is writ on Glory's scroll / In characters of fire"—it is surprising that he does not appear to call upon a specifically military pennant such as the one implied by Whitman's poem but instead calls upon a nationalistic banner of "blazoned folds." However, the word "blazoned" is carefully chosen. It carries a double sense, primarily meaning "displayed" but secondarily referring to heraldry. The association of Ethiopia with the "Lion of Judah" royal coat of arms was widely known outside of the country, the caricature in *La Lune* in fact depending upon a general readership's knowledge of this association. Furthermore, "blazoned" is hardly the poem's only reference to monarchism; the terms "majesty," "noble," "honour," and "glory" all attempt to ennoble the Race by using regal terms that would call both ancient and modern Ethiopia to mind.

The association of nobility with Ethiopia resurfaces in Dunbar's tribute to Frederick Douglass, but, even more than "Ode to Ethiopia," "Frederick Douglass" complicates the relationship between the sovereign and the people. During their first meeting in 1893, Douglass asked Dunbar to recite "Ode to Ethiopia," and, after Douglass's death less than two years later, Dunbar included a strategic mention of Ethiopia in his elegy: "Ethiopia, with bosom torn, / Laments the passing of her noblest born."[75] As with most poetic references to race-as-Ethiopia, she is figured as feminine, as materfamilias of the race, as she "weeps for [Douglass] a mother's burning tears." Yet she is also imagined collectively, as all black people (i.e., her own children): Douglass was "her champion" who lifted her "when Bondage held her bleeding in the dust." As in "Ode to Ethiopia," Ethiopia the mother has suffered (birth) pangs through slavery, producing a nation of "swarthy children" that is also "Ethiopia," essentially giving birth to itself. At the end of the poem it becomes clear that "Ethiopia" and "race," both figured as feminine, are synonymous. Reinforcing the connection, Dunbar ends the poem with a line that resonates with Ethiopia's biblical association: the race, not Ethiopia, "stretches out her bleeding hands to God" and, recycling the language of ascension from "Ode to Ethiopia," is "rising from beneath the chast'ning rod."

The abstraction opposing Ethiopia in the poem, another unified symbol out of a collective, is Oppression, which is imagined as masculine. Douglass attacks "the very den / Where grim Oppression held his bloody place / And gloated o'er the mis'ries of a race." His primary weapon in this fight is his voice, a "stirring cry," a "fearless clarion," a "voice . . . ringing o'er the gale." The voice is notably a martial one, becoming its most strident in its characterization as a "battle-cry." In fighting Oppression, Douglass prepares "the strong bow of his pow'r" and shoots "his arrows," dying "in action with his armor on." Even Dunbar himself gets caught up in the progression, allowing his language to become energized with militarism. He begins the elegy with a "hush," but, as the poem marches toward a close, increasingly he punctuates his lines with exclamation points, of which there are four in the last three stanzas.

Dunbar's banner in this poem—Douglass's battle cry leads us to "place our banner where his hopes were set"—is an imperial one; the flag of the black race is planted as if to represent an imperial claim. The flag functions to centralize a black nationality, as "Ethiopia," under a single authority. This Ethiopia was one that Dunbar, born four years after Tewodros's death, would have known as a paragon of black military resistance due in large part, as I've attempted to show in this chapter, to Tewodros's actions during the Anglo-Abyssinian War. In 1893, two years prior to the publication of Dunbar's elegy, an author writing in the well-known African American newspaper the *Freeman*, published in Indianapolis, uses nearly identical terms to invoke a metaphorical army of African Americans claiming black nationality under a unifying flag of "Ethiopia." She writes, in an apostrophe perhaps more inspiring than Dunbar's, "Oh Ethiopia! may thy future be bright and hopeful, as thy past has been dark and hopeless, for already we see . . . the young of this race girding on their armor and preparing for the conflict with odds and opposition, and we believe that they shall succeed in planting the banner of Ethiopia on the dizzy heights of distinction."[76] African American periodicals of the turn-of-the-century United States often reverted to a common lexicon when discussing Ethiopia and called upon the nation's metaphorical significance in order to appeal to their audiences. We will see, in the next chapter, how the *Colored American Magazine* packaged this idea of Ethiopia for its readership.

CHAPTER TWO

Pauline E. Hopkins and the Shadow of Transcription

The shadow of a mighty Negro past flits through the tale of Ethiopia the Shadowy and of Egypt the Sphinx.

—W. E. B. DU BOIS, *THE SOULS OF BLACK FOLK*

Consider . . . that in the heart of . . . Africa, whose institutions elsewhere are as shifting as the sands of her deserts, there is found a people the annals of whose unconquered national existence run back until they are lost in the darkness of legendary history.

—G. REYNOLDS, "ABYSSINIA AND KING THEODORE"

"PERHAPS NO DECADE is more important," Mark Christian Thompson writes, "for the development of Ethiopia as a rallying point in African American political thought than the 1890s," with the introduction of Ethiopianism not only as a new African Christian movement but also as a "mythological narrative through which African Americans could identify culturally and ontologically with Africans."[1] This expansive and vague mythology at the base of late nineteenth-century impressions of the nation, when additionally inflected by the detailed chronicled news of the contemporary nation at this time—most visibly, the news of the remarkable Italian defeat at the 1896 Battle of Adwa—presented a dichotomous version of Ethiopianism. As a source of ancestry, Ethiopia seemed simultaneously present and absent, an ever-shifting symbol of ghostliness. It was identified, paradoxically, by the shadow that it cast, as the epigraph by Du Bois illustrates. The literature of the period, in its treatment of

Ethiopia as symbolically fluid, illustrates Thompson's general point that "Ethiopianism was a mutable concept."[2]

Under Pauline E. Hopkins's editorship, the *Colored American Magazine*, self-described as "the only first-class illustrated monthly published in America exclusively in the interests of the Colored Race," promoted a documentary interpretation of Ethiopianism in their histories and biographies. By "documentary," I intend to evoke two senses of the *Oxford English Dictionary*'s definition of the adjectival form: both simply "Of the nature of or consisting in documents" (that is, written) and "Factual, realistic." In documenting "Ethiopia," with special attention to its monarchy, Hopkins asserted the value of a fact-based historical approach to imperial Ethiopianism that converged with existing myth. The magazine's content regarding Ethiopia, including illustrations, biographies, and fictions, conformed with what Hazel V. Carby calls the magazine's general "pedagogic function" and shaped how the community of readers created and fostered by the magazine conceived of a black pride that could be based in modernity.[3] Although the biblical Ethiopia that would "soon stretch forth her hands" would have been familiar to most African Americans, the *Colored American Magazine* presented a more grounded Ethiopia, one of secular contemporary events. At this time, the magazine published a significant serialized novel about Ethiopia that could be called a historical fiction, although, as a result of the mysticism at its heart, the text becomes somewhat generically indeterminate or even "generically radical," as Elizabeth Ammons describes it.[4] The novel is Hopkins's *Of One Blood; or, The Hidden Self*, published between 1902 and 1903, notably only a few years after the aforementioned Battle of Adwa.

If, as C. K. Doreski writes, the *Colored American Magazine* "offered a product-intense, textual world in which even biography and history might become marketable commodities," then this version of Ethiopianism was effectively being sold to the magazine's readers especially through nonfictional narratives.[5] Mentions of Ethiopia surfaced frequently in the magazine. In fact, the May–June 1903 installment of *Of One Blood*, during which the protagonist first meets the inhabitants of a hidden Ethiopian city, was immediately followed by the first installment in a series titled "Ethiopians of the Twentieth Century" (using "Ethiopian" in accordance with the general definition, as the subtitle announces that the piece addresses "Questions Affecting the Natives and Colored People Resident in British South Africa").[6] Carby finds that a "network of relationships between *Of One Blood* and other, nonfictional articles in the journal indicates . . . the extent of an intertextual coherence achieved under Hopkins's editorship,"[7] but I would argue that the confusion produced in the clashing of genres dismantled that seeming coherence, resulting in some conflicting messages about Ethiopia and its symbolic or exemplary value. Where history collided with fiction, producing imaginative histories and historical fictions, the magazine fell back upon a partly imagined Ethiopia. Just like Emperor Menelik's claims that he descended from King Solomon, the magazine's collective claims about Ethiopia in these hybrid genres could be entertained by readers precisely because they seemed factual but receded into a mythic, unfocused point in a distant past that was comfortably familiar. The simultaneous specificity and generality conjured a source of pride that didn't need to be—and could not be—absolutely pinpointed and yet was manifest and potent enough to be used in service of racial uplift. I use the word "conjured" here deliberately, as the amorphousness of the idea of Ethiopia inevitably led back to a sort of inventive mythic Ethiopianism. Mythmaking was already intrinsic to the ideology of Ethiopianism that was developing as early as the eighteenth century, as it had long been to Ethiopia itself. Ethiopianism, according to Wilson Jeremiah Moses's definition, "involved a good deal more than mere allusions to Ethiopia in the songs, sermons, and folklore of the African peoples. It was a historical mythology, presenting an exalted view of the black race and its cosmic messianic mission."[8] In the *Colored American Magazine*'s documentary mythmaking, the editors produced a paradoxical condition in which the idea of Ethiopia was presented to their readers as both familial and alien. The alien aspects of Ethiopianness often acquired an air of mysticism that the nonfictional texts in the magazine attempted to rein in. While John Cullen Gruesser claims that the generic hybridity of Hopkins's novel serves, in the end, the promotion of an African American exceptionalist view, I find instead that Hopkins's constant collapse into the fantastic when faced with Ethiopia betrays a belief in *African* exceptionalism, a fear that Ethiopia—whether understood as modern Abyssinia, ancient Meroe, or the continent of Africa in general—cannot be contained.[9]

Of One Blood is a good example of a fictional text that introduces the mysticism that the historical and ethnographic texts of the *Colored American Magazine* avoid while still participating in documentary Ethiopianism by sending its characters to Ethiopia, as Ammons puts it, "not in a mind trip but in a real trip."[10] While engaged in an archaeological expedition, the novel's protagonist, Reuel Briggs, discovers that he is descended from a royal Ethiopian lineage. The seemingly still-ancient Ethiopians (despite contact with the "outside" world) are living hidden in Telassar, a modern

Meroe, and they pass on to Reuel their culturally inherited knowledge, which is largely mystical in nature. But even before his trip to Ethiopia, Reuel exhibits behavior inspired by intrinsic mystical power supposed to be Ethiopian in derivation. It is through his mystical power that he is able to restore to health the apparently dead Dianthe Lusk, his future wife (and, as he discovers later, sister). His fellow medical students and physicians think that his reanimation-through-magnetism hypothesis "smacks of the supernatural . . . , charlatanism, or dreams of lunacy," but Reuel defends himself with the assertion that "the supernatural presides over man's formation always."[11] He succeeds in reanimating her, and she, in fact, walks zombie-like through her life from that point after. According to Reuel, she is the victim of a "dual mesmeric trance," requiring a year in order to recuperate and restore her memory, during which time she "may still be liable to the trances" (471–72). As a result of this susceptibility, she is easily manipulated by Aubrey, the villain of the novel and brother to Reuel and Dianthe.

"The Hand of Mysticism"

Although mesmerism—sometimes represented in the novel as a power a character exerts by holding a hand before another human being or animal—has received the most attention of the mystical elements in the novel, I focus here upon another "hand of mysticism": Ethiopic (and Ethiopianist) writing. A reimagining of the biblical hand of Ethiopia that promises to stretch forth, this "hand of mysticism" weighs heavily in the novel. As Walter Ong has written, "When a fully formed script of any sort, alphabetic or other, first makes its way from outside into a particular society, it does so necessarily at first in restricted sectors and with varying effects and implications. Writing is often regarded at first as an instrument of secret and magic power."[12] Much of the writing in *Of One Blood* is mysterious or magical in origin, allowing Hopkins to document the space between fact and fantasy. As Susan Gillman and Dana Luciano have pointed out, the character of Mira, an enslaved woman who is revealed to be the mother of the novel's three major characters, is responsible for making obscure texts legible, but it is worth examining more closely just how these texts are deciphered. One of the earliest examples in the novel of the written "hand of mysticism" comes from the scene that introduces the phrase and involves a ghostly Mira's appearance out of thin air, emerging from the floor of Dianthe's room, to mark a passage in the Bible before disappearing again:

> As the woman passed from her view, Dianthe rose and went to the table to examine the book. She did not feel at all frightened, recognizing instantly the hand of mysticism in this strange occurrence. There on the open page, she perceived heavy marks in ink, underscoring the following quotation from the twelfth chapter of Luke: "For there is nothing covered that shall not be revealed." On the margin, at the end of this passage was written in a fine female hand, the single word, "Mira." (506)

Writing about Shakespeare's plays, Marjorie Garber points out that "the appearance of ghosts . . . is almost always juxtaposed to a scene of writing," citing examples from *Hamlet*.[13] We see the same juxtaposition here in Hopkins's novel. Both Gillman and Deborah E. McDowell, in her introduction to the novel, characterize this moment of inscription as an instance of "automatic writing." I would argue, however, that it is not so much automatic writing as it is one of fully conscious annotation, Mira's version of biblical exegesis or gloss. Mira has power, but it is not, as McDowell suggests, a creative "literary power."[14] It is, rather, a clerical or interpretive power. The "heavy" underlining contrasts with the "fine" signature, speaking to Mira's desire to identify herself and yet keep the focus squarely upon her function as annotator. And, yet, I do not believe that Mira is "a surplus to the text," or even that Mira "mak[es] a space for herself in the words and texts of others."[15] Her name may be in the margins, but Mira is neither marginal nor present. Her signature in fact reinforces her ghostliness; as Garber writes, citing Derrida, the signature is "a sign of the simultaneous presence and absence of a 'living hand,' which stands for its signator in that person's absence. . . . A signature, then, is very like a ghost."[16] Mira's function—the actual marking of the text—is necessary and productive, and actually spawns another text for analysis. In both of the novel's descriptions of Mira's biblical marking, the marking itself calls out for further examination just as the passage called out for Mira's initial examination: first, Dianthe herself "examine[s] the book"; later, she asks her husband Aubrey (who has duped her into marriage), "Examine the book, and tell me, is that fancy?" (598). An oral account of Mira's appearance is not sufficient; she must prove the truth of her story through the written record of it, magically supplied by Mira.

Mira's "writing" requires her to suppress her selfhood precisely as Reuel is supposedly discovering his "hidden self." Her transparency is crucial to the scene that reveals Jim's treachery to Reuel. He sees Jim "draw from his vest a letter, seemingly hidden in a private pocket" (522). Suddenly,

Mira appears, and "twice did the shadowy finger of the shining apparition in the tent door point, letter by letter, to the pictured page of the billet, which Jim was at that very moment perusing with his natural, and Reuel Briggs with his spiritual eyes. When both had concluded the reading, Jim put up his letter" (522–23). In this weird scene of doubly doubled reading, of a letter doubly secreted (not just hidden in a vest pocket but a "private pocket"), Mira is nothing more than a human manicule (☞). She points not to Aubrey's letter but a cinematic representation of it. As if thrown by a ghostly film projector, "Jim—who sat directly behind [Reuel]—[was] placed like a picture on his very table" (522). As an autonomous character, Mira is completely absent from the scene; she is her function. As a matter of fact, a preface to this installment when it appeared in the *Colored American Magazine*, summarizing chapters one through eleven, describes the scene thus: "one night, by clairvoyant aid, Reuel reads a letter that Titus has received" (339). Her activity in the scene is completely obscured. An enslaved woman in life, she serves purely as amanuensis in a manner that evokes the word's etymological roots of "servant" and "hand."

As a pointing finger, Mira could be mistaken for a hieroglyph, but her appearance also, interestingly enough, recalls a particular contemporaneous impression of Ethiopic script, the invoking of which supports the *Colored American Magazine*'s project of documentary Ethiopianism. In *With the Mission to Menelik, 1897*, an English diplomatic travelogue Hopkins is likely to have read, Count Edward Gleichen compares Ethiopic script to "a complicated series of semaphores, with arms pointing in every direction, and dots, blots, and dashes in different positions on, or hanging to, those arms."[17] So, in other words, not only is Mira an annotator or interpreter of writing, she likely resembles for Hopkins—in her semaphoric pointing—Ethiopic writing itself. Consider another moment, late in the novel, when a scream awakens Reuel in the middle of the night: he finds the "shadowy figure" of Mira, who guides him with "uplifted finger" to a wall, which, predictably, confounds him. Then the wall slides away and he discovers the captured Charlie Vance and Jim Titus behind it. Mira's indexical index finger, which points out but also—in its shadowiness—mystifies the scenery to which she points, strangely recalls Ethiopic script *and* performs the stance of travel writing published by Europeans like Gleichen and tourist writing found in the "quality" mainstream magazines contemporaneous with the *Colored American Magazine*.[18] Through her body language, she reveals strange scenes and passages for her curious reader. Look, as her name suggests.

One might say that Hopkins, in these Mira scenes, dramatizes her own frequent "borrowings" as similar annotations. Several critics have addressed Hopkins's plagiarism, among them Daniel Hack and Geoffrey Sanborn. Hack, for example, has shown that several passages from *Of One Blood*—including these very moments of Mira's materialization—are taken from Victorian texts, in what he calls a "recurrent feature of Hopkins's compositional practice."[19] Following Sanborn's lead in understanding Hopkins's plagiarism "as an indication of the degree to which [Hopkins] hears in [writing] an unendingly nonsubjective voice," I turn here to the original sources of various archaeological and historical passages of the novel set in Africa in order to demonstrate how Hopkins made strategic use of these travelogues to complement the magazine's generic hybridity.[20]

Perhaps the most significant source from which Hopkins copies passages about Africa is G. A. Hoskins's 1835 *Travels in Ethiopia*. But Hopkins may have come across Hoskins's text in a 12 December 1835 "reprinting" in *The Mirror; or, Literature, Amusement, and Instruction*. This article, titled "Ethiopia," summarizes Hoskins's then recently published book and lifts, uncited, the following language, which Hopkins then lifts herself in a double plagiarism: "At the extremity of each portico, as before observed, is the representation of a monolithic temple, above which are the traces of a funeral boat filled with figures. . . . Diodorus mentions that some of the Ethiopians preserved the bodies of their relations in glass (probably alabaster) cases, in order to have them always before their eyes. These porticoes may have been used to contain such cases." These sentences are only slightly altered when they appear in Hopkins's novel.

Hoskins's text, as reproduced by Hopkins, pervades *Of One Blood*. Compare this lengthy passage from Hoskins:

> One who . . . had visited the chief galleries of Europe, gazed upon the breathing image of divinity in the Apollo of the Vatican, or the deep expression of the most poetical of statues, the Dying Gladiator of the Capitol; who had beheld and felt the pictorial creations of a Raphael and a Correggio, and, with delight, contemplated Grecian, Roman, and modern sculpture, could not be unmoved at finding himself on the site of the very metropolis where those arts had their origin. The traveller who has seen the architectural antiquities of Rome, and has admired the magnificent use that nation has made of the arch, making it the chief ornament of their baths, palaces, and temples, would be further deeply interested at finding here the origin of that discovery. . . . The beautiful sepulchers of [Meroe] afford satisfactory evidence of the

> correctness of the historical records. Where a taste for the arts had reached to such perfection, we may rest assured that other intellectual pursuits were not neglected, nor the sciences entirely unknown. Now, however, her schools are closed for ever, without a vestige of them remaining. Of the houses of her philosophers, not a stone rests upon another; and where civilisation and learning once reigned, ignorance and barbarism have reassumed the sway.[21]

to this one from Hopkins:

> One who had visited the chief galleries of Europe holding the treasures accumulated from every land, could not be unmoved at finding himself on the site of the very metropolis where science and art had their origin. If he had admired the architecture of Rome and the magnificent use they had made of the arch in their baths, palaces and temples, he would be, naturally, doubly interested at finding in desolate Meroe the origin of that discovery. The beautiful sepulchers of Meroe would give to him evidence of the correctness of the historical records. And then it was borne in upon him that where the taste for the arts had reached such perfection, one might rest assured that other intellectual pursuits were not neglected nor the sciences unknown. Now, however, her schools are closed forever; not a vestige remaining. Of the houses of her philosophers, not a stone rests upon another; and where civilization and learning once reigned, ignorance and barbarism have reassumed their sway. (538)

In truth, there are too many lifted passages to cite here. Nearly every factual description of Africa is taken in its entirety from various sources.

At the risk of subjecting Hopkins's plagiarism to too generous an interpretation, it is likely that she viewed the direct lifting of passages—at least those from travel essays and books about Africa—as serving the larger project of documentary Ethiopianism. One 1890 article criticizes the plagiarist's urge to steal from fellow authors, ironically, as an "imperial fancy," and we could say that Hopkins builds her synthetic texts in order to invigorate her imperial Ethiopianist drive.[22] Beyond simply "establishing shots or genre bits," as Sanborn puts it, these borrowed moments in *Of One Blood* transmit the profound intimacy of unfiltered firsthand travel accounts directly to readers of fiction who may be unfamiliar with historical and contemporary discoveries in Ethiopia.[23] Rather than citing sources as she might have in a nonfictional essay, she incorporates the facts she has discovered into her fiction, producing a bricolage from the results of her research.

The shadows and echoes of Hoskins's and others' texts in Hopkins's do not necessarily distinguish her novel from those of her contemporaries. As one writer sardonically remarked in 1890, "The plagiarist has been on promotion during the last dozen years. . . . For several years his way has been smooth, and his regular methods have not been varied under any pressure from society."[24] In fact, during the Victorian period, "'plagiarism' was substantially redefined as a necessity of literature, rather than a felony committed against it."[25] The impulse to plagiarize was explained away by one magazine writer in 1862 as an "instinct for the reproduction, in some shape or other, of every strong impression."[26] Certainly Hopkins's Ethiopianist project, which required her to conduct her own textual "exploration" mimicking those physical explorations by nineteenth-century adventurers whose texts she absorbed, was the product of the "strong impression" left upon her by her reading and the resultant desire to proselytize, so to speak, to her *Colored American Magazine* audience. Furthermore, as the novel was published in a magazine and not in book form, Hopkins's liftings in *Of One Blood* begin to resemble reprintings such as *The Mirror*'s: the unauthorized transferring of a book's text to the medium of the periodical in order to distribute it to a different audience.

One of the foremost writers of Hopkins's day, Brander Matthews, addressed a similar case in his "The Ethics of Plagiarism," published in 1888. He defends H. Rider Haggard, who had been accused of plagiarizing parts of *King Solomon's Mines* from travel literature about Africa (and, coincidentally, from whom, Sanborn tells us, Hopkins takes a few sentences that appear in *Of One Blood*). Although the charges never amounted to anything, Matthews argues that

> had he done what he was accused of doing, there would have been no harm in it. Mr. Haggard, in writing a romance of Africa, would have been perfectly justified in using the observations and experiences of African travellers. Facts are the foundation of fiction, and the novelist and the romancer, the dramatist and the poet, may make free with labors of the traveller, the historian, the botanist, and the astronomer. Within reason, the imaginative author may help himself to all that the scientific author has stored up. One might even go so far as to say that science—in which I include history—exists to supply facts for fiction, and that it has not wholly accomplished its purpose until it has been transmuted in the imagination of the poet. If Mr. Haggard had made use of a dozen books of African travel in the composition of that thrilling and delightful romance of adventure, "King Solomon's Mines," there

> would have been no more taint of plagiary about it than there was in Shakspere's reworking of the old chronicles into his historical plays.[27]

If we apply this perspective from Hopkins's contemporary to our reading of her novel, it becomes clear that her borrowings may not have been considered intellectually criminal at the time of publication, despite JoAnn Pavletich's assertion that they would have "been identified as a problem."[28] If anything, those who expose plagiarists are criticized more strongly by W.D. Howells, in an 1899 article, than the plagiarist himself: "they please their miserable vanity by showing their alertness, and are proud to bear witness against you in the court of parallel columns."[29] Moreover, just as Mira's role is to clarify and yet obscure, Hopkins's various sources bring to the reader a degree of immediacy and clarity she herself could not supply and yet the multiple voices produced in this din make it difficult for a reader to find the source from which this adventure originates. If we accept Sanborn's claim that Hopkins "wanted to cast, at times, a disintegrative haziness over her own authorial voice, to make it seem to emanate from something more than a single mortal self," then this intent behind her plagiarism collaborates with her desire to cast Ethiopianness as both shadowy and distinct simultaneously.[30]

We can, in addition, think of Mira's obscurantist but ultimately revealing stance as a representation of Ethiopic writing colored by Hopkins's training and occupation as a stenographer. Hopkins worked as a stenographer periodically throughout her life; her job was defined by her ability to accurately reproduce and transcribe the words of others. According to music scholar Alfred W. Cramer, stenography evolved in the nineteenth century as a technology that "operated somewhere in the space between language and hallucination," and this convergence supports the possibility that Hopkins could have viewed the phantom-writing aspect of *Of One Blood*'s plot through her own experience with stenography, as Mira also operates in the space between language and hallucination.[31]

The German inventor of shorthand Franz Xaver Gabelsberger was inspired, as Cramer puts it, by the hope "that stenography might permit direct expression of human thought and recover originary meanings of language that lay hidden in alphabetic script."[32] At the same time, the "search for ideal expression unencumbered and undistorted by the limitations of words" led many scholars in nineteenth-century Europe to look for a supposed "purity" in "Oriental languages (whose exotic forms and opaque meanings suggested higher worlds to Europeans)."[33] This coincidence, along with the perceived visual resemblance between the "dots, blots, and dashes" (to use Gleichen's description) of the two linguistic systems, suggests to me that it would not have taken much of a leap for Hopkins to connect Ethiopic writing to the code of shorthand. Moreover, Pitman's shorthand and many others are essentially alphasyllabaries, just like the Ethiopian and Meroitic scripts. In other words, both use diacritical marks in order to modify consonants with an accompanying vowel sound. Alphasyllabaries (termed "abugidas" by Peter T. Daniels in 1990, "from the Ethiopian word for the auxiliary order of consonants in the signary")[34] are relatively rare scriptive systems—used in certain South Asian and South East Asian languages, and in the family known as Canadian Aboriginal languages—so, again, this is likely more than a coincidence.[35]

As both writer and symbol of esoteric writing, Reuel follows in Mira's footsteps; he is referred to as "the scribe" even when he is engaged in the banal and individualistic activity of "making entries in his journal" (522). And the same lotus-shaped birthmark that signals him as the king of the new Meroe also marks the parchment obtained by Professor Stone with a seal "formed to resemble a lotus flower" (528), essentially equating Reuel and an important explicative mystical text in the novel. Although indelibly marked as royal, Reuel is also, paradoxically, as insubstantial as his mother is. Although Reuel appears to have found his "hidden self," that self is Ergamenes, a historical royal whose figure he only temporarily occupies. Incidentally, Hopkins praises the original, historical Ergamenes in her *Primer of Facts Pertaining to the Early Greatness of the African Race and the Possibility of Restoration by its Descendants—with Epilogue*, crediting him with overturning an "absurd custom" that allowed "electors . . . weary of their ruler" to demand their king's suicide, so it is not surprising that she should allow Reuel to serve as his second coming.[36] Reuel learns from Ai, his guide through his new kingdom, that reincarnation is a cornerstone of his people's religion and that "when the body of a good man or woman dies, and the Ego is not sufficiently fitted for the higher condition of another world, it is re-associated with another body to complete the necessary fitness for heaven" (562). It is implied that this reincarnated state is the position in which Reuel, as the latest Ergamenes linked to a queen who descends from a matriarchal line of women all called Candace, finds himself. He is a vessel for a king that possesses him. How else to explain his sudden ability to speak fluent Arabic, his increased mesmeric powers? As Ergamenes, he is a character from a book, walking around in the real world, such as it is. His magical abilities converge with the magical properties of the ancient texts in which his stories were told.

The Regalization Fantasy

When Reuel returns to Telassar after exacting vengeance upon Aubrey, he takes Aunt Hannah with him. Her position in the novel is unique as the only New World member of Reuel's family who appears to be black, and she is striking. After wandering in the woods in despair, Dianthe meets Aunt Hannah in a "typical Southern Negro cabin" (603) and is struck by a regal quality (specifically, an African one) that she perceives in the woman:

> Somewhere she had read a description of an African princess which fitted the woman before her.
>
> "I knew a princess; she was old,
> Crisp-haired, flat-featured, with a look
> Such as no dainty pen of gold
> Would write of in a fairy book.
>
> "Her face was like a Sphinx's face, to me,
> Touched with vast patience, desert grace,
> And lonesome, brooding mystery. (603)

The poem, misquoted and left uncredited in the novel, is Sarah Piatt's 1872 "The Black Princess," which Paula Bernat Bennett calls "a poem very popular in its own day if problematic in ours."[37] Although the lines remembered by Dianthe place Hannah outside of literature—"with a look / Such as no dainty pen of gold / Would write of in a fairy book"—if we read the rest of the poem, we discover that the subject of Piatt's poem is, in fact, inscribed within a story. She is "a slave—like one / I read of in a painted tale." And, in fact, the rest of the poem seeks to realize the fairy tale that the "dainty pen of gold" refuses to take up. The last five stanzas of Piatt's poem bear quoting:

> Nothing of loveliest loveliness
> This strange, sad Princess seemed to lack;
> Majestic with her calm distress
> She was, and beautiful, though black.
>
> Black, but enchanted black, and shut
> In some vague giant's tower of air,
> Built higher than her hope was. But
> The true knight came and found her there.
>
> The Knight of the Pale Horse, he laid
> His shadowy lance against the spell

That hid her self: as if afraid,
    The cruel blackness shrank and fell.

Then, lifting slow her pleasant sleep,
    He took her with him through the night,
And swam a river cold and deep,
    And vanished up an awful hight.

And in her Father's house beyond,
    They gave her beauty, robe, and crown:
On me, I think, far, faint, and fond,
    Her eyes to-day look, yearning, down.[38]

Piatt's poem disturbingly invents a story in which black skin can be the product of an evil fairy tale curse, and, when the knight rescues the princess, the "cruel blackness" can fall away. But the poem shares so many elements with the plot of *Of One Blood* that it is difficult to dismiss the similarities as pure coincidence. The strange appellation "enchanted black" could describe any of the main characters in the novel, and the "shadowy lance" that can be used "against the spell / That hid her self" could not be a more perfect description of the novel's many revelations of self (Mira's "shadowy" revelations to Dianthe and Reuel, Aunt Hannah's revelation to Dianthe, etc.). We even have what sounds strikingly like an indictment of Aubrey, who "took" Dianthe and "swam a river cold and deep." The reception the black princess receives at "her Father's house" is remarkably similar to what she would presumably receive at Telassar. However, the black princess's rewards received only in death in Piatt's poem can be actually hers in life in the world of Hopkins's novel, if we understand, as Dianthe does, the princess to be Aunt Hannah.

If Reuel can be a king, it makes sense that Aunt Hannah can be a princess. *Of One Blood* activates the fantasy in which anyone—and everyone—can be a historic king or, at the very least, descended from one. This implied tension between inclusivity (as a universally available fantasy) and exclusivity (as a fantasy that necessarily excludes others from similar exaltation) is in fact embedded in the Ethiopianist ideology. The shadowy mythology surrounding Ethiopian monarchism leaves room for fantastic claims to the throne, a quality that Hopkins exploits in her novel. As Martin Japtok points out, Reuel "only fully decides to embrace his African heritage once this heritage assures him an elevated social and economic position."[39] It would be unthinkable that Reuel would have remained in Telassar if it had been revealed to him that he was descended from an ordinary ancient Ethiopian. Furthermore, both European and African American impressions of Ethiopia often rested upon an understanding of the nobility as exceptional and the commoners as inferior and uncivilized. Expressing an apparently commonly held view, Gleichen distinguishes between Menelik and his people, claiming that "the difference in character between Menelik and his people is most marked, and is entirely in favour of the former. Perhaps in few countries is the contrast between the upper class, or aristocracy, and the proletariat so striking as here."[40] Access into the regal world Reuel discovers by accident is extremely limited. Telassar's vibrant activity is veiled and invisible to the rest of the world, with the walls of the city resembling the blind approach of Ethiopia's real-life rock-hewn churches. Although Ai tells Reuel that written language in the form of hieroglyphics was democratically accessible in ancient Ethiopia—"A knowledge of these characters in Egypt was confined to the priests, but in Ethiopia they were understood by all showing that even in that remote time and place learning and the arts had reached so high a state as to be diffused among the common people" (536)—he fails to mention that the competing script, on the other hand, was the exclusive province of the privileged few. Reuel himself is excluded as a reader of an ancient text he receives from Ai, which Ai calls "a record of the wisdom and science of your ancestors." When Reuel, seemingly in frustration, asks Ai, "What language is this? It is not Hebrew, Greek nor Sanskrit, nor any form of hieroglyphic writing," Ai responds, "It is the language once commonly spoken by your ancestors long before Babylon was builded. It is known to us now as the language of prophecy" (572).

Hopkins's descriptions of this writing sometimes point to Meroitic script and sometimes to Ethiopic (or Ge'ez), which reflects a long-standing general confusion surrounding the geographic and cultural discontinuities among all of the civilizations or groups of civilizations that have been called "Ethiopia" going back to classical antiquity: the Kush Empire seated in Meroe in modern-day Sudan, or what would become Abyssinia (more closely associated with the ancient Aksumite Empire), or Africa as a whole. Complicating matters further is the argument, summarized by Fikru Negash Gebrekidan, that, "rather than constituting two distinct empires, it is more likely that both Axum and Nubia belonged to a loosely federated political structure, perhaps tied by complementary commercial interests. When Nubia, with its capitals at Napata and Meroe, was the more powerful of the two, Axum paid homage and sent tributes; but when Meroe's fortunes fell, the highland province did not hesitate to take matters into its hands."[41] However, although the pre-Babylonian provenance may be anachronistic, the foreign language Reuel encounters—given that it is not "any form of hieroglyphic writing"—is likely that which Martin Delany transcribes under the heading "THE OLD ORIGINAL ETHIOPIAN ALPHABET" in his 1879 *Principia of Ethnology: The Origin of Races and Color*. In this text, Delany cites classical and biblical sources in his efforts to prove ancient Egyptian and Greek cultures' indebtedness to ancient Ethiopian innovation, including writing. His research, which was borrowed liberally by Hopkins herself for her *Primer of Facts*, reveals, citing Heliodorus, that "the Ethiopians had two sorts of letters, the one called regal, the other vulgar."[42]

Meroitic script, although indecipherable in Hopkins's time and still insufficiently translated in our own, is known to have been written in two forms: "a 'cursive' or linear version for general use, and a pictorial 'hieroglyphic' lapidary style for monumental purposes on temple walls and other royal monuments."[43] However, the non-hieroglyphic Ge'ez, reproduced by Delany in *Principia*, appears to be the "regal" script he has in mind as "the oldest, we believe, on record" and that "which none but the kings, priests, royal family and nobility were expected to learn."[44] Delany draws visual parallels between letters of the Ge'ez and Greek scripts, claiming that the latter was derived from the former, which makes Reuel's alienation from the writing all the more surprising, given his linguistic faculties. Furthermore, the Ge'ez script is used to transcribe modern-day Amharic and Tigrinya, and we would expect a scholar like Reuel to be at least passingly familiar with the written script used an area in which he is spending a good amount of time and is engaged in archaeological research, even if he cannot translate it. Unlike Mira's pointing hand, which corresponds to easily interpreted hieroglyphic and alphabetic writing, there is an unexpected lack of transparency to this regal "hand of mysticism" with which Reuel is confronted.

The Sages of Telassar, as Ai tells Reuel, must have "knowledge of two out-world languages" (561), and Reuel's faculty for languages—despite his inability to read Ge'ez—would technically qualify him for sagacity. This differentiates the nobility and clergy in *Of One Blood* from the common people: they move easily from one language to another. That Ai calls the foreign languages "out-world languages" emphasizes the fact that this capacity is not purely academic but practical, that the Sages aspire to circulate easily in the world beyond the kingdom. The fluidity and transparency associated with the polyglot's experience through the world are fundamental to the Sages' approach to knowledge.

Even Abdadis, who appears at first to be simply "an owner of camels who was used to leading parties into the wilderness," is revealed to be Telassarian royalty when Reuel sees him within the walls of the city, but we might have guessed at his royal status by his shadowy liminality (513). Although there is no evidence in the novel that he speaks "two out-world languages," it is clear that he has what we might call out-world experience. He functions as a mediator between the Africans and the Americans, and his name—as an Arabic/Amharic combination, "Abd Addis" would translate roughly to "new slave" or "new servant"—hints that he does not belong entirely to the ancient world. There may even be an echo of Menelik's newly founded capital, Addis Ababa, in his name.

But Hopkins's spelling of his name is inconsistent; he is called alternately "Abdadis" and "Ababdis," a confusion introduced in the original *Colored American Magazine* printing and one we might explain away as a misspelling. However, the alternate "Ababdis" spelling may have come to Hopkins by way of G. A. Hoskins's 1835 *Travels in Ethiopia*, mentioned earlier in this chapter. In it, Hoskins writes of "the Sheakh of the Ababdes, the tribe who provide camels to caravans and travellers for the journey between Assuan and Makkarif, the capital of Berber."[45] Contrary to John Lewis Burckhardt, author of 1819 *Travels in Nubia*, who, Hoskins writes, "speaks of the treachery of the Ababdes," Hoskins finds them "more grateful for kindness, more attached, more proud of their liberty, and tenacious of their character, and more disinterested, than any other of the Arab tribes."[46] He mentions also their practice of "occasionally sing[ing] to animate their camels," in which "one camel-driver sings a verse, then the others answer in chorus," which reminds Hoskins "of the Venetian gondoliers."[47] Hopkins lifts this account in her description of Ababdis's singing: "The singing reminded travellers of Venetian gondoliers. . . . There was generally a leading voice answered by a full chorus" (515). The Ababdes are also mentioned by Sir J. W. Dawson in his 1889 *Modern Science in Bible Lands*: in a chapter called "Egyptian Stones and Their Teaching," Dawson discusses a site at which flint flakes have been found that are "the work of the rude negroid tribes which, in ancient times, inhabited the region, and of whom the Ababdis of the Eastern side of the Nile are supposed to be descendants."[48] Edward Upham, in the notes to his 1824 *Rameses; An Egyptian Tale: With Historical Notes of the Era of the Pharaohs*, locates the Ababdes "between Higher Egypt, the Red Sea, the confines of Nubia, and Abyssinia," speaking both Arabic and "a language of their own, which [James] Bruce also pronounces to be the Geez or Ethiopic."[49]

Hopkins's naming of this character seems to have been influenced not only by the bilingual signification of the "Abdadis" spelling but also potentially by these descriptions of the Ababdes by nineteenth-century travel writers and archaeologists. In both cases, however, Hopkins seeks to underscore the liminality of the character through his name, whether as a bridge between Eastern and Western cultures or as a nomadic figure of literal transnationalism (i.e., crossing modern national borders of Egypt, Sudan, and Ethiopia). This typographical "error" succeeds in combining the features of both names that assert the character's role as mediator while simultaneously emphasizing the mystery and shadowiness surrounding him.

The Legend of Menelik

Ambiguous and amorphous—like the idea of Ethiopia behind Ethiopianist ideology—the Ethiopian royals imagined by Hopkins can fit anywhere. As Charlie Vance suggests to Ai when asked if Ai's dark skin would relegate him to second-class citizenship in the United States, "you could get there all right with your complexion in my country. We would simply label you 'Arab, Turk, Malay or Filipino,' and in that costume you'd slide along all right" (584). The costume would prove crucial. For example, the transformative "gorgeous robes of office" worn by the humble camel-driver Abdadis, who turns out to be a resident of Telassar, render him "almost unrecognizable" to Reuel (553). The actual king ruling Abyssinia at the turn of the century, Menelik II, was profiled in a December 1900 issue of the *Colored American Magazine* in a piece titled "Menelik, Emperor of Abyssinia" by S. E. F. C. C. Hamedoe, and the article was accompanied by two images showing him in his regal costume. One simple portrait shows him wearing a cross, but the other—an uncredited image from Gleichen's book, captioned in the *Colored American Magazine* as "Menelik Receiving the English Commissions"—shows him sitting on a platform under a canopy.[50] Hamedoe describes Menelik's attire in detail: "His dress is a long white muslin veil falling on the shoulders almost to his feet, bound to his forehead with green ribbons. He wears a velvet coat, trimmed with silver and the Legion of Honor and Grand Cordon of Catherine of Russia."[51]

Similarly, a photograph of Empress Taitu, reproduced from Gleichen's book and credited there to yet another source (*Une expédition avec le négous Ménélik: Vingt mois en Abyssinie*, by J.-G. Vanderheym), seems intended to display her striking regal costume and furnishings.[52] Although this photograph is not discussed in Hamedoe's essay, it is accompanied in Gleichen's book by a description of the luxurious surroundings pictured, recalling that "bright coloured carpets of French make covered the floor of the room, an immense gilt clock reared its length against one wall, and French Ornaments and curtains of dimity completed the furniture."[53]

FIGURE 2.1. "Reception of the Mission by Menelik," in *With the Mission to Menelik, 1897* by Count Edward Gleichen (London: Edward Arnold, 1898), facing p. 130.

Hamedoe's descriptions emphasize, as much as Gleichen's do, what he finds "curious" in the country's culture and its inhabitants' behaviors, and, indirectly, how the mystery shrouding the country—as "the traveler of today finds some parts forbidden, other parts accessible"[54]—will determine its availability as a locus of Ethiopianism. The subtitle of Hamedoe's article is "A direct descendant of Solomon the Great and the Queen of Sheba," which he promptly addresses in anticipation of the expected challenges to the statement: "The question arises as to the authority of this statement, and as the most ancient philosophers claim that it is impossible to cite ancient Abyssinian history, I shall not attempt it. Yet ancient and modern historians claim that the Negus is the direct descendant of this former union."[55] It is significant that Menelik's claimed inheritance is not simply genealogical and cultural but also biblical. As the living embodiment of biblical antiquity, Menelik was perfectly situated, from an external perspective, to be transformed into an already legendary figure (and Gleichen in fact calls his achievements "almost superhuman").[56] Apocryphal stories exist today about Menelik's alleged habit of eating pages from the Bible when he was ill for what he believed were its restorative properties. Rather than stepping outside of texts as Mira, Reuel, and Aunt Hannah do, Menelik is supposed to have attempted to take the writing into his body as if a textual sacrament and a physical incorporation of his biblical inheritance.

FIGURE 2.2. "Queen Taitu," in *With the Mission to Menelik, 1897* by Count Edward Gleichen (London: Edward Arnold, 1898), facing p. 146.

Menelik's mythical presence—even in his own day—is also noted by the original French source of the Empress Taitu photograph, which opens with an epistolary preface that remarks that, in Menelik, "there is something of the prophet . . . , of the mystic, and also of the modern man."[57] In conceiving of Reuel's double self, Hopkins must have known that the child of King Solomon and Queen of Sheba from whom Menelik descended was also named Menelik in the later Ethiopian tradition and, coincidentally, that Gleichen translates Menelik's name as "a second self."[58] Reuel's "hidden self" appears to have been modeled as much upon the modern-day king of Abyssinia as upon the ancient Ergamenes.

As I mentioned at the start of this chapter, Abyssinia's 1896 defeat of the Italians under Menelik had increased African American interest in the country. Hamedoe cites this event—"when the world was astounded by a Negro army . . . that humiliated one of the first powers of the world"—as the moment when this "almost unknown King" appeared on the world stage.[59] The humiliation noted by Hamedoe was a crucial aspect of the cultural interpretation of this event. Significantly, it appeared that the "Negro army" did not prove themselves merely equal to the Italian one but superior. Hopkins gestures toward the country's military strength in Dianthe's death scene, during which Dianthe is ushered into the Ethiopian royal line by an invisible pageant described as "a vast but viewless army"; even the dirgeful music accompanying the pageant's progress is said to be "of strong martial measure" (614). In addition to the Italian defeat, Menelik's role in consolidating Ethiopia contributed to his earning "the respect of the world by reversing what otherwise was deemed to be the natural order of white supremacy."[60] The *Colored American Magazine* profile emphasizes this resistance to white supremacy, describing Empress Taitu as a defiant pro-black heroine who "hates Europeans."[61] But Gleichen finds this attitude even more pronounced outside of the nobility. He writes that the ordinary Ethiopian "hates a white face, and is anxious to keep all Europeans out of the country."[62]

Because African American Ethiopianist discourse as it appeared in the *Colored American Magazine* and elsewhere depended in large part upon European accounts of Ethiopia (and both European and African American discourses upon classical sources), essays like Hamedoe's implicitly either confirmed or refuted the published impressions of the country that were already circulating at the turn of the century. Where Hamedoe sees virtue in the defiance and anti-European attitude of the Ethiopians, Gleichen, for example, sees foolish arrogance. The common people of Abyssinia, Gleichen writes, "imagin[e] that their victory has laid not only Italy, but the whole of Europe, at their feet, and their heads are proportionately elevated."[63] And, because these heads "have become considerably swollen with pride," they ludicrously believe that "political Missions to Menelik from European powers simply mean the bringing of tribute to the greatest sovereign in the world."[64] This attitude, of course, is disruptive from an imperialistic perspective, a perspective committed to the myth of progress that requires the Englishman to believe that he is bringing light to Africa. As Gleichen puts it, with some degree of astonishment, "we perhaps, who thought we were impressing the natives with the power and magnificence of Great Britain, were in their eyes merely an outward and visible sign of their own superiority!"[65] In spite of his people's nationalistic haughtiness that sometimes manifested as anti-European sentiment, Menelik was, according to Gleichen, "thoroughly alive to the necessity of keeping touch with European nations, if he wishes to be considered a civilised monarch" and "extraordinarily well-acquainted with what is going on in the world."[66] Gleichen's description of the empress takes pains to mention that much of her decor is French in origin, because he is determined to show the contradictions in the Ethiopians' Afrocentric position, even as he presents Empress Taitu's decor as evidence of her civilized and enlightened worldview.

The authority and respect accorded to the independent Ethiopian kingdom prompted Hopkins to ask, in a section of a series of pieces called "The Dark Races of the Twentieth Century" devoted to Abyssinians, why "the United States authorities maintain friendly relations with all independent black governments," as evidenced by a "treaty [that] has just been signed between the United States' government and 'Menelik II, by the Grace of God King of Kings of Ethiopia,'" all the while "dealing severely with its own Negro population."[67] She turns once again, as we have seen throughout this chapter, to the document—in this case, to a treaty with Abyssinia cited as textual proof of her own government's hypocrisy—in order to support her Ethiopianist argument. Hopkins does not, of course, mention that the respect given to Menelik and his court is never extended to the ordinary Ethiopian. In order to build bridges between Africans and African Americans, Hopkins urged African Americans to become "thoroughly familiar with the meagre details of Ethiopian history" and to develop "an international friendship with the Blacks of Africa" in order to "help forward the time of restoration,"[68] but these bridges, constructed through the *Colored American Magazine*'s imperial Ethiopianism, linked only to Ethiopian nobility. As a result, this confederation proposed by Hopkins could take unexpected forms; fraternity could be reconfigured as an unusual type of intraracial passing similar to the one Charlie Vance suggests to Ai. This type of passing required only the proper costume and linguistic facility, as we will see in the following chapter.

CHAPTER THREE

Fashioning the Imperial Self

Ah, Potentate! How greatly do I fear
(Knowing my Nordic brother and his way)
That, should that beard remove from off thy chin,

Thy rich dress change to occidental gear,
Some of those with thee might be heard to say,
"Now, who the hell let these damned niggers in?"

—P. J. WHITE JR., "VESTIS VIRUMQUE CANO: A SONNET ON AMERICAN OFFICIALS GREETING AN ETHIOPIAN POTENTATE"

IN HIS MEMOIR *The Big Sea*, Langston Hughes introduces a tailor, one of his companions on a transatlantic ship voyage to Africa, with, as Kenneth Warren writes, an "unmistakable air of ridicule." The tailor hopes to "teach the Africans to wear proper clothes, coats and pants" so that "they would be brought forward a long way toward the standards of our world." In this project, he is a failure; when Hughes encounters him again in Washington, D.C., a few years later, he admits "he had had no luck at all selling suits to Africans."[1]

The irony here is that, in the era of Jim Crow, reversing the costuming in the United States—importing African dress to a Western context—would permit African Americans to be "brought forward a long way toward the standards of our world," if these contemporary "standards" are those reinforced by the regimented and racist codes of segregation, as the exotic did not pose as many restrictions as the familiar. As Mary Church Terrell would argue in "What It Means to Be Colored in the Capital of the United States," African Americans were refused again and again from restaurants and hotels, but these restrictions often did not apply to "representatives of any other dark race." Terrell exploited this loophole in her unpublished story "Did Jeff Jackson Hear Caruso," as Elizabeth McHenry points out, by dressing a black character in a fez in an effort to pose as Turkish and gain admission to the opera: "In stories of light-skinned blacks who might pass as white or as 'foreigners,' Terrell discovered a fictional mechanism that enabled her to represent the absurdity of black-white relations, as well as the maneuvers to which African Americans resorted in order to gain basic access to the nation's institutions and services."[2] But these maneuvers did not even require interracial passing, as black foreigners were sometimes exempt from restrictions to which black Americans were subject.

That a fez is sufficient to transform a person from one to whom Jim Crow applies to one who has freedom of mobility illustrates not only the centrality of costume to the practice of passing but how costume was used specifically to ennoble in Orientalist ways, characterizing the relationship between Africans and African Americans as both one of affiliation (because identification could be as simple as donning an item of clothing) and one of difference (because the costume, seen as exotic, distinguishes the costume-wearer from those around him and from his previous identity). The paradox of Ethiopianist passing is that, rather than attempting to blend in, African Americans posing as Africans made themselves into spectacles, drawing the attention and scrutiny of those who would police their movements rather than deflecting it, throwing themselves into the public eye.

The visual representations of late nineteenth-century imperial Abyssinia in the British and U.S. media, particularly in photographs and illustrations of Tewodros and Menelik, presented potential intraracial passers with a formula for adopting a spectacular form of Ethiopianism. However, the pomp associated with Abyssinian imperial culture in situ would prove difficult to adopt convincingly. It would prove much more feasible for an Ethiopianist passer to present oneself as a Westernized royal, one with the ability to convey one's story in languages other than Amharic. When Tewodros's son arrived in Britain, accompanied by his flashy guardian Captain Speedy, the inventors of spectacular Ethiopianism had a viable example of what imperial Abyssinia in the West could look like. Rather than following in Tewodros's or Menelik's royal footsteps, they appear to have studied the well-documented lives of the young prince and his guardian, each of whom became spectacles for merging elements of the West with the splendor and formality of Abyssinian imperial culture.

Prince Alemayehu and Captain Speedy

One of the most recognizable Africans in the public eye internationally in the late nineteenth century was Prince Alemayehu of Abyssinia. Alemayehu, the son of Emperor Tewodros, was orphaned by his father's suicide at the conclusion of the 1867–68 Anglo-Abyssinian War and his mother's death from tuberculosis shortly thereafter. Oddly, he was taken by his father's adversary Sir Robert Napier and, ostensibly at his dying mother's request, placed under the care of the eccentric British explorer Captain Tristram Speedy. Speedy transported the young prince to the Isle of Wight and served as his guardian until he was enrolled in Cheltenham College a few years later, followed by stints at Rugby and Sandhurst. Not long after their arrival in 1868, Alemayehu and Speedy sat for photographic portraits by Cornelius Jabez Hughes, frequent photographer of Queen Victoria and other aristocratic figures, and by Julia Margaret Cameron, among others.

Between 1868 and his tragic death from pleurisy at the age of eighteen or nineteen in 1879, Alemayehu's likeness was captured in photographs, paintings, sketches, busts, miniatures, and enamel on porcelain by numerous artists. In a personal reminiscence titled *Anecdotes of Alamayu: The Late King Theodore's Son*, an author identified only as "C. C." first apologizes for exposing personal information about the prince but follows this apology by insisting that he "can scarcely be considered as a private individual: rather must he be regarded as somewhat of public property."[3] It is the rare image of Alemayehu that does not convey profound sadness and detachment. He is often described as fearful, anxious, and sensitive. He is a romantic and spectacular figure, displaced in unending exile, steeped in nostalgia and obsolescence, but also an example of successful assimilation of the exotic.

Requiring long sitting times, the vast majority of studio portraits in the early days of photography were staged in a manner that looks artificial and stilted to a contemporary eye, with the sitters often looking wistful. Cameron's series exaggerates the artifice of her poses by having her subjects dress in traditional Abyssinian clothes. With his fur coat and headgear, Speedy's elaborate dress looks more "exotic" than Alemayehu's. For a British public familiar with Thomas Phillips's c. 1813 portrait of Lord Byron in Albanian dress, Captain Speedy cuts a similarly romantic figure in his Abyssinian costume.

But Speedy's use of Abyssinian costuming was not limited to the photographer's studio. The spectacle Speedy invited offended some, such as

FIGURE 3.1. Julia Margaret Cameron, photographic print of Prince Alemayehu and Captain Speedy, late nineteenth century [1868]. © The Trustees of the British Museum.

Sir William Jervois, governor of the Straits Settlements, who wrote in an 1876 letter to Mr. Meade of the Colonial Office that Speedy "has apparently a delight in dressing himself in a gorgeous leopard skin, with a grand turban on his head, and still further exciting the curiosity of the natives by playing on the bagpipes, an instrument on which he performs with much facility."[4] He was said to be "a very unusual character with a great fondness for 'dressing up.'"[5] Even his name was translated to an Amharic one, Basha Felika, a sort of Abyssinian alter ego created by Tewodros. According to Speedy, the emperor, unable to pronounce his name, "determined to call me 'Fellika' which signifies in Amharic booth [*sic*] swift and flashing—the double meaning being appropriate both to my name and to the reflection from my spectacles, a glint of which had at the moment caught his eye."[6]

Speedy's assumption of Abyssinian costuming was far from casual. In an 1898 article titled "Abyssinia and Its People," he displayed his awareness of the semiotics of Abyssinian dress. As an example of "the dramatic habit of the Abyssinians of expressing their feelings by the way in which they wear their clothes," which he calls "unique and artistic," Speedy cites the practice in legal suits of knotting one's shawl, displaying it for the judge, and "laying a hand expressively on the knot [to] wager that he is speaking the truth." In addition, Speedy continues:

> To express scorn a man will take the end of the toga, or "shammah," and raise it to his face, drawing it lightly across his nose just below the eyes, and turn at the same moment with an indignant and haughty gesture from his opponent. The superiority of a chief when conversing with his inferiors in rank is shown by throwing the shammah over both shoulders, crossing it over the left, thereby indicating that no hand of friendship is to be offered. Equality is indicated by the shammah being thrown over the left arm only, leaving the right hand free to greet an acquaintance. Not infrequently when pleading his cause the accused, at the commencement of a trial, will draw his shammah before his face and, with expressions of humility and shame, state his defense, whether guilty or not; at the same time he will whisk one end of it into the semblance of a rope, and, passing it round his neck, exclaim: "Hang me, if I deserve it," or twisting it into the likeness of a sword, say: "Behead me, if I speak falsely," then, allowing it to fall to the ground, he will drop on his knee, adding: "But what I ask is justice."[7]

The theatricality and expressiveness Speedy associated with Abyssinian dress contributed to his exploitation of it in his public appearances. After returning to Britain, he lectured on the topic of Abyssinia while wearing variations on the national costume, dressing "successively as an Ethiopian priest, and [*sic*] ordinary Ethiopian 'citizen,' or peasant, and an Ethiopian nobleman."[8] As Richard Pankhurst writes, "One newspaper enthusiastically observed that his 'extraordinary height' appeared 'magnified' when he spoke in the 'voluminous and gorgeous' costume of an Ethiopian cleric, that his 'graceful manipulation' of the toga of an Ethiopian was 'something worth seeing.'"[9] Speedy felt no qualms about adopting the sartorial splendor of various manners of Ethiopian dress.

As for Alemayehu, his extraordinary arrival in England led many to wonder how he would "translate" into English culture. Although Speedy was his surrogate parent, he was more accurately a ward of the state, and it was left to the state to decide his future. As the *Brooklyn Daily Eagle* asked, "The Queen, having captured the Abyssinian curiosity, the question now is what will she do with him?"[10] One of the possibilities raised was to educate him at English schools before repatriating him to Abyssinia "to rule it in the interest of Great Britain" while at the same time benefiting Abyssinia by crowning "this English-speaking and cultivated young prince."[11] Another option was to train him to serve Britain as an army officer in India. In any case, Alemayehu's death at such a young age prevented any of these plans from coming to fruition.

Although Cameron's photographs pose Alemayehu in Abyssinian clothes, Jabez Hughes and other photographers sometimes photographed Alemayehu in English dress. Taken at Hughes's studio, an early portrait of an uncharacteristically cheerful Alemayehu pictures him in an American suit and a hat bearing the word "Urgent" on its band, presumably a reference to the HMS *Urgent* on which he traveled to England. Ironically, appearing in Western clothes rendered Alemayehu even more of a spectacle, as viewers delighted in the contrast between his ethnic identity and his adopted dress. For example, the *Brooklyn Daily Eagle* reported, with apparent surprise, that Alemayehu "wears knickerbockers and eats ices like any Briton."[12] Similarly, when Speedy and Alemayehu stopped in Suez on the way from Abyssinia to England to buy new clothes, one of their companions, the war artist William Simpson, noted that he "saw [Alemayehu] for the first time in elastic-side boots," which he deemed a "curious thing for a young savage."[13] Even before his arrival in Suez, the *Times* wrote that he had "taken very kindly to English customs, wearing a sailor's dress, of which he is evidently very proud, and handling a knife and fork at the dinner table with as much gravity and decorum as if he had been to the manner born."[14]

FIGURE 3.2. Jabez Hughes studio, carte-de-visite of Prince Alemayehu, 1868 (possibly photographed by Capt. Tristram C. S. Speedy). © The Trustees of the British Museum.

In fact, his apparently painful enforced separation from Speedy—against Queen Victoria's wishes—was part of a determined effort to graft Englishness successfully onto Alemayehu. On removing Alemayehu from Speedy's care, Robert Lowe, the Chancellor of the Exchequer, wrote to Gladstone that, while Speedy served overseas, the prince should be placed under the care of the headmaster of Cheltenham College rather than grow up in India and Malaysia. He worried about the soundness of an "Oriental education in an Oriental country" for this quasi-Oriental boy and, echoing the aforementioned *Brooklyn Daily Eagle* article, wrote, "it is possible that a day may come when the boy may have some part to play in Abyssinia and we should be inexcusable if we neglected even the remote chance of importing there some faint sprinkling of European culture."[15] Sir Henry Bartle Frere also suggested in 1876 that Alemayehu may become king of Abyssinia in the future, to which Sir Thomas Biddulph (Keeper of the Privy Purse), who observed that Alemayehu was "as gentle a child as is possible to see and appears to have little trace of his savage origin," wrote to Queen Victoria that "he had never heard anything more preposterous, that the boy was totally unsuited for such a position and had no wish to return to Abyssinia; he had quite forgotten his own language and had no wish to be anything but English."[16]

The queen, however, apparently never truly believed that Alemayehu had assimilated completely into English culture. Upon learning of Alemayehu's death, a "very grieved and shocked" Queen Victoria wrote in her diary, "All alone in a strange country, without seeing a person or relative belonging to him, so young and so good, but for him one cannot repine. His was no happy life, full of difficulties of every kind, and he was so sensitive, thinking that people stared at him because of his colour, that I fear he would never have been happy." Although she never received it, a letter to Queen Victoria sent from Alemayehu's grandmother nine years earlier had begged her to "look after him," believing that although "God deprived him of his father [and] his mother, He gave him you [instead]."[17] Given his wandering childhood, however, he appears to have never had a stable surrogate parent. He became a symbol of alienation and dislocation.

I give this extended anecdote of Alemayehu's brief life in England as a proper English boy, along with the reciprocal Abyssinian costuming of Speedy, as a means of framing this chapter's incidences of aristocratic imposture to follow. The theatricalized demonstrations of Abyssinian costume for which Speedy became known helped script the behaviors of those who hoped to similarly transform through Abyssinian dress. In addition, as restricted as Alemayehu's mobility was, others adopted Ethiopian royal identities in order to exploit an increased ease of travel, seeking admission to places they normally would not be allowed. As an international spectacle whose every move was tracked in the British and American press, who was forced to live the life of a "little captive prince" as if in retribution for his father's imprisonment of the British captives, Alemayehu provided a familiar image of Ethiopian monarchy upon which these imposters signified.[18] Through their impressions of royalty, they perform popular Orientalist conceptions of the Abyssinian imperial character.

Virginia Woolf's Abyssinian Blackface

The most notorious impersonation of an Abyssinian prince was not driven, in a strict sense, by Ethiopianism. A generation after Julia Margaret Cameron asked the young prince and his guardian to sit for photographs, Cameron's great-niece Virginia Woolf, seemingly inspired by those pictures, would take part in a practical joke through which she unintentionally inserted herself into international affairs. In a preface to *Victorian Photographs of Famous Men and Fair Women*, a 1926 collection of Cameron's photography, Woolf remarks upon the transformations of costuming that frequently took place at Cameron's home as she prepared for her work: "Boatmen were turned into King Arthur; village girls into Queen Guenevere."[19] The staged images of Alemayehu and Speedy—in concert, perhaps, with reports of a memorable assembly of Menelik's representatives who visited London for the 1902 coronation of King Edward VII—probably informed Woolf's sense of how to stage Abyssinian imperial culture.

In 1910, just as human character was changing, Woolf changed herself in order to participate in what became known as the infamous Dreadnought hoax. She, her brother Adrian Stephen, the artist Duncan Grant, and others disguised themselves in blackface and elaborate robes as Abyssinian princes and received a royal welcome onboard the British battleship HMS *Dreadnought*. Not only did they deceive the naval officers onboard the *Dreadnought*, Woolf seemed to believe that all of the passersby on the street assumed that they were true Abyssinians.

Most critics addressing this incident have seen it as broadly subversive and satirical, as the pranksters' overtly theatrical "attempt at impersonation was deliberately and nonchalantly amateurish."[20] However, the details surrounding their costuming suggest the opposite. With the help of theatrical costumer Willy Clarkson, Woolf and her accomplices were attired so convincingly that Clarkson said "when hed [*sic*] done with us, not even the Emperor himself would know the differcn [*sic*]."[21] This was no laidback and impromptu practical joke; an article in the *Aberdeen Journal* said that the ringleader of the pranksters "was absolutely reckless in his expenditure," buying £500 of jewels when the imitation jewelry proved unconvincing and "demand[ing] absolute accuracy in make-up" from the costumers.[22]

This attention to appearance extended to the care taken in conducting themselves in a manner supposedly in keeping with Abyssinian imperial culture. The fairly recent memory of Alemayehu's presence in Britain shaped Woolf's impressions of behavior expected of an Abyssinian prince. She bows but she does not smile, because "native princes should be very severe and dignified."[23] When interviewed by the *Western Gazette*, Woolf (identified as "the young lady who shared in the hoax") said that she worked hard "to preserve [her] Oriental stolidity of countenance" during the experience.[24] Although her story involves many comical close calls with exposure and bungling—worrying about fake beards that nearly detach; speaking not Amharic but a weird amalgam of Latin, Swahili, and nonsense, and sometimes resorting simply to "Bunga, bunga"—it is clear that she thinks her impersonation approximates the real thing and that she sees her disappearance into the Abyssinian character along the same lines as did her great-aunt's photographic subject, Captain Speedy.

Once exposed, the outrageous Dreadnought hoax gained notice in newspapers across the United States and Britain, and even throughout Africa. A theatrical production went so far as to incorporate a reference to the event into its performances:

> A roar of laughter was raised at the Weymouth Pavilion Theatre on Monday night in the course of a variety entertainment, when one of the comedians worked into one of his songs the following, to the tune of "The girl he left behind him":
>
> I've just been on a Dreadnought ship;
> Some thought me a costermonger;
> Said I, "I'm an Abyssinian Prince,"
> And I shouted "Bunga, bunga!"[25]

The Dreadnought hoax likely captured the imagination of the writers and performers in this variety show because the theatricality of the hoax itself mirrored their own escapades; it was, in essence, a variety show sketch taken offstage. Woolf christened herself "Prince Mendax," a name suitably burlesque. Anyone with rudimentary familiarity with Latin might have realized that she was not genuinely trying to hide the deception, despite the enormous expense, preparation, and attention to comportment. As Elisa deCourcy points out, the photograph of the Abyssinian imposters that circulated in the press was "akin to a curtain-call line up . . . , impl[ying] to the newspaper readers the conclusion of a performance" and gesturing toward "something obviously, rather than subtly, theatrical and thus faux about the assembled cast's 'royal' status."[26] As elaborate and detailed as their costumes and behaviors were, their goal was to render themselves public spectacles along their route to the ship. Woolf remarks that, as they boarded their first-class train car, "everybody took us seriously. . . . I saw people staring very respectfully at us."[27] Upon boarding the train again after the hoax was concluded, she notes the cumulative effect of their warm reception—both by the navy and by passersby—upon the imposters' own sense of authentic representation: "this time we carried ourselves like princes ind eeed [*sic*]. The people stared. A faint cheer was raised. And we lined up outside teh [*sic*] carriage door and bowed deeply, to the citizens of Weymouth."[28] An Orientalist bow, to be sure, but one that also anticipates the curtain-call postures deCourcy recognizes in the staged photograph of the imposters.

But to argue that the imposters' "perceived triumph in their masquerade was not so much located in their closeness to a legitimate Abyssinian royal typecast but indeed, their distance from one," as deCourcy does, presumes that the imposters understood the culture of Abyssinian royalty itself to be distinct from an ornately wrought public spectacle.[29] Woolf's 1940 speech about her participation in the Dreadnought hoax concludes smugly with the claim that the "real Emperor of Abyssinia," during a visit to London immediately following the hoax, "complained that wherever he went in the street boys ran after him calling out Bunga Bunga."[30] As Emperor Menelik was gravely ill at this time, it is possible Woolf has in mind instead the 1911 delegation who attended the coronation of King George V, sent by Lij Iyasu. In any case, just as Prince Mendax's reception had been informed by the antecedents of Alemayehu and the 1902 retinue attending King Edward VII's coronation, the public's reception of actual Abyssinian noblemen in 1911 was likely informed by the earlier response to Prince Mendax and his associates, whether or not the noblemen were taunted by jeers of "Bunga, Bunga."

Panthea Reid argues that Woolf "chose the Abyssinian masquerade as an expression of solidarity" or "political commentary" prompted by her own personal identification with Alemayehu and by her father's vocal protests against the Anglo-Abyssinian War in the press, respectively.[31] According to Reid, Woolf and her accomplices were so committed to the idea of presenting themselves as Abyssinian princes in particular that they rescheduled the hoax for a time when an Amharic-speaking officer was not onboard the ship. Although Reid's view of Woolf's intentions is more generous than mine—it is difficult to ignore the mockery she makes of Abyssinian imperial culture—Woolf's desire to represent Abyssinianness specifically is indisputable.

Spectacular Ethiopianism

Woolf's impersonation was spectacular, and it expresses a fascination (and possibly sympathy) with imperial Abyssinia, but it was not Ethiopianist. Sharing elements with Woolf's impersonation but presenting an unmistakably Ethiopianist perspective was the extended hoax perpetrated by Isaac Brown, a Jamaican man who successfully passed himself off as Emperor Menelik's nephew at the turn of the century. As Robert A. Hill recounts in a fascinating essay, he was not unique but a "member of *Æthiopis vagantes*, . . . a group of wandering 'Ethiopians,' consisting largely of West Indians, who, along with a smattering of African Americans and continental Africans, traversed the Atlantic world promoting their special 'Ethiopian' lineage and pedigree."[32] Like Woolf's Prince Mendax persona, Brown did not attempt to hide entirely the artifice of his assumed identity. One of his pseudonyms, Makaroo, "is an Arabic word," Hill points out, "deriving from the root *makara* (they cheated; they deceived; they planned)."[33] Yet his trickster-like impersonations cannot be interpreted as mere larks; he was driven by ostensible self-interest, admittedly, but through a clearly articulated Ethiopianist ideology.

It is instructive to trace the development and refinement of Brown's career as an Ethiopian imposter. The earliest of his appearances cited by Hill dates from 1904, when Brown posed as a prince of Ceylon in Jamaica. Within a week he was found out, predictably after people who knew him "when he wore ordinary clothes" identified him. Realizing the necessity of costume, Brown later tricks a tailor into helping him accomplish his deception, telling him that "if he could only get a suit of clothes covered with gold tape and brass buttons he would make the one who aided him immensely wealthy when he heard from father."[34] (Needless to say, this reward never materialized.) As in the cases of Woolf and Speedy, the sartorial spectacle is essential to Brown's performance of imperial culture, but the Prince of Ceylon incident cannot yet be considered properly Ethiopianist. As Hill points out, Brown identified variously as royalty from West Africa, North Africa, Zululand, Ceylon, and so forth, but it was through his Abyssinian royal identity that he was able to achieve his Ethiopianist goals. Recognizing that the nation had not been colonized, Brown deduced that the Abyssinian royal he impersonated would have access to the land and wealth necessary to dupe his victims.

A December 1907 *New York Times* article reported the efforts of Brown, posing at the time as a Prince Ludwig Menelek of Ethiopia, to sell 150,000 acres of Abyssinian land to a wealthy American capitalist. Rather than

Europeans, who are "not altogether disinterested," an American investor, he argued, would not carry the same threat of "endangering the safety of his uncle's throne." Linking himself to Menelik but claiming to be more far-seeing, Brown credits Menelik with being "patriotic [and] progressive, but [he] lacks the co-operation of a sufficient number of similarly enlightened men to work out the ambitious plans he cherishes for the regeneration of Abyssinia."

Two years later, Brown no longer targets wealthy American capitalists but African Americans of all classes. In a 1909 letter published years later in a 1935 issue of the *Chicago Defender*, the newly renamed Prince Johannes (for the first time using a convincing Ethiopian name) offers to "give six million acres of land to all the Colored people that will come home" if only he can secure $5,000 to get started, with the assurance that contributors will get a return on their investments ("Ethiopia is too rich"). Presenting the opportunity as an Ethiopianist project, he says, "If you people will cooperate with us, in five years we can put all the Europeans out of Africa" and that "this plan must be kept private by all colored people."[35] Whether or not Brown imagined his appeal to the public to have been Ethiopianist all along, his project becomes more explicitly so over time. Even in his early imposture as a prince of Ceylon in 1904, he is quoted as desiring "to address the black people this evening on how to ameliorate their present condition," but the full-fledged Ethiopianist plan proposed in the 1909 letter both signals the future exaltation of black people intrinsic to Ethiopianist ideology and summons them to their homeland.

As a representative of Abyssinian imperial culture, Brown imagined himself as a tether connecting the black peoples of the world to their native land; although supposedly rooted in Abyssinia, he was a worldly figure who saw himself as the country's ambassador. As if inspired by the translation of Alemayehu's name—"I have seen the world"—Brown says in a 1908 article, posing as "Prince Hendrix Hull Polawharoo, crown prince of Abyssinia and the destined successor to Menelik," "A prince should know the world and should know languages." He emphasizes his worldliness, claiming that he has left Abyssinia to travel internationally on two occasions, the first being coincidentally in 1896, the year of the Battle of Adwa. Interestingly, Brown repeatedly depicts Menelik as insular and parochial—"my first cousin, does not like me to go about, but I do"—contrary to contemporaneous accounts that emphasize Menelik's openness and desire to engage the rest of the world.[36]

As Hill writes, "We do not have to choose between the imposter as prodigy and the imposter as deceiver"; instead we can consider the imposter to be "a political actor who performs important work."[37] This is especially clear in the case of Prince Joseph Emanuel Blayechettai, another such imposter whose political work involved traveling the United States as a successful lecturer at churches and colleges, and who in the 1920s published two booklets, *The Pen of an African* and *The Hidden Mystery of Ethiopia*. He was even more persistent than Brown in his promotion of Ethiopianism. An article printed in the *Chicago Defender*, credited to the *El Paso Times*, introduces Blayechettai as a student of "foreign lands with a view to assisting in the restoration of his people to the position they once held in world affairs." In other words, the abstract goal of Ethiopianism—restoration—is here made concrete by a supposed future ruler. Interviewed by the journalist, Blayechettai turns on a rushing stream of Ethiopianism: "'They taught the Chaldeans astronomy,' he declared. 'The Ethiopians were the architects who measured the space and laid the foundations of the pyramids and put the finishing touches on the face of the Sphinx.'" He concludes with the following prophecy: "Ethiopia shall be rebuilt. Her marble pillars shall be repolished and reset and the foundations upon which they once stood shall be strengthened with the gospel of the Son of God."[38]

Blayechettai claimed to be the kidnapped son of a king of Tigre, an Ethiopian province. Seemingly borrowing from Alemayehu's story of British adoption, he claims to have been rescued from Ethiopia as a child due to a precarious situation involving royal succession and "taken to London and educated by an English nobleman, spending eight years in Oxford."[39] In one iteration of his story, Blayechettai claims to be a grandson of Menelik's and says he "fled to the forests and lived the wild life of a native to escape cruel treatment from an aunt."[40] Alternate versions of his personal history claim that he was kidnapped by "the Gallas [*sic*] tribe" (although the caption to the frontispiece of *The Pen of an African* says that he is of the "Frank-Galla tribe") or "the Dervishes tribe" and that a "Methodist missionary in Abyssinia saw promise in the lad, who was sent to England."[41] In a brief letter to the editors of the *California Eagle*—written in response to a challenge submitted by a skeptical former president of the Los Angeles Universal Negro Improvement Association (UNIA) titled "L.A. Man Seeks Truth"—Blayechettai defended himself, stating, "When the white man took me away from Abysinnia [*sic*], I was visiting the Father of Ras Tapari [*sic*] in Harrar and the day of our departure I was told by the white man that my mother was the sister of King Menelik."[42] He insisted that he was "not frauding anyone but am living as a respectable Christian Gentleman."[43]

Before being singled out by "the white man," however, Blayechettai was first identified as exceptional by a fellow Abyssinian. He introduces his tale with the familiar trope of the royal mark, as seen in Pauline Hopkins's *Of One Blood*. The *Chicago Defender* interview mentions the miraculous identification of the kidnapped orphan by a passerby:

> On the morning of May 6, 1893, I was sitting in front of a little wooden house, covered with straw, when a priest from Haddis Hababa passed. He stopped, and when I drew near him he saw that I had a mark on my left hand which identifies me as belonging to royalty. He questioned me and then took me to Haddis, where we met a white missionary, Sir H. Hamilton of England. The priest turned me over to him, and he took me to England, where I resided with him for three years.[44]

Unlike Reuel's mark in *Of One Blood*, which indicates a hidden inheritance, Blayechettai's mark identifies him as having once actively participated in a noble community. His being recognized as such activates an individualized version of the restoration narrative that is part and parcel of Ethiopianism. The *Chicago Defender*'s interest in Blayechettai's story is somewhat ironic, given the newspaper's criticism a few years earlier of an event involving another self-identified Abyssinian prince: the Star Order of Ethiopia demonstration in 1920, addressed in this book's introduction. In both cases, the Abyssinian princes filtered personal narratives of regality through abstract Ethiopianist ideologies, but Blayechettai's autobiography allowed the newspaper to present a restrained, conservative, and scholarly perspective that saw value in what the Western world could teach Africa. Like many Ethiopianist imposters, he claimed to speak over a dozen languages and was said to be a well-traveled "man of wide experience and broad education"; according to reports, he was "pursuing courses in philosophy and journalism at Harvard university" in 1928, but Harvard University Archives has no record of his attendance.[45]

Unsurprisingly, critics and historians such as Dennis Hickey, Kenneth C. Wylie, and Stephen Howe cast doubt on his story of his past—as Howe points out, it is difficult to believe that an Ethiopian would preach for the conversion of his countrymen to Christianity when Ethiopia's Christian history was integral to its mythology—but Blayechettai appears to have succeeded in convincing his audiences of his invented identity. E. D. Cannady, for instance, publisher of the *Portland (OR) Advocate*, hosted a "tea for Prince and Princess Blayechettai of Abyssinia" on 21 November 1925, which was duly reported in his newspaper, and *The Pen of an African* is prefaced by dozens of testimonials from ministers, university officials, and newspapers singing his praises, one of which stated that he would be returning to Abyssinia in May 1927. We even find a newspaper fragment advertising a lecture by Blayechettai among the Du Bois Papers at the University of Massachusetts–Amherst.

As Blayechettai reportedly said in one of his lectures, "that what a man thinks he is, that he will be."[46] Although he intended with his statement to argue for the unrecognized potential of African Americans in the United States, he gestures toward his own successful reinvention, as he also does slyly in the opening sentence of the introduction to *The Pen of an African*: "Princes are coming out of every hill and every plain." To describe the awakening of Africa prompted by the coming of Christianity, he writes that "the empire of disobedience is shaking off the old Coat, and dressing up herself in the new." This new coat, however, is only a return to an originary sartorial aristocracy, as he argues that the African peoples "once weaved into beauty the royal robes of kings, queens and princes."[47]

So well did Blayechettai play the role of the refined Westernized African that the press could not help but picture him costumed as the most celebrated black character on the stage. In a newspaper article quoted by Blayechettai in one of his pamphlets, the *Monrovia (CA) Daily News* wrote, "While the Prince has many of the features familiar to us as associated with the Ethiopian race, he is a stalwart, broad-shouldered, striking figure with strong face which reminds one of the stage figure of Shakespeare's Othello, the Moor of Venice. One could easily imagine him as a regal character when arrayed in the barbaric habiliments of his people."[48] The "barbaric habiliments," a required aspect of the mobility afforded by Ethiopianist passing, are readily transported by the viewing public into the realm of the fabulous—whether imagined as Shakespearean, classical, biblical, or otherwise—even when they are not actually viewed. I have come across no clear evidence that Blayechettai dressed in Abyssinian clothes for his public appearances, but his self-presentation as Ethiopian royalty apparently prompted his audiences to imagine the implicit spectacle.

Similarly, Brown refrained from dressing in Abyssinian clothes, or even, as Woolf did, "exotic" clothes intended to read as Abyssinian. Commenting upon a photograph accompanying Brown's 1909 letter printed in the *Chicago Defender*, Hill claims that his clothing "suggests that he was anything but Ethiopian."[49] Earlier articles appearing between 1904 and 1907, all cited by Hill, variously describe Brown as follows: a "tall, well-groomed, frock-coated, silk-hatted colored gentleman," "in tall hat and fashionable cut clothes," "arrayed in a tweed frock coat, tall black beaver and black kid gloves, and carrying a formidable looking stick."[50] The strategy he employed to convey nobility depended largely upon elements of foppishness. Although one article observes that he "was wearing a miniature of some order on his right breast," rarely are there references to specific items of clothing or accessories indicating royalty.[51] However, like Blayechettai, Brown relied upon the royal mark trope when his usual indicators of nobility were unavailable. When deceiving a tailor into making him a suit of clothes, as I mentioned earlier, he "gave as proof of his identity a tattooed chicken on the back of his neck," which was all that was needed for the tailor to "f[a]ll for his line of heated atmosphere."[52]

In citing Natalie Zemon Davis on imposture, Hill writes that "the Ethiopian prince was nothing if not prodigious in the sense of the strange, the marvelous, the bizarre."[53] Hill finds evidence of this prodigiousness in his multilingualism and his worldliness but neglects to mention one of the most notable physical proofs of the Ethiopian prince's prodigiousness: the royal mark. Inscribing their bodies with nobility, Brown and Blayechettai incorporated themselves into a long-standing mythology. According to Marc Bloch, literary and historical sources dating at least as far back as the medieval period describe heirs to various European kingdoms as bearing some royal mark: "a skin-blemish or *naevus* in the form of a cross," or fleur-de-lis, or sword, and so on, that serves as infallible "proof of royal blood, a certain pledge of future accession to the throne."[54] Although Bloch admits that "the idea of a royal or racial sign would seem to belong to nearly all periods and countries," having been "born spontaneously in different civilizations, from similar ideas concerning the miraculous character of certain lines, in particular those from which the rulers of a nation were descended," it is likely that Brown and Blayechettai realized the expediency of the royal mark through exposure to European, rather than African, mythologies.[55]

Ironically, regal identity was in actuality much more fluid in Abyssinia, as we have seen in the case of Emperor Tewodros, whose mother sold *kosso* (a remedy for tapeworm) to support her family after the death of her husband. To quote Teshale Tibebu:

> Noble status was a free-floating status in which anybody was a potential candidate for membership. Noble status was not hereditary. . . . A person like Emperor Tewodros II, coming from a humble background, could seize hold of the throne by simply *claiming* to descend from an imperial line. There was no need to "verify" the claim since it was might that secured right to the throne.[56]

Ethiopia's national epic, too—the *Kebra Nagast*—was used in order to substantiate claims to the throne. In other words, one could argue that manufacturing a claim to the throne, as Brown and Blayechettai did, was not conceptually at variance with actual practice in Abyssinia.

In its ability to provide increased access and mobility, allowing one to transcend the limits of Jim Crow, the invented Ethiopian royal mark is the inverse of the racial sign (for example, the myth of the blue fingernail half-moon discussed by Werner Sollors in *Neither Black Nor White Yet Both: Thematic Explorations of Interracial Literature* [1997], a supposed giveaway of black ancestry in those who are passing for white). Displaying one's royal mark delivers one from one's existing circumstances, authenticating a personal narrative that would otherwise seem fantastic. It is a physical embellishment that goes beyond the clothes or jewels one wears, locating noble ornament in the body itself.

When Captain Speedy was traveling on his honeymoon, the author of *Anecdotes of Alamayu* hosted Alemayehu in his guardian's absence with "pleasure, mingled in no small degree with wonder." Observing the boy, he "fe[lt] that it was a page of wonderful romance, of which it might truly be said, 'Truth is stranger than fiction.'"[57] The deceptive stories invented by Blayechettai, Brown, and Woolf were believed because imperial Abyssinia, following the tragic life of Alemayehu, never ceased to be a "wonderful romance" in the West. The resulting popular phenomenon of the Ethiopian royal imposter and, as we will see in the following chapter, the transformations sought by mariner Harry Foster Dean and banker William Henry Ellis in their attempts to found Ethiopian empires are two sides of the same coin.

CHAPTER FOUR

Imperial Embellishment

Why gazeth thou?
*See thou not that I am of Etheopean [*sic*] lineage?*

—HARRY DEAN, UNTITLED POEM

ALTHOUGH ISAAC BROWN and Joseph Emanuel Blayechettai, presumably motivated by relatively modest personal gain, lacked the ambition to actualize the power of imperium, two other men—Harry Foster Dean and William Henry Ellis—did strive in earnest to found Ethiopian empires of their own. Like the numerous Ethiopian royal imposters who emerged early in the twentieth century, Dean and Ellis depended upon illusory and mercurial self-definition to fuel their imperial dreams. However, while the Ethiopianist imposters constructed imperial selves who were exiled royal ambassadors, the personal stories of imperial Ethiopianism created by Dean and Ellis were only the first steps toward claiming genuine empires in Africa. Their narratives—their yarns—weave tales of men who believed that inventive self-presentation was the key to becoming a self-made emperor.

Harry Foster Dean, author (with Sterling North) of *The Pedro Gorino: The Adventures of a Negro Sea-Captain in Africa and on the Seven Seas in His Attempts to Found an Ethiopian Empire* (1929), begins his maritime adventure with the grandiose aspiration to single-handedly found a black empire in Africa, one that would extend from South Africa and include contemporary Lesotho and Mozambique—with no mention of Abyssinia. "To Dean," according to North, "all of Africa was 'Ethiopia,' and every black man an 'Ethiopian,'" and Dean made no secret of his plan to reclaim it.[1] His power was considered such a threat that one of the major British participants in the Scramble for Africa allegedly called him "the most dangerous 'negro' in the world."[2] However, as with Brown's and Blayechettai's stories, the suspicion of fabrication taints Dean's text, particularly when it comes to his links to imperial power.

The autobiographical *Pedro Gorino* follows Dean's Ethiopianist journey toward the restoration of an empire in Africa. His special fate, authorizing him to do so as he sees it, is preordained by a familial inheritance: he counts Paul Cuffee among his ancestors, and boasts that he can trace his lineage directly to Africa on both sides of his family. In his youth, he leaves the comfort of a black middle-class household in Philadelphia in order to join the crew of his uncle's ship and circumnavigate the globe. It is on this trip that he first articulates his fantasy of a maritime solution to Ethiopia's diminished status. Upon hearing a story from his uncle about a Dutch sea captain's deception of an African king in order to kidnap the community's boys and girls, thus sparking the transatlantic slave trade with his quick escape by sea, the young Dean decides he would "some day build a fleet for the Ethiopian race and thus help them to free themselves from bondage" (56). Years later, he buys his own ship—his beloved *Pedro Gorino*—with an eye to "instigate a movement to rehabilitate Africa and found such an Ethiopian Empire as the world has never seen" (67). He comes close to succeeding on several occasions but is thwarted in the end by the clandestine efforts of African colonial governments that sabotage his project. Dean concludes his story in Madeira, dejected, having lost his ship and all of the wealth he had amassed.

John Cullen Gruesser refutes as spurious Dean's claim to be the descendent of Cuffee, an assertion that I would argue is strengthened by the fact that Dean wrote an article years before writing *The Pedro Gorino* in which he recounts the story of McKinnon Paige (spelled here "McKennon Page") and Said Kafu, and the role of Paul Cuffee in African emigration, without once mentioning any connection to his ancestry.[3] Even Dean's contemporaries, including W. E. B. Du Bois, expressed skepticism about various aspects of his account. Just as Du Bois wrote of Garvey that "dream, fact, fancy, wish, were all so blurred in his thinking that neither he himself nor his hearers could clearly or easily extricate them," so, too, does he believe of Dean that "perhaps his dream goes in some respects beyond the facts."[4] *Time* magazine wondered if the book, like *Trader Horn*, was "another dubious 'autobiography.'"[5] Prolific writer and mariner Charles J. Finger claimed that he knew *The Pedro Gorino* was a "false adventure book" when he read "some silly statement about how a ship had tried to turn the corner at the Horn three times (it had to be the magic three)."[6] The little scholarship that has been written about Dean's autobiography tends to revolve around its authenticity and the degree to which Dean embellishes his stories. The word "embellish" emerges again and again in discussions of *The Pedro Gorino*, and it is as if the literal embellishments adopted by the imposters discussed in the previous chapter—in the form of decorative costumes or bodily markings signaling their African nobility—now figuratively adorn Dean's tale to facilitate his passing. The narration itself becomes costume. As the *Time* reviewer writes, *The Pedro Gorino* appears to be decorated with a "dark embroidery."[7] Arthur A. Schomburg, in the same vein, calls the narrative "a piece of lace."[8]

"Some Dark Incantation"

It is unsurprising that readers have doubted Dean's claims. In fact, Dean anticipates that there will be challenges to the truth of his unbelievable story. Twice, he embeds letters in *The Pedro Gorino* (one from John Cuffee to his father, Paul, and the other from Dean to a friend named Alfred) in what appear to be attempts to authenticate his account preemptively (12, 177). In addition, more than a few readers have pointed out that the transparent title of the British edition of his book, *Umbala*, means "it is true." The title comes from one of Dean's anecdotes:

> One man at the hut of this chief said nothing but "Umbala." Every time the chief spoke this man uttered his single word until it grew to an enormous and terrible significance. It seemed like some dark incantation. At my first opportunity I asked Emtinso the meaning of the word. He said that it meant, "It is true." It seems that it was a rather general custom among the kings and chiefs to hire these hypnotic artists who continue to say, "It is true, it is true," until the natives believe every word their rulers tell them. (162)

Rather than underscoring the truth of his book, as George Shepperson and others have argued, the title—viewed through this anecdote—appears to reveal that truth can be willed into existence. It is only natural that we will now read Dean's own story as if it is accompanied by the same insistent, persuasive assertion of truth in the face of seeming falsehood. In other words, it is almost as if he wants to throw doubt on his story as one that becomes true only through "dark incantation," an incantation that Dean's narration renders with "an enormous and terrible significance." Just before the introduction of the word "Umbala," Dean recalls another storytelling incident punctuated by another performative declaration of truth: "At the conclusion of this story most of the audience shouted, 'Icoona,' meaning

'It is the truth,' or 'I understand'" (149). What distinguishes this story from the chief's is the challenge faced by the storyteller. "Icoona" is not chanted by "hypnotic artists," and there is a listener in the crowd who counters the agreeing members of the audience with "'Amaguthly,' meaning 'I doubt it,' or 'Go on with you'" (149). Dean understands "Amaguthly" as an invitation to dialogue—that it was "merely a matter of form," a code indicating that the listener "had a story to tell which he considered infinitely more entertaining" (149). Not only does Dean introduce this element of dissension into the text, but he also gestures, self-reflexively and knowingly, toward the entertainment value and the mythic improbability of his own story.

One of the most unbelievable episodes in Dean's account involves a near-death experience that follows his mysterious ejection from his own ship while sleeping by a group of treacherous Englishmen to whom he had rented it. When he somehow survives and returns to Knysna, no one recognizes him and, he says, "One and all discredited my story," anticipating his future readers' distrust of the book as a whole (107). Adding to the irony is the fact that he ends the chapter, titled tellingly "The Phantasy at Knysna," with a remark acknowledging that the very first readers of his story assumed it was an untruth: "All that ever came of the affair was a short, semi-humorous article in one of the local papers that took it all as the fabrication of an old salt which might entertain their not-too-serious readers" (109).

Presumably this newspaper is neither the *South African Spectator* nor *Izwi Labantu*, newspapers edited, respectively, by Dean's friends F. Z. S. Peregrino and Allan Kirkland Soga. The connections he pursued with Peregrino and Soga indicate that Dean knew the importance of print journalism for legitimizing his pan-Africanist project. As Shepperson writes, Peregrino "set up webs of business and political connections which were useful to Harry Dean."[9] In tracing those mutually beneficial networks in his book, Dean "unveils to his readers an embodied Africa and modern African literati engaged in periodical culture and translation."[10] Dean would put Soga in touch with Pauline E. Hopkins, who published Soga's letter to the editor, in which he called for Africans and African Americans to "co-operate by extending hands across the sea," in the *Colored American Magazine*.[11] (Hopkins would later turn to Soga as "the corner stone of [her] 'international policy.'")[12] And, in planning a "suitable reception" for his fellow African American countryman Bishop Coppin, Dean first contacted Peregrino. But his connections with African journalists were not the only ones he cultivated. In a remote Boer village, Dean runs into an old friend who happens to write for a London newspaper. He accompanies him on his assignment as a war correspondent and witnesses a war between the Swazis and the Zulus after which the exhausted victorious army is slaughtered by the Boers (231). Later, after returning to the United States and only a few years before writing *The Pedro Gorino*, Dean worked as a subscription agent for the *Favorite Magazine*, edited and published by Fenton Johnson. A certificate authorizing Dean to "transact business" on behalf of the magazine during the course of a lecture tour linked Dean's cause with the periodical's more general aim of "fighting to make the world safe for the Negro."[13]

Dean had an abiding faith in the transnational potential of periodicals, particularly those conceived in the service of racial solidarity. In fact, he even attempted to start his own magazine. A 1920 FBI file on Dean documents his plans to start a magazine based out of San Diego called *Habasher's Promised Land*. The author of the file, advising that Dean "be kept under surveillance as to radicalism and agitation among negroes," writes that he "claims that 'Habashero' and not 'Negro' is the true name of persons of African descent" and is likely "one of the usual negro fakers 'African Princes.'"[14] Despite the skepticism evinced by this FBI report, Dean views the textual support supplied by print media as a means to establish and ground himself in the reality of his imperial dream, similar to the manner in which he uses the documentation of his embedded correspondence.

But it is not only his dream that needs grounding; he needs also to assure himself of his own reality and the reliability of his senses. He finds himself susceptible to "mirages [that] bewilder the unaccustomed eye" (150). Upon regaining consciousness on the beach after being thrown overboard from his ship, he perceives the woman who helps nurse him back to health through a misty veil: he says, "through my dreamy senses she seemed some dusky goddess" (106). She and her fellow villagers were, to Dean, "less real than any [people] I had ever known" (106). Even after recovering and returning to town, he says, "I no longer could distinguish the real from the unreal nor the truth from the fabric and weave of my fevered mind. My waking hours were filled with dreams, and at night my dreams echoed my waking hours" (108). This blurring of the boundaries between day and night is intensified by the even more profound loss of Dean's sense of time in general, as he succumbs to the familiar stereotype of an Africa frozen in time. He thinks that his protracted recuperation in the Africando village has lasted the entire summer, but only two weeks have passed.

Having passed into this dream-like atmosphere, Dean himself becomes "less real": "now I was more like an image of death than a living human being" (107). He is, quite literally, no longer himself. Recalling "stories of men who had come back to earth in other forms," Dean wonders, "Was

I really so different from what I had been?" (108). Not "who" I had been but "what"—even his quiddity is in question with this transformation. Fittingly, just before being rescued, Dean remembers the following lines from *The Tempest*, a textual recollection he finds "infinitely soothing":

> Full fathom five thy father lies;
> Of his bones are coral made;
> Those are pearls that were his eyes:
> Nothing of him that doth fade
> But doth suffer a sea-change
> Into something rich and strange . . . (104)

Dean's transformation—his "sea-change / Into something rich and strange"—renders him almost inhuman. His restoration to health is essentially a resurrection from the dead, one prefiguring the anticipated Ethiopianist resurrection of his African empire; he recalls that, as he lay washed up on the beach, his "legs seemed rigid and frozen and my arms lay stiffly at my side," as if rigor mortis has already set in (105). If the Africando woman who heals Dean appears to him as a "dusky goddess," it is as if her godliness is transmitted to Dean himself.

Furthermore, this Africando woman is hardly the only figure in *The Pedro Gorino* whose godliness attaches to Dean. Of Segow Faku, King of the Pondos, Dean writes in eroticized awe:

> I perceived such a picture of majesty as one could not easily forget. Twenty feet before me on a huge cowskin, squatted like the Buddha, was Segow Faku, King of the Pondos. His face was handsome, his skin shining black. His body was enormous and beautifully muscled. He was almost naked, his bright robe thrown to one side. He wore only a breech-clout, a single necklace of teeth, and a bracelet of ivory on one arm. An ostrich plume adorned his hair. (164)

The comparison to Buddha is not simply incidental. Just before meeting the king, Dean confesses, during a conversation with Bishop Coppin, that he is not a Christian but rather "inclined more toward Buddhism" (143). Rather than casting Segow Faku as a religious figure that would be exotic and alien to him, he views him as a representation of divinity according to his own belief system.

Segow Faku returns Dean's admiration; welcoming him to the village, he presents Dean ceremoniously with a chicken. Just as the godliness of the Africando woman adheres to Dean, Segow Faku's act not only is "as decorous as the bestowal of knighthood," it bestows Dean with a supernatural quality. The villagers, having never seen such a thing, view Dean "from that moment forth [as] something superhuman" (165). Two chapters later, he delivers a persuasive speech that succeeds in preventing a war between the Pondos and the Pondo Mesis, thereby accomplishing a "superhuman feat" (182). On a large-scale mission to kill a lion tormenting the Pondo Mesis, Dean, improbably, is the one who delivers the fatal shot (193). The lion, described as an "old monarch," is dethroned by Dean (192), and, like Reuel in *Of One Blood*, he has a power over the lion that the Africans do not. Here, Dean appears to have absorbed a superstition regarding "the supposed respect shown to the royal blood by lions" referenced by Marc Bloch, who cites Friar Francis's remarks to the doge of Venice: if Philip of Valois "would expose his person to hungry lions and could escape unscathed from their claws," Edward III would recognize him as the king of France because "lions never harm a true king."[15]

In beginning with his genealogy—linking himself to Paul Cuffee and, through him, to Said Kafu—Dean believes himself to be just as regal and legendary as the African kings he meets. Despite assertions by the *New York Times*, the *Baltimore Afro-American*, and other periodicals that Dean descends from a long line of kings, and North's claim that Dean introduced himself to him as "a prince in my own right back in Africa," Dean himself admits that he "could make no claim to royal blood" (xviii, 249). However, he celebrates the innate regality of his ancestors the Cuffees and Deans, with both maternal and paternal lines leading him directly back to Africa. As sailors and seafaring merchants, his ancestors are figuratively royal, as he claims that "maritime people are aristocrats wherever they go" (7). Recalling a childhood visit to his aunt in New Orleans, he says, "I lived the life of a young prince" (29). Twice in his youth, while sailing with his uncle, Dean met kings whom his uncle could count as intimate friends: King Kalakaua of Hawaii and the King of the Herreros in Saldanha Bay (35, 52). As a child, he is trained to believe that he is in his element when among royalty and to imagine that he is capable of leading an empire himself. "Even at that early age," Dean writes, "I was dreaming of an Ethiopian Empire" (56). When Dean's uncle begins to educate him in astronavigation, it is fitting that "the stars that stirred [his] imagination most were those in Cepheus, Cepheus, King of Ethiopia" (34). Later, he even credits this mythical celestial king of Ethiopia with orienting his ship: "Finally one night we got sight of Cepheus and got our bearings" (128). It is no surprise then that, in his eulogy for Dean, North calls him "the stuff of which Negro emperors are made."[16]

But Dean differentiates himself from the godlike monarchs he meets in Africa by positioning himself in the shifting role of mediator, one who can settle differences from a superordinate position and is able to see the "big picture." In other words, he sees himself as the proverbial "King of Kings," a title assumed by Ethiopian emperors to indicate their sovereignty over regional Ethiopian "kings." Over the course of his journeys, he finds himself more than once in the position to unite feuding African kingdoms, bringing him closer to his dream. He eliminates the long-standing feud between the Pondos and Pondo Mesis by emphasizing the "same blood" running through their veins (and, by extension, his own) (183). Later, when a group of African kings visits Cape Town to meet with the Prince of Wales, Dean wonders, "Why not utilize the opportunity and bring them together in one great meeting?" Dean sees himself as the catalyst necessary for black union, even as he admits—contradicting his earlier speech to the Pondos—that these are "feuds which ran back to the very dawn of time" (251). His self-aggrandizement renders him nearly supernatural; the success of his speech leads him to claim (somewhat modestly using the passive voice) that "war had been averted by a miracle" (184). He acquires "an enormous and terrible significance," much like "Umbala" itself.

However, despite Dean's emphasis on consanguinity and solidarity, he believes himself to be different from Africans. As Gruesser points out, citing a passage about a foolish "native Somali" who would take three cents of shell money over a thousand sovereigns, Dean often "engages in the exceptionalism and paternalism that so many earlier black American Ethiopianists exhibited toward the continent's inhabitants."[17] Even his comparisons that depict Africans in a good light are tinged with condescension, as when he compares South African huts favorably to the cabins in which African Americans live in the South (161). When he meets the Prince of Wales, he says, in a remark intended to surprise the reader, "for all his braids and fine demeanor, I thought him no more royal or aristocratic than Segow Faku, his shining black body adorned with nothing but a breech-clout, an ostrich feather, and a necklace of ivory" (248). Although Dean advertised his lectures as an attempt to "refute the psuedo [*sic*]-scientists, so-called anthropologists, who view the African life through their standards and ideals," he is frequently guilty of the same.[18] When Bishop Coppin leads a group of African kings in singing a hymn of his own composition, "Ethiopia Stretch Out Thy Hands," it begins soberly but eventually "the harmony grew wilder and more wild, the rhythm more and more barbaric. They drummed upon the table, they sang weird minor strains" (252). Dean's reaction suggests his estrangement from the scene, but his imperial presence is necessary to contain it.

In his persuasive speech to the Pondos, Dean reminds them that the elderly men in the tribe knew a time before the disaffiliation of the Pondos and Pondo Mesis. Viewing intraracial tension as the culmination of the gradual effects of deracination, Dean's visions of empire rest upon an originary argument that is essentially Ethiopianist. His "dreaming" is restorative:

> Once more Mashonaland was Ophor, and gleaming black bodies brought gold from the mines. The ruins of Zimbabwe were no longer ruins, but stately masonry. . . . And those dark descendants of the Phoenicians, still worshiping the crane and the ram, reattained the genius of their ancestors, sailing their ships to every country, bearing the wealth of Africa. As in the ancient days, precious stones and metals poured from Sheba northward through all Arabia, and westward down the wide rivers of the jungle. (155)

Everything in Dean's future-Africa is determined by ancient Africa. At times, Dean is vague about the greatness he hopes to restore, but here he makes it clear that "gold from the mines" and "precious stones and metals" are the throughline holding this future-Africa together. Dean's career as a pan-Africanist is undergirded by a quest for wealth, by commerce. When he visits the De Beers offices, he is shown a tray covered with diamonds that he says "was wealth enough to found the Ethiopian Empire of which I had dreamed so long" (226). After acquiring a fortune in ostrich feathers, he realizes that "within the year I could buy Lorenço Marques" (255). Dean's first attempt to purchase this territory (currently the city of Maputo in Mozambique) from the Portuguese rested upon his appeal to wealthy and well-known African Americans for funding, an appeal that ends up entirely unsuccessful. He shames them in an apostrophe ("Why did you not respond, men of my race?"), arguing that they have "forgotten their motherland as completely as if their forbears had not spent their lives in her jungles" (124, 123).

Dean even goes so far as to imagine an antediluvian, Pangea-like empire, uniting various peoples of color. Observing that Soga's father, Teo Soga, has a Japanese-sounding name, Dean cites a story told to him by the son: "before the cataclysm South Africa, Madagascar, Sumatra, Java, and even Korea and Japan were all connected by land and formed a great, illustrious, and powerful empire. The people were highly cultured, and the rulers rich and wise. When the great flood came over the land it left only the remote provinces" (93–94). Shepperson and Gerald Horne read this anecdote, respectively, as evidence of Dean's interest in Asia and of his belief in a link between Africans and Asians—and it is both of those things—but even more noteworthy, I think, is Dean's desire to believe in an originary *empire*, and his unique ability and responsibility for uncovering and stimulating its root.

Vagrancy and the Flow of Ethiopian Empire

In his disheveled state after his near-drowning, Dean notes with surprise that he is mistaken by his friends for "some old beach comber or beggar" (107). However, throughout his book he links his imperial ambition, ironically, to homelessness. The beginnings of his Ethiopian Empire can be traced to the multiethnic, mostly black crew of his ship—a model of black internationalism—linked only by a necessarily nomadic and shifting space, a virtual space only summoned into existence through ideality. As Gruesser points out, the *Pedro Gorino* is a perfect illustration of the ships that symbolize Gilroy's Black Atlantic, those "micro-systems of linguistic and political hybridity."[19] Dean writes of his crew, "We were dark brown Vikings on an African coast ready for wind and rough weather, yet to the prosaic men with whom we did our business we were nothing but a tramp ship on the Indian Ocean" (90–91). An ocean tramp, as defined by the *Oxford English Dictionary*, is "a cargo vessel, esp. a steamship, which does not trade regularly between fixed ports, but takes cargoes wherever obtainable and for any port." Certainly, this is the sense of the term Dean intends, but the implication of vagrancy is unavoidable. Sterling North's preface even introduces Dean (who was elderly and destitute at the time when the book was written) as a "sea tramp," and his quotation marks around the word suggest that this is Dean's own description of himself (xvii). He seems to be evoking what Michelle Ann Stephens calls the "classic image of the black mariner as a drifter."[20]

After identifying the *Pedro Gorino* as a "tramp ship," Dean mentions a group of Africans who were traveling as passengers on the ship. He calls them disdainfully an "unsophisticated lot" who "tried to gorge themselves at every meal" until he trains them to be sailors (91). Dean's attitudes toward Africans throughout the book, despite his stated intentions to unify all black people, betray a belief that empire, ideally, will be led by New World Africans—ones who would, to paraphrase Du Bois, Americanize Africa. Even the appellation "dark brown Vikings" (leaving aside the fact that Vikings are usually depicted as an "unsophisticated lot" themselves) suggests that Dean's crew are culturally both European and African. Moreover, though these black Vikings are sailing under the Norwegian flag on a Norwegian ship originally called the *Pellar Guri*, the ship is rechristened *Pedro Gorino* by Sydney Wilson, Dean's West Indian cook, who announces that "Pellar Guri no name for black man's ship" (72). He mishears a Spanish name because, Dean claims, he "had been under Spanish influence all his life," and Dean's interpretation of Wilson's misunderstanding thereby ascribes the ship's renaming to the residue of European imperialism, rendering this renaming at odds with Dean's stated goals of founding an Ethiopian Empire (71). Ironically, if they had instead kept the original name, the ship could have been an even more perfect symbol of Dean's efforts at empire-building:

> In the early part of the fifteenth century, Norway was under the sway of independent robber barons. There was one tyrant who became so cruel and greedy that the people drove him from the land. He escaped to Scotland where he bribed a Scottish chief named Sinclair to assist him in conquering Norway. Together these schemers gathered a huge army and descended upon the unsuspecting Norwegians. There was a peasant girl named Pellar Guri living in one of the valleys. With great courage and spirit she rallied all the peasants of Norway and drove the robber and his hirelings from the land. From this united effort rose the Kingdom of Norway. (71)

It is no accident that Dean chooses to tell this nationalistic story. What sounds at first like a story of democratic, proletarian revolution ("all the peasants of Norway . . . drove the robber and his hirelings from the land") instead ends up the advent of a monarchy. Just as Pellar Guri's mobilization of her people resulted in both their liberation and their transformation into imperial subjects, Dean dreams that his race will come together in a "united effort" to support an Ethiopian Empire of his design.

At first, Dean's belief in African American exceptionalism seems borne out by the fact that he and his countrymen disrupt the system of racial classification in South Africa. Dean writes, "The class distinctions and stratifications when I was in Cape Town were so numerous as to be utterly bewildering" (118). He is surprised to find, as Langston Hughes would find later in *The Big Sea*, that his light skin put his racial status in question in Africa; in Dean's case, Africans acknowledge him as black but the local government fails to do so. This instability, Dean says, leads him to "realiz[e] the danger of my position" but also to recognize an opportunity upon which he would later capitalize: he would "locate in the very midst of the imperialists and learn their game at first hand" (79). Meanwhile, his fellow countryman, Kid Gardener, is jailed when he enters a bar and thus flouts the segregationist practices of Cape Town social life but then is grouped with European rather than African prisoners because he is American. Kid Gardener himself objects to being classified as "black," as it is understood in Africa; when the bar owner says, "Get out, swartz," Kid replies, "You trying to class me with your Cape Town nigguhs? I'm from Texas, and I ain't to be tampered with."[21] Dean implicitly agrees with the Kid, deciding that his "one chance" lies in his U.S. citizenship, which Dean recognizes can trump his racial identity in Africa. His attempts to involve the American Consul, however, prove fruitless.

Kid Gardener's racial status in Africa is not as flexible as Dean's, nor as flexible as that of his partner in crime, the "mysterious" and "uncanny" Haji Hassan, whose regality allows him to defy categorization. Dean finds Hassan's persona immediately intriguing, particularly the rumor surrounding him that he was a Somali prince. Before learning there is truth to this rumor, Dean identifies Hassan as a "princely looking black-skinned fellow" (81). Despite his skin color, however, his ethnicity and race are not so easy to place: he is also believed by some to be an "Arabian scholar." Dean even compares him to a cat, saying that his eyes contained an "iris encircled with a yellow ring, the pupil dark and piercing," leading Dean to claim, "I knew that I was dealing with no ordinary man" (82). He is not easily classified—not even as a human being, putting him in a league with Dean himself.

Although he is a prince, Hassan has abdicated his position because he "had decided to see more of the world" (83). In doing so, he becomes a man of the world, no longer of fixed nationality. This nationlessness allows him to bond with the Kid—"it seemed quite natural that the absolutely fearless, handsome, mysterious Somali should have taken a fancy to the recklessly daring, brilliantly foolhardy, Texas cowboy" (83)—and positions him as an ideal citizen of Dean's transnational black empire.

These successful intraracial connections, again, are undermined by Dean's occasional lapses into cultural relativism. Dean is conflicted, torn between Eastern preservation and antiquity on the one hand and Western progress on the other. As Gruesser points out, citing Dean's satisfaction upon learning that he cannot afford to install an engine in the *Pedro Gorino*, "Dean's resistance to modernization in regards to his ship, the most powerful symbol of his dream of an 'Ethiopian Empire,' accords perfectly with the tensions inherent in the Ethiopianism invoked by the first generation of twentieth-century black American writers to depict

Africa."[22] In his first articulation of his imperial dream, Dean claims that his Ethiopia "would be greater than the empires of Africa's past" because he "dreamed of an empire infinitely more cultured" (67–68). In the same vein, although he admires Segow Faku's breech-clout, he makes a point to note that King Lerothodi "was a stately looking, middle-aged man dressed in European fashion" and Queen Baring "wore Parisian dresses of pale yellow and green silks" (209).

Even as Dean's description of Segow Faku—similar to his description of his ancestor Said Kafu during his time in England as a "slim Mandingo boy attired in the finest Arabian costume" (5)—exoticizes him, neither can Dean see European dress on an African as anything other than a costume, hiding his true self. During the meeting with the Prince of Wales, Dean notes that the African kings are "dressed as carefully as English gentlemen, with high top hats and Prince Albert coats" (251). However, "their retainers and heirs apparent were arrayed in all their barbaric splendor," leading Dean to claim "how thin the veneer of European culture actually was, and how thoroughly these people retained the characteristics of their race" (251).

African characters in Dean's book are always moving back and forth between "cultured" and "barbaric"—most often with a simple wardrobe change—but at base maintaining their so-called racial traits. This phenomenon is exploited by Haji Hassan, in a diamond-stealing scheme that Dean thinks ingenious:

> Shortly before the recruitment in any particular kraal Haji would plant several of his confidential men, strip them of all outward signs of civilization, array them as the natives themselves and leave the rest of the deception to their own intelligence. These men could appear every bit as unsophisticated as the natives, and although the De Beers agents were continually on the watch they were deceived over and over again. (224)

Because the imperialists (including economic imperialists such as De Beers) clearly expect more "trouble" from "civilized" Africans, Haji takes advantage of their prejudices. In fact, Haji strips himself too by posing as an "illiterate Malay" (221).

Africans who show no evidence of civilization are apparently incapable of deception. They are instead naive tabulae rasae ready to be influenced. On the other hand, in his apostrophe scolding his fellow African Americans, Dean accuses them of rejecting his plea "because of the centuries during which [they] have labored under the hypnotic influence of false ideals, false logic, false education, and false code of morals" (124). Who is subject to the right influences and who to wrong influences is a frequent topic of discussion for Dean; in both cases, it concerns the power of a hierarchical superior to control another. Just after learning about the practice of the Umbala chant, Dean says, "It came to me at this time that the native Ethiopians' naïve confidence in their leaders might, if used to the right ends, prove their most valuable asset, but if abused as it has been in the past would surely keep them in an abased and lowly position" (162). Later, in response to the fear of his power among the British colonials, Dean says, "They could not undermine the influence I was already gaining with the natives. They could not undo my work once I had instilled the desire for liberty in those fertile Ethiopian minds" (208). Then again, during the meeting of the African kings, Dean says, "Here if only the right words might be spoken and the right influences brought to bear, Ethiopia might be reinstated in all her former glory, or even better, lifted to a level of civilization more cultured, prosperous, and powerful than ever before" (251). It is almost as if Dean imagines a literalization of the word's etymology, pouring his ideas into the Africans he meets and allowing those ideas to flow through them, and through the circulatory system of his proposed polity.

A government with a top-down system of "influence" is in keeping with Dean's paternalistic ideas about empire. Although Victoria J. Collis argues that Dean "does not always define empire as a type of government at the head of which there is an emperor or supreme ruler" and that "Dean makes clear to his reader that such a union [between the Pondos, Pondo Mesis, and Basutos] would be democratic, even socialist,"[23] I argue that what seems democratic in Dean's dream empire is more akin to feudal reciprocity. Democratic thought seems irrelevant to the governmental structures in place, and it appears that Dean respects the existing structures. When the king of the Pondo Mesis holds a banquet, Dean tells us "the king did not eat; he was host" (194). The people celebrate him, in tribute, and he pays for these compliments through food and drink.

Though Dean scolds the recipients of his funding request for falling prey to the wrong influence, it is evident that the influence he hopes to wield over the Africans is a Western one. This is despite the fact that he clearly admires the African cultures and governments about which he learns. In his desire to unite the kings, the privileging of Westernness as a common ground upon which these kings (including Dean) can meet puts Dean at the center and leads to a cultural dissolution in the name of racial union. After spending the entire book detailing specific African cultures,

Dean ultimately can only imagine his pan-African empire as one that eliminates difference, as a general "Ethiopia" rather than a syncretic one.

Interestingly, there is a period in Dean's life in Africa that is, as Shepperson says, "veiled in mystery."[24] North, in his eulogy of Dean, said:

> When we were writing the book, Dean would not allow any mention of his "Twelve Black Years." But no harm can come of telling that story now. Dean went native. He went up the Congo with a trading party, married a native chieftain's daughter and became the "Admiral" of the tribe's war canoes.
>
> Ten children were born to that strange union. Then some tragedy of which Dean would never speak brought him back to civilization at the age of 30.[25]

If the story of Dean's "going native" is true, why would he leave it out of his narrative? Wouldn't it further legitimize his claims to imperium and naturalize the Ethiopian identity he claims? It is possible that the desire to avoid reliving "some tragedy," perhaps involving his large family, silences him, but his reluctance could also be explained by his apparent view that by "going native" he allowed the influence to go the wrong way. As much as Dean wants to preserve aspects of the existing Ethiopia, his goal is to build a new one that contains it, supersedes it, and depends upon his own values as much as African ones.

Later in his life, Dean reassumed an African identity. In 1923, while living in Liberia, Dean apparently identified as Liberian. Offering to import specimens of a breed of miniature deer to the United States, he says in a *Baltimore Afro-American* article, "We have them for pets on my place. They are a replica of your deer in everything except size."[26] The modern nation of Liberia, rather than the center of Conrad's so-called Heart of Darkness, may have offered Dean the second-generation Africanness closer to the one he idealized: a New World African identity filtered through Americanness. Even as a child, traveling with his uncle, he identifies Liberia as "the one bit of land in all Africa still held by its rightful heirs"—by which he means, I assume, both native Africans and diasporic Africans—and therefore an appropriate "base for operations" for his future Ethiopian Empire (56).

The actual Ethiopian empire, then led by Menelik, is a strange absence in Dean's book. It is almost as if he views the empire's existence as a threat to the argument of the book itself. It is fairly obvious—based on Dean's subtitle alone—that his use of "Ethiopian" connotes the general sense to mean "African" or "black," as critics have been quick to point out. In fact,

Shepperson writes that Dean's dream empire "had nothing to do with the country of Ethiopia."[27] Practically speaking, yes, this is true. One review of *The Pedro Gorino* lists "Abyssinian chiefs" among those Dean meets along his journey, but this is inaccurate.[28] The book never mentions stopping in Abyssinia, and Dean's best chance for an empire, according to *The Pedro Gorino*, was in Lorenço Marques. However, the country generally known as Abyssinia at the time of his sailing *was* an empire, and Dean, as informed as he was, could not have ignored the significance of an existing independent African empire for his plans.

Besides Liberia, Abyssinia was a place where Dean ended up "many times during his life," according to North. Dying on the cusp of the Italo-Ethiopian War, Dean was concerned about the imminent crisis: North said, "If there is any justice in the next world, he will lead in the spirit, as he promised to lead in the flesh, the black boys from Chicago who will go to join Haile Selassie."[29] Dean educated himself thoroughly about the country, even making bizarre claims such as one reported in a 1920 article advertising an upcoming lecture: "Most people do not know that the French cooking is just a degeneration of the Abyssinian style of cooking."[30] Both Dean's aforementioned planned magazine, *Habasher's Promised Land*, and the nautical college he founded, Habashi Nautical College, presumably take their names from "Habesha," the Arabic etymological source for "Abyssinia." An obituary in the *Kansas City Plaindealer* noted that Dean had left behind a manuscript about Abyssinia that was expected to be published posthumously.[31] Another obituary, appearing in the *Chicago Defender*, claims that Dean "evinced a keen interest always in the ancient empire, that is right now the center of world discussion," and identifies him as a "personal friend of the late King Menelik of Ethiopia."[32] Years earlier, a 1912 *Indianapolis Freeman* article advertised a lecture Dean would deliver titled "Marcus a Prince of Abyssinia."[33]

It should not surprise us by now that Dean would befriend an Ethiopian king and present a lecture about an Ethiopian prince. He pursued monarchy wherever he went. (Dean also supposedly "held letters from the Japanese royal family instructing Nipponese everywhere to extend the possessor the utmost of courtesy at all times," additional evidence of his interest in Japan.)[34] The question is, does place matter when founding a racial empire? When he first arrives in South Africa, Dean says, "I realized that the cape was the most strategic point in that part of the world and was bound to become as important as the Golden Horn in ancient times" (79). At another point in the narrative, when Queen Baring offers him a concession in Basutoland (Lesotho), he "dreamed of a center from which culture could radiate to every corner in Africa" (211). When the Portuguese offer him the opportunity to buy Lorenço Marques, he imagines "a new center of culture for the colored race" serving as a "foothold [from which] an enterprising colony might expand until it had recaptured the whole continent" (116). The starting point almost seems irrelevant; the only goal is to make all of Africa "Ethiopia."

For this reason, it is all the more surprising that Dean ends his narrative with his expulsion from South Africa, having failed after several attempts to found an empire. We know that he returned to Africa between this expulsion and the writing of his narrative. Instead, however, Dean ends, as Stephens puts it, "bereft of both his visions of statehood and the vehicle that could have gotten him there."[35] The ship he boards destined for London stops in Funchal, Madeira, and Dean disembarks, finding himself "part of a motley crew of pirates, fugitives, and seamen, without nationality yet still working together to imagine and create communities.[36] His narrative ends where it began—in Funchal, where Said Kafu and McKinnon Paige stopped before heading first to London and then to the United States—with a purgatorial symmetry. Now as nationless as Haji Hassan had appeared to him, Dean strangely seems to conclude that nation makes no difference in the end: in Funchal, he "haunted the resorts of seamen that lie along that dirty, lively, wild, crescent bay, seeking passage aboard any ship for any country whatsoever" (262).

This ghostly haunting recalls a story Dean tells—like *The Pedro Gorino* itself, initially greeted with skepticism by those who hear it—about a mythical elderly woman with white skin living in Pondo Land. She is the subject of gossip and speculation, and "a hundred stories centered about her" (169). Upon meeting with her, Dean discovers that she is the descendant of an English woman shipwrecked along the southern coast of Africa in the eighteenth century. The men onboard the ship strike out for help, never managing to reunite with the women and leaving them to fend for themselves. Almost all of these women married local men. As the elderly woman tells Dean, "As lotus-eaters they forgot their native land and were happy here" (174).

This anecdote, aside from casting the hospitable Africans in a positive light, sounds oddly allegorical. Earlier, Dean had launched a diatribe against the wealthy African Americans whom he approached for funding for falling prey to the "hypnotic influence" of the West and "forgetting their native land," and yet here he lauds the English women's ready acceptance of resettlement and integration. Describing them as lotus-eaters, he suggests that Africa had some sort of hypnotic or soporific effect upon them—a variation on Dean's own dream-like state after being thrown overboard—leading them to follow the example of fellow mariner Odysseus's men in losing all desire for homecoming. The well-read Dean was likely also familiar with Tennyson's account of the land of the Lotus-eaters as a "land where all things always seem'd the same!" Odysseus's sailors give in to "the influence of mild-minded melancholy," unwilling to return to their families because

> . . . all hath suffer'd change:
> For surely now our household hearths are cold,
> Our sons inherit us: our looks are strange:
> And we should come like ghosts to trouble joy.
> . . . .
> Let what is broken so remain.[37]

This assertion is the rejection of the nostalgic impulse: the wistful desire for home that drives repatriation is abandoned, with the recognition that the home to which one returns is never the home one left. In comparing the English women to lotus-eaters, Dean introduces the paradox at the heart of his Ethiopian Empire. One must forget one's native land, because it changes, but the imperial project can only work if one believes Africa to be changeless. Dean cannot commit fully to either vision.

It is fitting, therefore, that Dean frequently resorts to the figure of the metaphor, in which *The Pedro Gorino* abounds; aside from its decorative qualities, crucial to embellishment, it allows sameness and difference at once. The beach of Florida looks "like a white ribbon" (25); the sea is "as blue as indigo" with the sky "curv[ing] over us like a silver bell" (26); near the Sandwich Islands, the water was "so hot and glaring that it might have been molten metal"; and "the ship lay like a tired bird on glassy water" (35). These examples come from a random ten-page stretch of the book, and there are many more I could have given in its stead. These are unlikely to be North's additions because he quotes several of Dean's metaphors in his praise of Dean's "delightful script": "as they were in a sea of glass"; "like clipping the wings of a brilliant cock"; "mounted the waves like a Guinea goose"; "as thickly scattered as dewdrops on a field of clover"; and so on (xxiv). Dean's penchant for metaphor aligns with his fascination with transformation in stasis, old identities showing through new ones like palimpsests. When he washes upon the beach near Knysna, he is transformed but, to again cite *The Tempest*, "Nothing of him . . . doth fade."

The Man Who Would Be King

Rather than seeming under the influence of the lotus, William H. Ellis—like Dean, a man who dreamed of a black empire—was said by a bookseller from whom he allegedly bought thousands of dollars' worth of books about Abyssinia to be acting "as if he had been eating hasheesh" when talking "about that unknown and shadowy part of the Eastern Hemisphere."[38] Surpassing Dean in hubris and ego, Ellis was a colorful African American businessman known alternately as the "Moor of Wall Street," the "Hawaiian Count of Monte Cristo," and the "Colored Moses of Texas." Both Dean and Ellis set their sights on Africa but also conceived colonization projects in the Americas: in 1933, Dean attempted an all-black farming colony in Washington State,[39] perhaps inspired by Ellis's Mexican agricultural colony a generation earlier. Like Dean, Ellis reportedly befriended Emperor Menelik of Ethiopia, visiting him in 1903 and 1904.

Fantastic controversies and rumors marked Ellis's life, as Karl Jacoby's recent biography details. Even his mythic beginnings sound like the stuff of legend. His bravado spurred him to take advantage of miraculous turns of fortune, and he became renowned for "attacking and overcoming obstacles which to others seemed insurmountable."[40] Upon his death, the writer Prosper Buranelli declared, "A prodigious fellow has left the earth."[41] As a figure, in fact, Ellis is best understood as a prodigy or marvel—one article about him was titled "Ellis the Marvel of His Time"—in the vein of the Ethiopian-imposter-as-prodigy described by Robert A. Hill in his article on Isaac Brown.[42] Ellis was said to have "figured strangely, perplexingly in a dozen famous and sometimes dark affairs in the high world of gold and diplomacy, and seemed to have the magic of touching with a dreamy, fabulous glow every object of money or state that his fiery ambition encompassed."[43]

Just as Dean wandered dream-like after being rescued from near-death, Ellis constructed a life—or series of lives—that felt like a dream, marked by numerous rebirths. He moved swiftly from identity to identity, transforming himself sometimes so astoundingly that the list, according to Buranelli, "reads like the composition of a sick fancy—cowboy, colonizer of negroes, stalwart of old time politics in Texas, aspirant opera singer, wealth speculator in Wall street, diplomatic emissary of the United States government, friend and adviser to King Menelik of Abyssinia, Duke of Harrar and Hawash, 'the man who would be king,' magnate of Latin-American rubber concessions and, finally, bold and powerful manipulator of troubled Mexican politics."[44] His most successful invented identity was that of Guillermo Enriques Eliseo, a Cuban "gentleman." As Eliseo—a man who could pass—he would capitalize upon his gift for making money, often through his ability to win people over. Gaudy and flashy in displaying his wealth, he "wore many diamonds, dressed conspicuously and cut a wide swath in Wall str."[45] In order to pass as a gentleman, he also spent money "schooling himself in the arts of worldly gentility, in elegance of manner, aristocratic poise, suave persuasiveness of speech."[46] His wife, a white woman, was also an enigma. One article remarks, "She dresses gorgeously. Her antecedents are not known."[47] Soon, however, articles identified her as a "woman of culture and refinement," a "grandniece of a one time baron of the exchequer."[48] This noble identity was, again, probably a ruse.

Newspapers again and again describe Ellis's life as "stranger than fiction," and, as one journalist in his Texas hometown observed of Ellis's biography, "there is considerable fiction in the narrative referred to" and "he might even play the role of the Lost Dauphin, or the Man in the Iron Mask, if he ever heard of those personages."[49] This mocking dig at Ellis is hardly an exaggeration; in his multiple identities, Ellis clearly had a flair for the dramatic. He was rumored to be "planning an opera troupe with a professional woman singer" in which he would "sing the Verdian role of Otello to her Desdemona," but this troupe apparently never materialized.[50]

Clearly, he was a larger-than-life figure. Articles frequently obsessed over his physicality, describing him as a "striking figure, standing over six feet in height and giving one the impression that he possesses great muscular power."[51] Another article says that he is "tall, powerful, black mustached and brown of complexion," and ultimately "a very ambiguous figure," one whose "racial antecedents were doubtful in a region where racial antecedents count for so much."[52] Ellis exploited and cultivated this ambiguity. He flouted and transcended the limitations of Jim Crow by staying at segregated hotels and riding in Pullman cars. In fact, this is yet another similarity between Ellis and Dean: both men sued or threatened to sue for discrimination when they were asked to leave white-only spaces (in Dean's case, an elevator, and in Ellis's, a train car).[53] Dean's lawyer based his case upon the fact that his client had traveled extensively in Africa and thus "was more susceptible to a damage to his feelings through refusal of a ride in the elevator than the ordinary person." Both prodigious men assumed extraordinary and exceptional status.

Passing as Cuban—and, at other times, as Hawaiian—Ellis presented himself as an ethnically liminal or fluid figure similar to Dean's friend Haji Hassan. However, rather than obscuring his national origins as Hassan does, Ellis doubles down on them. His knowledge of Spanish allows him to impersonate a Cuban more persuasively, and his supposed plantations in Hawaii would appear to reinforce his identity as Hawaiian. No one had any reason to doubt him, and one article published in an African American newspaper notes that he is "of even darker complexion than his noted countrywoman, ex-Queen Lil," without speculating about his racial background.[54] In 1903, before he was widely known, he is even identified in an African American newspaper specifically (and parenthetically) as "white," lest a reader assume otherwise.[55]

When he was revealed to be African American, the general public response in the media, predictably, was outrage. Carrying the offensive headline of "The Hawaiian Croesus Was Just Plain Sambo," one article complained that Ellis stayed at the Raleigh Hotel in Washington, D.C., and, while there, "lived like a Prince."[56] Even more than his successful crossing of the color line, Ellis's reinvention of himself as royalty is seen as an affront; it is as if his attempt to regalize himself is the most outrageous aspect of his passing. In Menelik he saw not only a monarch but a peer, a powerful black man who essentially stood as representative of the black world, one who was poised to lead not only Abyssinia but "Ethiopia." Like Benito Sylvain, an advisor to Menelik originally from Haiti who urged Menelik "to not only embrace his endowed role as 'the greatest black man in the world,' but also to embark on a program 'for the general amelioration of the negro race,'" Ellis saw potential in the concept of a black imperial leader.[57]

Ellis's assumed regal identity combined with his genius for an American style of salesmanship allowed him to come closer to actualizing his dreams of empire than Dean did. His colonization plans were considered feasible and not just a pipe dream. One periodical speculated that Ellis could "become to Abyssinia what Cecil Rhodes"—the villain of Dean's autobiography—"was to South Africa," laying bare Ellis's imperial intention but divorcing it from race.[58] However, in asserting his racial connection to Menelik, Ellis was willing to relinquish his non-black identity. As Jacoby writes, "Ellis's greatest gift lay in identifying—and, more often than not, exploiting—the unexpected porousness of the color line and borderline," but Ellis displayed simultaneously "an almost extravagant disregard for his carefully crafted new identities by periodically engaging in projects relating to African American politics that raised awkward questions about his identity."[59] The *World's Work* claimed that "the Abyssinian project is not a fanciful one" particularly because Ellis appealed to Ras Makonnen, father of future emperor Haile Selassie, whom he met in London during

King Edward's coronation, as a "man of his own colour who talked big things in a big way."[60]

Although *The Pedro Gorino* is concerned with commerce from beginning to end, Ellis's financial goals were even more direct, and his calls for investment anticipate Isaac Brown's of a few years later. As Karen Sotiropoulos puts it, Ellis was "motivated more by business interests informed by the age of imperial expansion than by the goals of nineteenth-century emigrationists."[61] His visit to Menelik was equivalent to his "dash[ing] away to look at plantations in Mexico or mines in Arizona, because there seemed to be a field there for profit"; Ellis

> packed up plans for the First National Bank of Abyssinia, had specimen coins struck off for a circulating medium, filled note-books with commercial statistics, ordered a thirty-five-hundred dollar Mexican saddle made of elaborate workmanship, and had jewel-studded revolvers and cunning mechanical devices built to order as presents for the African King. Thus equipped he marched on the stronghold of Menelik with a caravan 200 strong.[62]

In preparation for his trip, Ellis brought gifts "four times as great in value as those sent by the Government, and he received in return presents of far greater value than those which he gave," apparently trying to convey to Menelik that he was more impressive than the official U.S. representation.[63] In addition, his arrival with an enormous caravan was designed not only, as one article suggested, "so that the tribesmen may get an idea of the wonderful importance of the stranger who goes among them" but also, I would argue, to connect his lineage to the Queen of Sheba just as strongly as Menelik did.[64] A 1903 article in the *Topeka Plaindealer* quotes Ellis as he recounts the visit of the Queen of Sheba to King Solomon: she "packed her caravan, camels, etc., loaded them with rich presents, jewels, olive oil, etc.," for a trip that resulted in her pregnancy with Menelik I, first of the Ethiopian monarchical line. It appears that Ellis sees himself as another figurative regal descendant of Sheba, arriving in Ethiopia with his caravan, camels, and expensive gifts, reversing her pilgrimage. In modeling himself after Sheba, Ellis anticipated that his momentous meeting with the king would bear fruit.

Impressing Menelik with his wealth, Ellis expected a transfer of wealth beyond the gifts Menelik gave him. The true purpose of his trip, as Sotiropoulos points out, is commercial, as Ellis claimed that he obtained "full concessions for all the diamond mines" in the country, hundreds of thousands or millions of acres (depending upon the source) on which to grow cotton, and the right to establish the Royal Bank of Abyssinia, allowing him to "control the finances of the country."[65] For Ellis, royalty is inseparable from the idea of financial success. Numerous articles make note of his seemingly immeasurable wealth as a sign of his regality. One writes that Ellis "had a collection of shining gems worth the ransom of a king," making the connection explicit.[66]

Ellis's attempts to regalize himself, again, were marred by controversy, and he often found himself at the center of intrigue. The most significant of these was the suspicion that surrounded him when Kent J. Loomis, brother of then assistant secretary of state Francis B. Loomis, fell or was thrown overboard during a ship voyage to Abyssinia. Loomis was the official American representative, but his mysterious disappearance left Ellis to complete the former's assigned task of delivering a signed treaty to Menelik. When Loomis's corpse washed ashore, the implication that Ellis, his cabin-mate onboard the ship, was somehow involved in his death was all over the newspapers, even though Loomis's brother "took occasion to deny very emphatically" that Ellis had murdered him.[67] Numerous articles also suggested that Ellis was sick with worry—"almost in an hysterical condition"—regarding the accusations.[68]

And yet, a *New York Times* article titled "Boast by W. H. Ellis: He Claims Credit for Treaty between America and Abyssinia" suggests that Ellis relished the opportunity to serve as the true mediator between the two countries. Newspapers were quick to observe that Loomis's disappearance was all too convenient, considering Ellis's goals. Refused a formal diplomatic role, Ellis seized the chance to aggrandize himself in the eyes of Menelik and, *The Week's Progress* noted, "would not be averse to having Menelik believe that the American government was right behind him (Ellis) in his business venture."[69] For its part, the U.S. government repeatedly distanced itself from him, tried to delegitimize his role, and essentially treated him in the press as a courier. He was said to be "proceeding to Abyssinia on personal business in which this Government has no interest and with which it has no concern" and that "the bearer of the treaty, whoever he was, would have no official or diplomatic character whatsoever."[70]

An earlier visitor to Abyssinia, Oscar T. Crosby, suggested that Menelik did not have a real grasp of where the United States was or what it represented when he visited him in 1900, mistaking the American Crosby for an Englishman. Ellis agreed that Menelik's "knowledge of America was deficient," but the king, according to Ellis, appreciated and valued the "attitude of the Americans."[71] In response to Ellis's claims that the soon-to-arrive mission from the United States was interested in a relationship that "would help trade and was not coming to try to get land," an "overjoyed" Menelik responded, "I will welcome them in God's love. That is what I long for—connection with a nation that is not looking to get some of my territory."[72]

Menelik found a surprising affinity in the United States' status as a nation "born in independence"; as he said prophetically, "Abyssinia will always be independent."[73] National independence, for Menelik, was of course distinct from democracy. According to Ellis, Menelik referred to Theodore Roosevelt, respectfully, as a king. One of his first requests of Ellis was to "tell him about the greatest men America has produced." To this, Ellis replied, "Washington saved his country from the English, Lincoln set the black man free and united the country, and Roosevelt is making a hoop about the country to keep it united"—all three descriptions cannily refer directly to recent Abyssinian history and the achievements of Tewodros and Menelik (in the case of Lincoln, the reference to national union only and not to the abolition of slavery).[74] Ellis knew instinctively how to appeal to Menelik and what sorts of strength and reverence he would value in another nation's narrative. For instance, an anecdote Ellis sent back to the Roosevelt administration reveals Menelik's and Ellis's shared respect for the U.S. flag:

> I then asked permission to deliver to him the Treaty, which I had carefully roled in an American Flag. I rose and with the Box contining the Treaty steped in front of the King, Bowed and began to slowly unful (old Glory) the Flag at the Glimps of our flag, he bowed twice and pulled off his Kingly hat and wached the old flag as it gradually fell from around the Box containing the Treaty.[75]

This show of flag worship recalls the 1877 Italian expedition mentioned by Chojnacki and cited in chapter 1, during which Menelik supposedly asked, upon receiving his visitor's flag, "why Europeans have such a respect for that object." By the time of Ellis's visit, Menelik was well acquainted with the flag's symbolic connection to sovereignty. Menelik, reportedly, was equally moved by a speech Ellis made during a dinner in his honor, in which he said, "As our American motto is, America for Americans, Monroe Doctrine, so I hope your motto will soon be 'Africa for Africans, Menelik Doctrine, and Europe for Europeans.'"[76]

Ellis's understanding of the Monroe Doctrine aligns with the more aggressive and vigorous interpretation known as the Roosevelt Corollary of 1904, Theodore Roosevelt's "big stick" practice of policing the Western Hemisphere, cited by the president himself as the justification behind the

U.S. intervention in the 1898 Spanish-American War in Cuba. With this addendum, Roosevelt inverted what was ostensibly an anti-imperialist document into a more transparently imperialist one: Monroe's pledged protection of the emerging New World nations from European intrusion evolves into Roosevelt's defense of extending and expanding the U.S. influence throughout the hemisphere. The more muscular version developed by Roosevelt appealed to Ellis's strongman sensibilities. However, he introduced yet another revision of the Monroe Doctrine: the Menelik Doctrine, though as simultaneously imperialist and anti-imperialist as Monroe's and Roosevelt's, differs from the American versions in that it is also monarchist.

Ellis's speech may have been disingenuous, because he appears to have believed most heartily in an Ellis Doctrine. The aforementioned failed colonization scheme in Mexico was his first international attempt to expand his sphere of influence. According to one obituary, "Ellis saw a happy land, a new Ethiopia, in the beautiful valleys of Mexico that he knew well," shepherding African Americans there to "reign over them and be a king among them."[77] An advertisement for his Mexican Colonization Company emphasized the opportunity to escape Jim Crow, as he had through passing, by adopting a new citizenship: "We wish to impress on your minds that the great Republic of Mexico extends to all of its citizens the same treatment—equal rights to all, special privileges to none."[78] Instead, emigrants claimed that Ellis and others exploited and abused them. According to an article reprinted throughout the United States, "Reports have appeared in American newspapers that some of the colonists escaped from the farm, were pursued by W. H. Ellis, the colored man who imported them, and that thirty-two were shot down, while the survivors were captured, taken back to the colony and subjected to harsh punishment."[79] One colonist "claimed that Ellis lassoed him and dragged him through the colony so as to intimidate potential runaway black colonists," and threatened "that he intended to have [him] and his children all murdered before they got out of the Republic of Mexico."[80] Another claimed that Ellis forged letters to the loved ones of illiterate colonists depicting a rose-colored view of the colony.[81] Eventually investigations dismissed these accusations as false, but the U.S. government brought the colonists back to the United States in any case. Even after the failure of this colony, Ellis was quoted in the *San Antonio Daily Express* as saying, "I have not abandoned the idea of Mexican emigration for the negro."[82]

Nevertheless, his attentions shifted mainly to Abyssinia, which he hoped to transform into a "modern Ethiopia, where negroes of the world will find refuge among their own."[83] This colonization plan constituted Ellis's attempt, in language echoing Du Bois's, to "solve the great race problem once and for all, drawing the world's color line about the boundaries of Abyssinia."[84] In an effort to perhaps make the country seem less alien, he claimed that it was "just as safe for a foreigner as Broadway is" and that Americans soon, with his efforts, "will know as much about the history, the people, the resources of Abyssinia in a few years as they now know of New Jersey."[85] At a banquet with Menelik, he observed that, although the Abyssinians "ate raw meat," he "was provided with a regular American dinner."[86] He "was emphatic in declaring that there is nothing suggesting barbarism at Menelik's court," with its European architecture and furnishings, and noted that Menelik "wears European clothes and a felt hat of American shape," while his wife "dressed in Paris modes," much like Dean's description of Queen Baring in *The Pedro Gorino*. The people of Abyssinia generally, according to Ellis, "are willing to adopt western materials and dress if they can be obtained."[87] Unlike Dean, who believes the African's adoption of Western dress to be superficial, Ellis, in light of his own experience of complete reinvention, believes the African identity to be entirely mutable.

In this Western influence—most visible in the Abyssinians' adopted dress—Ellis saw yet another field of financial opportunity in which he could insert himself into a position of power. He said that "the Abyssinian has discarded his leather clothes, and now stands robed in American cotton goods, but all of it passes through three or four hands, and finally reaches the Abyssinian at about four times the real value."[88] By eliminating layers of middlemen, Ellis (as a representative of the United States) could locate himself as the sole mediator. His ability to place himself at the center of power, just as Dean did, contributed to Menelik's inclination to treat him as a fellow royal. The emperor allegedly said to Ellis, "You have told me of the greatness and grandness of *your* kingdom" (emphasis added).[89]

Three Abyssinian flags, "said to be the first that have ever been taken out of the country," accompanied Ellis on his return trip to the United States.[90] It is tempting to interpret this gift as a signal from Ellis that he was reversing his diplomatic journey, now visiting the United States as a representative of Ethiopia. During his visit, Ellis claimed, Menelik named him the Duke of Harrar, the province governed by Ras Makonnen, whom Ellis had met in London. As unlikely as this seems, Ellis apparently did chaperone El-Hagg Abdullahi Aly Sadiq Pasha, a leader from Harrar, when he visited the United States with presents for Roosevelt in 1905, so it is possible that he had some official jurisdictional connection to Harrar.[91] A few years later, however, Ellis was somehow referred to as "the Duke of Abyssinia" in a 1912 letter from Charles William Anderson to Booker T. Washington.[92] In addition, a newspaper article about Ellis's second visit to Menelik claimed that Ellis "was called 'Duke of America'" by the emperor on his first visit.[93] The last of these emphasizes how large Ellis loomed in Menelik's imagination, but Ellis's shifting royal jurisdictions generally illustrate both his slickness and the insignificance of place in Ellis's project of Ethiopianist empire-building; he simply sought any opportunity for territory over which he could rule. He was said to have "exerted a wonderful influence" over Menelik, and even after the emperor's death Ellis believed that his duchy was "secure" and he "expect[ed] to end his days on his Abyssinian possessions."[94]

It was from this position that Ellis was poised to usurp Menelik's throne. As deferential as Ellis may have seemed in the presence of the Ethiopian emperor—in a letter to the Roosevelt administration, Ellis describes how he "advanced to his Throne smiled, . . . *bowed* Kissed his hand"—a 1923 obituary in the *Boston Globe* claimed that Ellis had the "ambition to be King of Abbyssinia [*sic*] and make it a nation of negroes equal to European powers" and described the motivation behind his visit with Menelik as "the first step in a plan to oust Menelik."[95] As the *World's Work* wrote, "He invaded the country like one great man come to confer with a brother."[96] Under the subheading "Menelik under His Thumb," one article claimed that Ellis said "he was able to do anything he pleased with Menelik."[97] Other articles claimed he was "exercising a strange influence over the King who is now quite old and feeble" and has the habit of "exerting an hypnotic power over others."[98] According to Buranelli, Ellis "had Menelik under his spell" and his usurping of Menelik was simply a matter of Ellis's salesman-like power of persuasion: rather than defeat Menelik, he would convince him to choose him to succeed him on the throne, just as he had, early in his career, "obtained such an influence over the widow of Hiram Hotchkiss, an inventor, that he managed the vast estate with a profit of $500,000."[99] Similar to the "hypnotic artists" described by Dean as influential members of some African kings' courts, Ellis employs his own version of "dark incantation" to give shape to his imperial goals.

It was reported that Ellis's plan to become emperor of Ethiopia was nothing new; he had been planning it for years before his trip. He was said to be "a man having unbounded confidence in himself and in his ability to accomplish whatever he sets his mind upon."[100] A fanciful description by Buranelli deserves quoting at length:

> A strange fire of ambition leaped in this brown, burning eyed fellow. His dreams rose out of a barbaric imagination—to spread banquets for duchesses and glittering actresses, to bow to the acclaim of admiring crowds, to snort commands before which all necks would bend, to walk in purple through a land and sit on a golden throne. For these things he yearned, and he hoped for them with a child-like faith. He had friends, he felt, in the supernatural world. He prayed always. With an intoxicating confidence he begged God to perform offices for him in enterprises at hand[,] to strike an antagonist with a fatal illness, to compel the weather, cause it to rain or shine or hail on a critical day.[101]

An even more outrageous imagining of Ellis's fantasies of conquest depicted him as if a boy playing conqueror, dreaming of discovering King Solomon's mines and amassing wealth the world had never seen. Enacting his anticipated adventures, he would

> draw pictures of that country's mountains while sitting abstractly in his office. At home he made miniature caves. In these he would pile hundreds of gold pieces. He would surround them with tiny hills of onyx, of coal, of tin, of silver. Around these and sunk in the earth were diamonds he had bought in the rough from Tiffany. Then he would light a cigarette, tilt far back in his chair and smile.[102]

As one article noted regarding Ellis's belief that Menelik would name him successor, "There is food for the richest kind of romance in all this."[103] The fictions created by Ellis in his attempts to transcend the barriers facing him as an African American at the turn of the century were now exceeded by the fictions that proliferated in his wake. He became a mythical character of sorts. As Ambassador David H. Shinn writes, Ellis was said to have met Eugene O'Neill in Mexico, who then based the character of Emperor Jones on him (although this origin is refuted by O'Neill biographies).[104] In addition, as Sotiropoulos writes, Ellis was the inspiration for a character in Ernest Hogan's *The Oysterman* who "lands on an island, discovers gems and gold, takes possession of the island community, elects himself king, and becomes wealthier than before."[105] It seems Ellis's stranger-than-fiction life begged to be dramatized. He was the sort of romantic character around whom fantasy and rumor endlessly circulated. One article published in 1910 reported that Ellis served as commander of the Abyssinian forces during the 1896 Battle of Adwa, despite the fact that there is no evidence he visited the country before 1903.[106] It is difficult to know where the truth lies in Ellis's story.

As late as 1919, Du Bois was writing to Ellis to ask for an introduction to three visiting Abyssinian dignitaries. He wrote:

> Dear Mr. Ellis,
>
> I am not sure of your address, but I assume that this is the Mr. Ellis who once made a pilgrimage to Abyssinia.
>
> As you know, three Abyssinian commissioners are in the country. I want very much to have them get in touch with the best colored people, and the opening wedge might be through the means of a dinner.
>
> I have written to the head of the Commission, but, of course, he does not know me and a mere letter will not carry much weight.
>
> I write to ask if you can help me in any way. I shall be greatly obliged.[107]

Clearly Du Bois presumed, even after all of the controversy surrounding Ellis and rumors of his desire to oust Menelik, that an association with him *would* "carry much weight" among the Abyssinian visitors.

Relying as they do upon a traditionally mythic conception of Ethiopian empire, the "true" ambitions of Ellis and Dean inevitably end up collapsing into half-truths and deceptiveness. It is no accident that Ellis and Dean would have settled upon imperial Ethiopia as a model—Dean abstractly (as his book's subtitle suggests) and Ellis literally. Their attempts to inflect imperialist hubris with Ethiopianist principles ultimately failed to find purchase, despite the fact that the shapeshifting quality of "Ethiopia" as figurative and literal, synecdochal and specific, appeared to mirror their own transformations in self-invention. Abyssinia was itself undergoing considerable territorial expansion and redefinition under Menelik. In other words, Ethiopianism is at base both fantasy and reality, and these oppositional poles between the idea of Ethiopia and the reality of Ethiopia pulled against each other with incredible force in the last decades of the nineteenth century, when Dean and Ellis were dreaming of empire.

CHAPTER FIVE

Empire on the World Stage

Robinson MacLean had lived up to my highest expectations. He will live up to yours. He registers with minute detail the kaleidoscopic pictures of Sheba today. As one marvels at the craftsmanship which co-ordinates the contrasting colours, presto! they are discovered to be a background for an action film of that figure which intrigues the world—Haile Selassie I—that medieval-modern chipping of flint whose encounter with a dictator's steel may end our age in a red roar of flame.

—C. H. J. SNIDER, FOREWORD TO *JOHN HOY OF ETHIOPIA* BY ROBINSON MACLEAN

IN PLANNING THE 1936 show of his musical revue series *Scandals*, Broadway producer George White decided to rechristen three featured dancers—known as Tip, Tap, and Toe—by restoring their given names Sam, Ted, and Ray in order to get away from the "variety connotation." Still, he and his writers struggled to come up with a concept "to take the team out of the vaudeville category" until he "chanced on a photo of Haile Selassie and he knew his labors were over." As White's work was ending, however, the work was just beginning for Sam, Ted, and Ray. The dancer in the Selassie role "studied photographs of the Ethiopian king for two weeks before he managed to successfully simulate the likeness of the African warrior."[1] He appeared in the show outfitted in Selassie's "sun helmet, black cape, gold-braided tunic and umbrella," while the other two dancers wore "neat Ethiopian regimentals."[2]

The "Selassie and His Army" scene was a great success. One newspaper reported that the dancers "'broke it up' as street lingo would have it."[3] Several others noted the amount of applause and the number of encores the scene received, even citing White's praise of Sam, Ted, and Ray as "the greatest trio of dancers ever to grace the stage."[4] The sound of their feet tapping on a drum-like stand, according to one reviewer, evoked the percussive sonic atmosphere one would expect of the Italo-Ethiopian War.[5] Many others, however, did not find the performance to be so dignified or complex. One newspaper said of the scene, it "may not strike you as being just the thing—if you are pro-Ethiopia—but you'll think it very funny."[6] A more outraged reviewer attacked the show generally as exceptionally offensive: "Not content with portraying Emperor Selassie as a buffoon and a minstrel clown, an impersonator of Mussolini declaims that the 'Italian race' needed a place in the sun and 'that's why darkies were born' "; furthermore, "the insulting epithet 'darky' is used throughout the song."[7] White, apparently, was not entirely sincere about abandoning vaudeville and the accompanying implications of blackface minstrelsy.

Just as White's show was starting its run for the Christmas season, *Time* magazine selected Haile Selassie for its coveted "Man of the Year" cover. Curiously, the first page of this profile pictured not Selassie but Sam, Ted, and Ray. As they appeared to be "clogging for dear life atop a small dais,"[8] the dancers' seemingly desperate performance stands in for the monarch's futile attempts to defend his nation and his sovereignty. Judging from the article's dialectal quotation from *Scandals*, again cited in part in the caption under the photograph—"Boys, our country am menaced! What is we gwine do?"—the brilliant performance of these tap dancers was also supposed to remind viewers of so-called "Ethiopian minstrelsy." In fact, one review calls the performers "three Ethiopian hoofers," gesturing toward both senses of the word.[9]

Perhaps because the set piece by Sam, Ted, and Ray was considered the "high point of the performance,"[10] the dancers reprised the roles of Selassie and his soldiers for a 1937 film titled *You Can't Have Everything*, starring Alice Faye as a playwright who sees her serious script transformed, to her dismay, by a Broadway producer (and love interest) into a musical. The Selassie tap-dance routine is inexplicably inserted without comment into this show, whose plot—thin as it is—revolves mainly around an arctic adventure. Flanking Sam, Ted, and Ray are women in vaguely ethnic but unplaceable costumes that do not appear to be African; the women, however, are certainly performing Orientalism, with veils and diaphanous dresses, gesticulating in a manner reminiscent of the Egyptian Sand Dance. Although the dais is present, the "Ethiopia" banner visible in the *Time* photograph is missing from the film. Even without these decorative flourishes, however, audiences in 1937 certainly would have recognized Selassie without any context and without his being explicitly

FIGURE 5.1. Film still of Sam, Ted, and Ray, in Norman Taurog, *You Can't Have Everything* (20th Century Fox, 1937).

identified. The performance depends upon their recognizing him. Rising from his throne, the Selassie performer throws his regal cape from his shoulders and takes center stage.

There was an inherent theatricality surrounding "Ethiopia," and particularly Abyssinian imperial culture, in the United States in the 1930s. The association with blackface minstrelsy, reinforced by the visual spectacle and impression of sartorial extravagance, made Selassie seem destined for the stage. Moreover, if we broaden our scope to include theatrical representations and caricatures of Menelik and other Ethiopian royals earlier in the century, we can see that the intersection of various cultural forces or tropes—Abyssinian imperial culture, media celebrity, and the "noble savage" stereotype foremost among them—resulted in the production of appealing stage characters. The last of these, the "noble savage," is inflected by the other two to form a variation I call the "Savage Statesman." Through concurrent attractions to ancient pomp or ritual on the one hand and progress and modern innovation on the other, the Savage Statesman is intriguing to theatrical audiences, who are drawn to him as a paradoxical embodiment of the past and the present, of barbarism and civility, of technology and tradition. He might use a telephone to order a thief's hand be cut off, for instance. It is easy to see how such a figure can be exaggerated into caricature, as in *Scandals*, but Selassie's ubiquitous periodical presence also led to his representation in a theatrical subgenre based in social realism: the Living Newspaper. This attempted authentic version of Selassie, perhaps not surprisingly in light of the appeal of the Savage Statesman caricature, was the only one to be suppressed from public view, as we will see in this chapter.

Selassie's Modernity

Given Selassie's inclusion in the *You Can't Have Everything* variety show and *Time* magazine's quotation from *Scandals*, it is clear that, in the American public eye, the emperor's nobility and antiquity were countered not just by modernity but by an exaggerated colloquial slickness: his supposed "compelling sales talk, the morals of a patent medicine advertisement, a grasp of both savage and diplomatic mentality, and finally . . . plenty of what Hollywood calls IT."[11] This is an unfamiliar Selassie—the American, the entertainer, transposed upon the noble and ancient emperor—but it is one who, in his perceived duplicity, perhaps corresponds with the leader who (also according to *Time*) had a "peculiar genius for browbeating Ethiopians while he charms foreigners."[12] As *Time* and other periodicals argued, Selassie found himself in the unenviable position of straddling the distance between his enlightened perspective and that of his "backward" subjects. According to his French physician, Dr. Sassard, the emperor had "inherited a savage country" and acknowledged that he "will never be . . . the chief of the wild hoards that his predecessors were."[13]

Leavening his bold and enterprising Americanness was a distinctly continental European quality. The emperor's ability to charm foreigners was helped undoubtedly by his ability to speak French, and the charmed Sassard found him to be "so different from those who surround him and from his own people," and "so superior to them."[14] A good deal of the *Time* article, like most coverage of Ethiopian emperors, focuses on the differences between the emperor and the typical Ethiopian. This view recalls in some ways what Lisa Siraganian, citing sociologists Everett Stonequist and Robert E. Park, refers to as the hybrid and modern "Marginal Man," who is situated between two cultures perceived to be mutually incompatible: "Trumpeted in American media as a cosmopolitan African reformer with a Judaic-Christian ancestry and a European royal costume, Selassie is even a Marginal Man par excellence."[15]

By emphasizing what was oddly modern and Americanized about him, some of the coverage of Selassie sparked readers' sympathy for a figure who was in some ways like them. Emperor Menelik had begun this transformative work of eliciting sympathy from the West through his Swiss advisor Alfred Ilg, who set out to paint Ethiopian landscapes as European, "tout[ing] mountainous Ethiopia as 'Africa's Switzerland,' a representation boosted in a postcard campaign" that depicted the Ethiopian *tukul* (a traditional thatched house) "with suspiciously Swiss orderliness."[16] As with Menelik, who was awed by early encounters with the automobile and the phonograph, Selassie's efforts to modernize the country through the adoption of Western technologies and the trappings of contemporaneity were frequently noted by the U.S. press. In fact, Selassie's self-conscious attempts to display modernity precede his reign. A *New York Times* article anticipating his 1930 coronation stated that he would arrive in a Rolls Royce with his officers trailing him in motorcycles (in contrast to his ascension to Negus three years earlier, when he rode astride an ass accompanied by subjects on foot).[17] Even shoes "were symbolic of modernism": according to Richard Pankhurst, photographs taken in the 1930s juxtapose a barefoot Lij Iyasu, "the 'conservative,'" with a shod Selassie, "the 'progressive.'"[18]

However, the modern qualities associated with Selassie in the media to which I want to draw attention here are considerably crasser and less idealized than a pair of shoes. According to Dick Welland, the protagonist of a novella by George S. Schuyler discussed later in this study, something valuable had been lost in the attempted modernization of what was once the "admiration of the ancient world." As he says with marked disappointment, watching his accomplices face a firing squad, "I see civilization has at last reached Ethiopia."[19] Dick's romantic Ethiopianism finds a tragic incompatibility between a vulgar modernity and "uncivilized" Ethiopia. Selassie's dichotomy—a technologically savvy intrepidness undergirded by an ancient and conservative primitivism—looks, to the West, either like chaos or play-acting.

Upon his death in 1975, the *New York Times* claimed that his reign "recalled the splendor and opulence of Suleiman the Magnificent or Louis XIV, with the difference that he lived and worked in a modern atmosphere and journeyed abroad in a commandeered Ethiopian Airlines plane."[20] What was perceived as an awkward disjuncture between traditional ways and contemporary innovations was further emphasized after his restoration, following the Italian occupation, when his renewed efforts were ostensibly informed by exposure to British culture during his exile. As *Life* magazine argued, in a 1947 article titled "Ethiopia Goes Modern: Since Returning to Power Haile Selassie Has Introduced Western Ways in His Ancient Land," the supposed "progress" made by the emperor only amounted to the "superimpos[ition of] a facade of modern methods upon an essentially primitive nation."[21] Underneath the façade, an Ethiopia frozen in time remained.

Menelik's Toys

Perhaps the first internationally reported incident linking an Ethiopian monarch to modernity is Tewodros's suicide by pistol, discussed in this book's first chapter—the bleak conclusion to "Tewodros's unrelenting quest for European technical assistance"[22]—but *To Menelek in a Motor-Car* may be the first extended English-language treatment of an Ethiopian emperor's fascination with modern technologies.[23] Determined to present an automobile to Menelik, Bede J. F. Bentley, a British adventurer traveling through the rough terrain of Abyssinia, Somaliland, and Djibouti, arrived to find an emperor who was "a man possessed with a quite remarkable passion for machinery, and gifted with intelligence to take pains to study and understand it."[24] During Bentley's visit, the two conversed "about motor-cars, traction-engines, railways, guns, engines, phonographs, and other novelties which he had introduced into his country of late years."[25] In addition, Bentley was granted a rare audience with Menelik's wife, Empress Taitu, who asked him to fix a "Biograph apparatus" upon which she proceeded to project a couple of films for her visitor.

By the time of Bentley's visit, Menelik was already widely known for his interest in modernity. Menelik acquired the country's first film apparatus—perhaps the one used by Taitu in the preceding anecdote—in 1898.[26] In 1904, the *Indianapolis Freeman* called him "a progressive monarch under whose reign telegraphs, telephones and manufacturing enterprises have sprung into existence."[27] When William Henry Ellis met Menelik, he said that he "found the telephone in use extensively in Abyssinia." In all of these cases, we might call Menelik an early adopter.[28]

Even so, reports could not resist suggesting that technology was somehow incompatible with the hidebound Ethiopian environment. Empress Taitu's retinue had apparently been instructed on how to use the film apparatus but "had promptly forgotten."[29] P. H. G. Powell-Cotton, in his 1902 *A Sporting Trip through Abyssinia*, noted that Addis Ababa's telegraph-telephone station resided in a "large circular tucul" where one

FIGURE 5.2. Photograph of Menelik, in *To Menelek in a Motor-Car* by Clifford Hallé (London: Hurst and Blackett, 1913), 260.

would "find the latest invention of telegraphic and telephonic apparatus lying on tables made of rough packing-cases, side by side with a few *amolé* or salts and a pile of cartridge cases (both empty and full), which have been received as payment for the messages sent." This juxtaposition of modern and traditional artifacts, combined with evidence of barter rather than a more abstract form of commerce, is presented by Powell-Cotton first as a "curious spectacle [of] the mixture of science and barbarism"—as if to suggest, oddly, that old and new forms of knowledge do not coexist in every culture—but finally as an inevitable failure. The attempted synthesis manifests in disarray, an anarchic breakdown or dissolution in which "materials of all sorts are scattered about—cells, insulators, receivers, callbells and so on."[30] This is hardly the orderly *tukul* of Ilg's postcards. Another visitor to Ethiopia remarked in 1900 that although the existence of telephones in the country "seems very civilized and un-Oriental," it is only the precarious telephone wire itself—under constant threat of "being cut and stolen" by the Ethiopians—that is a "sign of civilization," as the stations are described as "dirty Oriental hut[s]"; placing a telephone call under such circumstances requires one to give "the absurd instructions: 'Ring up Addis Abeba.'"[31] Similarly, a 1904 article appearing in the *Boston Daily Globe* reported that "Abyssinia is being 'wired'" and, although "the work is no joke," the Abyssinian effort is said to collapse into buffoonery and caricature. The wooden telephone poles are knocked down by the rain; then, they are eaten by ants; when iron replacements are ordered, the "simple native" steals them; when Menelik threatened death to any telephone-pole thieves, people left them alone but elephants used them as scratching posts and monkeys swung on the wires. The brief piece, reprinted from *Everybody's Magazine*, concludes with the following sentence: "Thus does civilization provide home comforts for the jungle people."[32] Leaving aside the fact that the "jungle people" here appear to be not human beings but elephants and monkeys, as they are the ones using the poles and wires as "home comforts," the article jokingly illustrates how the Abyssinian desire for technology is a farce, because technology cannot ever be adapted to the African scene.

The inevitable failure that results from grafting modernity onto imperial Ethiopia is a constant trope. Situated against the backdrop of ancient imperial culture, and impeded by the masses (who are said to lack his vision), the Savage Statesman treats "civilization" as a thing of amusement or play. Canadian journalist Robinson MacLean wrote of Selassie in his 1936 book *John Hoy of Ethiopia*,

> he lives two lives that can never be brought together. His one life is lived in lion skins, in the pomp and pageantry of the court of a lost tribe. His other life, choked back within him, always subordinate to his imperial existence, is the thwarted enthusiasm of a boy given toys and forbidden then to play with them. His toys are the radio stations, the cars and tanks and aeroplanes, the sports and clothes and carefree manners which have been born to our world after twenty centuries of birth pains.[33]

Much like MacLean and Langston Hughes, whose "Broadcast on Ethiopia" mocks Selassie's "second-hand planes like a child's," many remarked upon Menelik's curiosity with an infantilizing and condescending tone. The author of *To Menelek in a Motor-Car*, for example, compares Menelik's interest in technology to a "child-like inquisitiveness into the working of each new serious toy."[34] Bentley's first drive with Menelik contrasts the emperor's innocent attitude—he is delighted and intrigued by the new machine, urging his driver to go faster—to that of his men, cowering in the backseat. In 1965, T. R. Nicholson even titled his account of Bentley's turn-of-the-century adventure *A Toy for the Lion*. Technology is the emperor's plaything rather than a symbol of modernity.

Upon hearing a phonographic message from Queen Victoria in 1898, newspaper reports claimed that Menelik was "as pleased as a child with a new toy" or "a baby with a new rattle."[35] She sent the message by envoy, and he marveled that he could hear her voice as if she "were beside" him.[36] He responded by recording his own message to her. The content of each message, wishing growing friendship between the two empires, is scripted, empty, and formulaic—although politically significant, as England was advancing in bordering Sudan and the queen's message may have been intended to assuage him.[37] The greater significance of the correspondence for my purposes lies in the novel mode of communication and its reception by both Menelik and the press.

Although the account of the incident in the newspapers tended to be condescending, more careful and nuanced accounts come from an 1899 article in *Windsor Magazine* by Cleveland Moffett and Montagu Sinclair Wellby's 1901 book *'Twixt Sirdar and Menelik*. In the former, Moffett mentions that the envoy tells Menelik that he would have liked to bring an X-ray machine but feared that religious figures would forbid it, to which Menelik countered, "I should be glad to have such an apparatus; we are no longer where we were twenty years ago."[38] (Here, Menelik may be referring to the introduction of the telephone following Ras Makonnen's 1889 trip to Italy, which local priests deemed to be an instrument of demonic possession, a response that led Menelik to call them "cretins" whose superstitions might drive him to take up Islam.)[39] Moffett also cites Menelik's reaction to hearing the Queen Victoria recording, which he "studied with the greatest interest": "'This brings Europe into Africa,' he said, much pleased; 'this is a new way of writing, so that you read with your ears instead of with your eyes.'"[40] Far from childlike, Menelik's is a rather sophisticated response, recognizing the new mode of mechanical reproduction with which he was confronted as fundamentally inscriptive. This is in sharp contrast to the "exclusionary trope" identified by Lisa Gitelman, found in turn-of-the-century travel literature, comics, and periodicals, in which "racially distanced 'natives' play the bumpkin's part, fooled by their own reflections in a mirror or . . . by voices emanating from a phonograph."[41]

Wellby's first-person account likewise describes Menelik's response as serious and studious, rather than one of childlike curiosity:

> A table was then set in front of the king, and on this the phonograph was placed. With the exception of the gurgling sound produced by the instrument, dead silence pervaded the tent. The Negus was highly gratified with the message, even standing up that he might the more distinctly catch the words, for he was much struck with their clearness and firmness. He listened to the Queen's gracious words time after time, and readily consented to my attempting to photograph the scene.[42]

In other words, not only does Menelik appreciate the revolutionary nature of the invention, he also participates in the layering of another scriptive technology—photography—onto the scene. As he listens to Queen Victoria's words, now made historical, he facilitates his own historicization, through both Wellby's photograph and his own phonographic reply to Queen Victoria. Menelik's understanding of photography and phonography complicates the dichotomous Abyssinian model that Powell-Cotton found so unsuccessful. The technologies of the present freeze and solemnize past moments in time.

However, there is something else that all of these technological advancements—the automobile, the telegraph, the telephone, the phonograph, and so forth—share in common that has particular relevance to the case of imperial Ethiopia. They level space and eliminate distances. Each of these inventions allows for a network that can foster centralization. As communication technologies, the telegraph, telephone, and phonograph-as-correspondence permit the entire empire to be connected via networks that find their center in the capital. Even the automobile (along with the attendant development of a system of modern roads), while encouraging travel from one end of the empire to the other, ultimately proves that all roads lead to Rome—or, in this case, Addis Ababa. In other words, the imperial government can, and did, leverage technology to serve as a means of enforcing power centralized in the seat of the new modern empire. The technological networks themselves support the work of the emperor, violently stitching together disparate corners of his empire.

As Peter Garretson writes, the telephone and telegraph systems introduced during Menelik's reign "increased the monarch's power."[43] In addition to the centralization of infrastructure, the direction of information flowed toward the emperor, weakening the relative autonomy of the empire's peripheries. Menelik used the telephone to "exercis[e] his day-to-day supervision over his governors," who "had to telephone him about even relatively minor matters."[44] Comparing the telephone system to "a giant spider web with the emperor at the center," Garretson writes that it "could be used for centralization only if there was a powerful emperor in Addis Ababa to exercise authority."[45] Sure enough, when Menelik's health began to fail, the telephone and telegraph systems continued to grow but became less centralized and more regional. By 1928, Ras Tafari Makonnen (later known as Haile Selassie) "resorted to the radio when he began recentralizing Ethiopia."[46] Even film passed through the emperor's domain before being distributed throughout the kingdom: *Time*'s Man-of-the-Year profile calls Selassie "the world's only enthroned cinema censor."[47]

Savage Statesmen

Nevertheless, the concept of a strongly centralized imperial government is missing from the early African American libretto *Abyssinia* (1906), which features an antimodern Menelik. This is despite the fact that the imagery used in the show's songbooks centered upon a coin picturing Menelik surrounded by Amharic text, ably reproduced by the illustrator. Just as Ilg had contributed to Menelik's public relations campaign to promote the country's position in the world at the end of the nineteenth century, he "also secured the key markers of durable sovereignty so rare in Africa—postage stamps and coins—embossed with Menelik's likeness."[48] As a result, the image of Menelik circulated through the reproduction of these new artifacts in the American and European media, augmenting his international celebrity. In other words, the Menelik coin helped make the emperor a familiar face, but, more important, it was a symbol of both modernity and enduring consolidation.

Starring celebrated blackface performers Bert Williams and George Walker, Jesse A. Shipp and Alex Rogers's *Abyssinia*, according to David Krasner, "is located on a cultural divide separating early black musicals and more politically oriented black theatre."[49] The show was extremely popular as it toured the United States. In Washington, D.C., they sold out three nights in Convention Hall, a venue said to be the city's largest with a maximum capacity of five thousand.[50] Williams and Walker play Jasmine Jenkins and Rastus Johnson, respectively, the latter of whom has won a lottery and spends his winnings in traveling to Abyssinia with his friend. Jenkins and Johnson enter an Abyssinia lacking a strong sense of centralization.

FIGURE 5.3. "Where My Forefathers Died" [song], in *Abyssinia* by Jesse A. Shipp and Alex Rogers (New York: Gotham Attucks, 1906). Library of Congress.

Menelik is seen throughout the play dealing with a "rebellious chief," and Jenkins and Johnson themselves are misrecognized as minor royals: Rastus as a *Ras* and Jasmine as a "Jas," or (presumably) *Dejazmatch*. Regal identities are evidently so ubiquitous that their first names are mistaken for titles.

In addition, the fictionalized Menelik of *Abyssinia* is much more intimidating and violent than the version presented in *To Menelek in a Motor-Car*. For the most part, he is depicted dispensing justice in a particularly cruel and vicious manner. When the aforementioned "rebellious chief" is captured, Menelik vows to "send him back piece at a time and when all the parts shall have arrived in the public market place of his native village, I wish my own hand, shall feed his body to the Hyenas, as a warning to any and all who shall attempt to defy the mandates of Menelik, the second King of Kings of Ethiopia."[51] When a merchant is "convicted of dishonest dealing," Menelik decrees that his "right hand will be severed at the wrist" (as Bentley observed passively in *To Menelek in a Motor-Car*, amputation "seemed to be a favourite form of punishment in the country").[52] This traditional and immediate form of judicial violence is all we see from Menelik in *Abyssinia*. Abyssinian modernity is represented instead by the structured and Westernized military training of the younger generation: the character of Tegulet remarks that his nephew Bolasso, who has studied abroad, is teaching his soldiers "something modern in the way of European tactics." Bolasso recognizes that the Abyssinians' "proudest boast is that our institution [*sic*] have remained unchanged since the days of her Imperial Highness, the Queen of Sheba," resulting in a nation that is "many centuries behind the civilization of the present age."[53] Rather than present an image of a forward-thinking monarch, as *To Menelek in a Motor-Car* attempts to do, *Abyssinia*—the popularity of which may have lent increased force to its ability to shape impressions of the emperor—gives us a Menelik characterized by an Orientalist barbarism.

Impressions of Tewodros, even more than those of Menelik, conform to the sort of Oriental savagery associated with the Abyssinian monarchy in the late nineteenth century, as I suggested in chapter 1. The *Brooklyn Daily Eagle* reported toward the end of the Anglo-Abyssinian War that "Theodorus' defiance of England was the wanton act of an ignorant savage," demonstrating that Ethiopians cannot be said to "approach nearer to the standard of civilization than any other nation except Egypt and Morocco, on the African Continent," as was sometimes claimed.[54] Similarly, *Putnam's* rejected Tewodros's expectation of parity and participation on the world stage: "He overrated himself . . . and the relation of Abyssinia to the rest of the world," an indication of "oriental arrogance."[55] Perhaps attempting to deflate this egotism, *Punch* facetiously floated a plan to capture Tewodros—effectively reversing Tewodros's own violation in imprisoning the British legation—and display him in England as a "circus African" in order to make up funds lost in fighting the Anglo-Abyssinian War. The proposal, as Jeff Rosen writes, would turn Tewodros into "the centrepiece of a live exhibition that would tour the country":

> First catch your Negus, of course; but having caught him, bring him away and constitute him an exhibition. In so doing there would be no

> need to keep him in a cage or den; he might be made perfectly comfortable, only open to public inspection during certain hours daily at the Egyptian Hall, Piccadilly, or some other place equally commodious.[56]

He would be displayed in his "natural habitat," so to speak, to perform at certain designated times of day. Tewodros's suicide prevented this proposed spectacle from coming to pass.

It was because Abyssinian monarchs were portrayed in the media as exaggerated, pompous, and cold-hearted that they were ripe for melodramatic portrayals. One review noted that R. Henri Strange, who played Menelik in *Abyssinia*, displayed "fine dramatic ability" in an emotionally charged role that was "the dream of the Negro actor."[57] In 1868, there was even a rumor that Adah Menken would appear onstage in Paris in the role of Tewodros, printed with the reporter's joke that the emperor was lucky to have died before Menken could have "insisted on marrying him as one of the few remaining men of note who had not shared her nuptials."[58]

This melodrama is a natural outgrowth of the ostentatious and unruly resplendence associated with Abyssinian imperial culture, as we see when the tap-dancing "Selassie" throws off his cape. As W. B. Carnochan puts it, Selassie himself, in planning his coronation, "understood the allure of imperial display—the more spectacular the better."[59] Likewise, the 1911 coronation of Britain's King George V was attended by extravagant Ethiopian envoys whose "lion-skins and cloaks of gilded feathers," according to Osbert Sitwell, "impressed [him] more than anything [he] saw that morning."[60] In his awe, Sitwell reveals the commonly felt sense of acute spatial and temporal disjuncture between Abyssinian antiquity and Western modernity: "it was almost the first time that, thus watching its living representatives drive by and dismount, I realised the continued existence of Ethiopia into the modern world."[61] The previous British coronation, of Edward VII in 1902, had been attended by Ras Makonnen, a member of Menelik's court. A *Boston Globe* article with the subtitle "Gorgeous Ras Malsonnen [*sic*], the Victorious General of Menelik of Abyssinia, Attracts All Eyes—" reported:

> None of the special envoys who arrived here today, though they included princes of the greatest European dynasties, aroused as much interest as did Ras Makonnen, the victorious Abyssinian general and special representative of King Menelik.
>
> In picturesqueness and barbarian splendor the Ethiopian commander and his suite paled even the brilliancy of the oriental princes to whom London has become accustomed during the past week.

> Makonnen, who has black, curly hair and a beard, wore a haik (cloak) of white silk, pantaloons, a shoulder cape of heavy white satin bordered with gold and a broad-brimmed green felt hat.
>
> Three native chiefs who accompany him were scarcely less gorgeous in their apparel, while an African priest, carrying a heavy silver crozier, was the general's constant companion. Ras Makonnen's native followers carried guns and spears.[62]

Only a few months later, the same newspaper reprinted a short piece from the *New York Tribune* on the "barbarian splendor" of the Abyssinian imperial wardrobe. Titled "Royalty in Abyssinia: Bizarre Costume King Menelik Wears on Christmas Day," the article cites an awestruck recent visitor to the country who noted the emperor's "long coat of fantastic colors covered with gold lace," which, he says, "was bad enough, but the straw that broke the back of royalty, so to speak, was the rest of the outfit—white trousers and patent leather shoes." Concluding with a description of eclectic and bejeweled ornament clearly violating Coco Chanel's rule about accessories—"Perched on his head above a piece of white muslin drawn tight about his brow was a big gilt panama hat, the band literally covered with rubies and sapphires. There was a diamond stud in his left ear and a red silk umbrella deeply fringed in gold was held over his head"—the visitor asks, "If that isn't royalty, what is?"[63]

Imperial Celebrity and the Hollywood "IT" Factor

Viewers like the reporters for the *Boston Globe* and *New York Tribune* interpreted Abyssinian imperial dress as an invitation to spectate through the lens of African Orientalism. The sartorial excess of Ethiopian royalty even spilled over into women's fashion. In late 1935, newspapers from Biloxi, Mississippi, to San Bernardino, California, heralded the exotic "Haile Selassie Frock," a loose-fitting robe for women said to be a "new fad" emerging from Bermuda that "combines cool comfort with simple practicability," allowing women anywhere to play the role of emperor just as easily.[64] An article in the *Baltimore Afro-American* titled "Ethiopian Brown Newest Color to Dominate the Styles of London" announced "the birth of a new color for women's stockings—'Negus brown,' described as the same shade as an Ethiopian warrior's skin." (A color known as "Ethiopian brown" described women's clothing items for sale in advertisements printed in the *New York Times* and the *Los Angeles Times* at least two decades earlier, but I find no earlier reference to "Negus brown," which

FIGURE 5.4. "The 'Haile Selassie Frock' Is Introduced in Bermuda," *Wilson Daily Times*, 4 January 1936, newspaperarchive.com.

would suggest an association with Selassie's popularity as a public figure.) The color is said to have "already fascinated women who like to be in the fashion" and "is a seductive color that attracts attention immediately." In addition, the article reports an "overwhelming demand" for floor-length "Haile Selassie" cloaks among fashionable women, adorned with Ethiopian symbols and worn over formal dresses.[65]

As the example of Sam, Ted, and Ray illustrates, Selassie was understood to be both a performer and a performance. In *Amiable with Big Teeth*, a novel by Claude McKay addressed later in this book, a promoter expresses an eagerness to market a "Selassie" performance starring the emperor himself. When an Ethiopian nobleman tries to find employment for an Ethiopian princess as a performer in the United States, he is informed by this "high-powered salesman of modern amusement" that he would need to produce the then-exiled emperor instead, who, he insists, "could make up for the fortune he had lost to Italy, if he would consent to appear in a dervish dance on the American stage." Insulted, the Ethiopian royal refuses haughtily, to which he replies:

> "Don't stand so pat on your Ethiopian dignity, my good fellow," he said. "We have had the Queen of Romania, the granddaughter of Queen Victoria herself doing her stuff on the vast American stage. Your Emperor has a chance to make his now, while Ethiopia is still half alive. Colored people are all natural born actors. Better for Haile Selassie to become a dancing dervish making good money in America than to stay in Jerusalem, where he may eventually be reduced to the status of a street Arab hanging around the Mosque of Omar."[66]

In other words, Selassie *belonged* on the stage. He would lose whatever nobility he had left ("reduced to the status of a street Arab") if he didn't seize the opportunity to perform it. Like the *Time* magazine article, the "impresario" of *Amiable with Big Teeth* finds in him "plenty of what Hollywood calls IT." In a reciprocal relationship, Selassie himself embraced film and popular culture—*Time* writes that "the wall behind the Emperor's throne conceals a cinema projection booth"[67]—just as he was embraced and incorporated into pop culture. His name evidently invited rhyming. One popular song, "Shanty in an Old Shanty Town," included the lyrics "I'd be sassy as Haile Selassie," and the *Scandals* show mentioned at the start of this chapter featured "Mussolini" singing "I Love Selassie" to the tune of "I Love a Lassie."[68]

In 1935, Paul Robeson declared his intention to "present the life of Menelik II on the screen" to the *New York Amsterdam News*, saying that it would have to be filmed in England and Europe because "could you imagine a Black King being treated seriously in Hollywood?"[69] Incidentally, Selassie's visit to Hollywood a few years later proved Robeson correct. In an uncanny association of Selassie with American popular culture, a meeting between Selassie and a costumed Marlon Brando at 20th Century Fox Studios was captured on film. Brando was filming *Desirée*, in which he played Napoleon. A similar photograph appeared in the "Entertainment" section of a 1954 issue of *Jet* magazine, where it was titled "Reel Emperor Meets Real Emperor," accompanied by the following caption: "Ethiopian Emperor Haile Selassie is greeted by 'Emperor Napoleon.'"[70] The men are mirror images, turned toward each other in identical postures, each

FIGURE 5.5. Photograph of Marlon Brando and Emperor Haile Selassie, 1 May 1954, alamy.com.

wearing a jacket adorned with gleaming buttons and medals, gazing past each other across a century.

Apparently the film's producer, Darryl F. Zanuck, was aware of Selassie's admiration for Napoleon and invited him to visit the set to "witness the scene in which Napoleon crowns himself emperor in front of at least a thousand fancily dressed extras pretending to be at the cathedral of Notre-Dame in Paris." While Zanuck may have taken Selassie seriously, Brando used the opportunity to poke fun at his fellow emperor. Attached to Brando's Napoleon costume was a single medal; Selassie wore many. In French, Brando said to him, "It looks to me like you won more battles than I did, and I conquered Europe!" According to Brando's costar Cameron Mitchell, the disrespected Selassie was "furious, insulted, whatever," and "pointedly ignored Brando" from then on. Later that day, when Brando initiated a water-gun fight on set as a prank, Mitchell said, Selassie "got the hell out of there." The comic scene that ensued made a mockery of the imperial culture that Selassie held dear.[71]

Ethiopia as a Living Newspaper

Does the strangeness of the Selassie/Brando photograph reside in the impression that a "reel" emperor can approximate a "real" one to such a degree that an encounter between the two can be framed flippantly as the meeting of two living heads of state—and Brando's "method acting" would in fact demand embodying Napoleon—or that a "real" emperor feels sufficiently like a fictional character that he can coexist with an invention? Newspaper and magazine readers would have been as familiar with cartoons of Selassie as they were with photographs, and even those photographs were usually carefully staged. A celebrated propagandistic photograph of Selassie behind an anti-aircraft gun, printed widely in newspapers, appears to have been staged. It was difficult to know what was real.

In 1936, a "living newspaper" by Arthur Arent, titled *Ethiopia*, represented the Ethiopian conflict with an approach informed by social realism. Arent's play, the "first representative of a unique and dynamic American genre of drama," was directed by Elmer Rice of New York's Federal Theater Project and was a production of the Works Progress Administration (WPA).[72] It is unclear whether Rice or Hallie Flanagan, National Director for the Federal Theater, was ultimately responsible for the concept of the Living Newspaper: simply, to dramatize the news, with the New Deal goal of providing work for unemployed theatrical professionals and even newspaper journalists during the Great Depression.[73]

Rice called the Living Newspaper an "animated newsreel."[74] Initially, the idea was to splice together various scenes from the news of the day. However, Rice's enthusiasm for Arent's brief treatment of Italy's invasion of Ethiopia, written to serve as a single segment of the proposed show, led Rice to abandon that plan for an extended single-themed play.[75] The Living Newspaper that developed as a result was "the dramatization of a *problem*" as opposed to *The March of Time*'s characteristic "dramatization of . . . a [single] news event."[76] Regarding the technique of this genre, Arent claims that "the first thing to consider is not style, which is the manner of doing a thing, but content, which is the thing itself," and that "*Ethiopia* decided for all time the question of Living Newspaper content."[77] Fidelity to the truth was the motivating impulse.

In what William R. Scott calls "the first theatrical treatment of an important international issue," world leaders such as Mussolini, Selassie, Anthony Eden, and Pierre Laval were quoted verbatim, with news updates providing the play with a different ending every night.[78] Composed of short interrelated scenes, jumping with dizzying speed, the play circumnavigates the globe to listen in on speeches and actions taking place in Addis Ababa, London, Rome, Paris, Washington D.C., and Geneva (home of the League of Nations). Each scene begins with a "teletype" that functions as a newspaper headline. For example, "ADDIS ABABA, ETHIOPIA. . . . HAILLE [*sic*] SELASSIE DEFIES IL DUCE" introduces Scene 4.

Considering the apparent popularity of newsreels about Ethiopia, one could have predicted the dramatic potential of the Ethiopian Crisis for such a journalistic-theatrical treatment. A few years prior to the creation of *Ethiopia*, Rayford W. Logan—the historian perhaps best known for designating the turn of the century in the United States as the "nadir" of race relations—witnessed and described audience reaction to an actual newsreel about Ethiopia. "When the pictures of the coronation, recently, of Ras Tafari as joint ruler with his aunt, Empress Zauditu of Abyssinia, flashed on the screen of a northern theater," he writes, "one could distinctly sense the shock that disorientated the audience." Logan registers the viewers' response upon seeing a black emperor surrounded by his black subjects, and a black army that did not conform to the stereotypes of barbarism common to filmic representations. Although he admits that the soldiers lacked the modern weaponry used by Western armies and "of military formation there was none," he romanticizes the manner in which "rifles, borne in the easy fashion of our frontiersmen, glanced in the sunlight" and "cavaliers rode with the nonchalance of Cossacks." Several years before the Italian invasion of 1935, the casual display of strength and natural vitality to which audiences were exposed in this newsreel planted the seeds for the enthusiastic support that would resurge with the start of the Italo-Abyssinian War. As Logan writes, "The newsreel was not a vitaphone, but no great stretch of the imagination was needed to hear the old Galla cry, '*Ebalgume, Ebalgume!* Mow 'em down, Mow 'em down!' "[79]

Arent's *Ethiopia*, unlike the silent newsreel described by Logan, is an amalgam of voices. As Dan Isaac writes retrospectively, decades later in 1968, the play "looks like nothing so much as a modern piece of intermedia under the combined influence of McLuhan and Artaud."[80] The scripted teletype, originally intended to resemble "that on the Times Building," was abandoned for being "impracticable, because it necessitated a constant shifting of the eyes and head from the scene on stage to the moving ribbon of light above."[81] A loudspeaker was introduced to take its place, adding yet another voice to the din. As the form of the Living Newspaper evolved with subsequent plays, the loudspeaker "began to take on individuality and coloration," but its inchoate use in *Ethiopia* as what Arent calls "a kind of non-participating dateline," an objective mediator between scenes, evokes other scripted sonic continuities in the play.[82] Illustrating how a seemingly minor far-off skirmish can have reverberations throughout the world, Arent's auditory effects link eclectic moments and places involved in the Ethiopian Crisis: for instance, Scene 1 ends with the first audible gunshots of the war in Walwal, Ethiopia ("*the sharp rat-a-tat-tat of a machine gun*," followed by the "*regular beat of rifle fire*"), while Scene 2 opens in Geneva, with the chairman of the League of Nations banging a gavel that "*has carried the beat without a break from Scene 1*."[83]

The conflations stop, however, with Arent's representations of the two figures at the center of the play. *Ethiopia*'s stage directions generally depict Selassie favorably. He is first presented as follows: "*Lights up on Haille Selassie seated at desk. His manner is calm, scholarly*."[84] Mussolini, in contrast, is "*standing behind desk*" and "*wear[ing] the uniform of a corporal of the Fascist Militia*." Rather than a "*scholarly*" approach, Mussolini demands masculinist action. Although he claims that "Italy can and will present a whole library of documents and photographs bearing out our claims against Ethiopia," he insists that "the accelerated pace of Ethiopian military preparations renders it necessary for us to proceed with further measures of a military character."[85] This dismissal of documentation is obviously maligned by a play whose main generic distinction lies precisely in its documentary nature.

Arent juxtaposes the respective countries' calls to arms in order to underscore a collectivity in Ethiopia missing from Italy, led unilaterally by an authoritarian leader. Selassie's chancellor, Haille [*sic*] Wolderoufe, commands, "Now sound the war drums! Let each chief step forward and give the signal that will be picked up on every mountain crag, on every arid desert, and there sent on to the farthest extremes of the Empire, from Egypt to Kenya, from Somaliland to the Sudan! *LET THE DRUMS SPEAK!*" In response, "*Three or four of the chiefs step out from their men, and one by one go up and take a whack at the drums*."[86] Mussolini's call to arms, on the other hand, shows him "*standing on the balcony, alone*," in a "*strong shaft of light*" and surrounded by "*microphones and loud speakers*." Below him "*are massed his countrymen*."[87] Wolderoufe says that his people are "united under the chieftains, obeying them with one heart" just as Mussolini says that "twenty million Italians are gathered in the squares of Italy with one heart, one will, one decision."[88] The language is almost identical, but the Italian masses are indistinct, lacking individual will, where the Ethiopians visibly enact their will by hitting the war drums. Although Selassie never speaks—the "mobilization speech" is read by Wolderoufe—the scene highlights instead Mussolini's indirect connection with his people, facilitated by mediating technologies. His communication with the crowd is one-way, whereas Wolderoufe requires his chieftains to actively indicate their assent. The impersonality Arent attributes to the loudspeaker and related technologies—as opposed to the corporeal lion-skin drums—extends to Mussolini, whose call for Italians to respond with "one heart" sounds peculiarly heartless.

Arent's mobilization speech scene hews fairly closely to the description of the mobilization found in the *New York Times*, if less florid. Here, the journalist notes the "rhythmic booming of Haile Selassie's lion-skin mobilization drums" that were "taken up by professional drumbeaters on the crests of mountains surrounding the capital" and "reverberating across the roof of Africa, penetrating the frontiers of Egypt, the Sudan, Kenya and Somaliland, and re-echoing across the Red Sea." All Ethiopians, from all corners of the country, regardless of religion, are said to be joining together to repel the enemy. Recalling the silent implied war cry heard by Logan while viewing the 1929 newsreel, the *New York Times* records another call to arms: "The word throughout the empire was the Emperor's Amharic word, 'Kitet!' which means, 'Close ranks, unite!'"[89] As in Arent's play, the mobilization projects the image of a coherent empire.

Selassie may have wanted to present Ethiopia as a rapidly modernizing nation, but Arent's play emphasizes the sharp differences between the countries' technologies even in the contrast between the microphone and the drum. In fact, Arent quotes the Ethiopian Hawariate's speech to the League of Nations, in which he declared that "at this very moment, the Italian government is rolling up the most highly perfected engines of death and destruction that have been imagined by the most advanced civilization, engines of whose existence the people of Ethiopia never even dreamed."[90] Twentieth-century Ethiopia, a hybrid of modernity and tradition, is a seeming paradox that Arent cannot accommodate through a fact-based realism.

The Living Newspaper, as Arent characterizes it, intersperses what he calls "non-factual" additions or elaborations among the news events to illustrate its central problem. Without these "non-factual" additions, he claims, "the human element is missing."[91] For example, rather than a politician or some other figure whom Arent could quote from his newspaper sources, he might instead invent a plainspoken character who would better serve as "the audience's identification, the bridge that leads to an understanding in human terms of the subject of the debate."[92] It appears that this evolution in his poetics had not yet emerged in *Ethiopia*, which exhibits a stricter documentary style. *Ethiopia* depends upon a "rigid adherence to the use of the direct quote," which he claims, in retrospect, ironically gives the play a sense of "unreality and stiffness."[93] According to Arent, the only scene departing from direct quotation is the final one, which consists of a dizzying series of exclamations, resembling the fragments of the "teletype" script shouted by the loudspeaker. Uniformed representatives from Russia, Japan, Germany, Rumania, Poland, France, England, Italy, and Ethiopia stand abstracted on the stage, each spotlighted as he cries out, as the world approaches the cusp of war. The teletype setting the scene reads "WAR DRUMS BEAT OVER EUROPE" and the stage directions call for the unrelenting sound of marching feet to be played over the sound system. The voices of Italy and Ethiopia, the ostensible "problem" of the play, are stifled in this din, as a small imperialist war ignites into an international conflagration. The fragments Arent assigns to Ethiopia's representative in this scene—"A rifle for every man!" and "Fight to the death!"—differ dramatically from those assigned to the representatives of other nations. While most of the world is depicted verbalizing expressions of either warning or support, Arent never forgets that Ethiopia is fighting for its life.

Although these lines are "non-factual" additions, it is especially in this scene that we notice the absence of the "human element" that Arent claims is a necessary addendum to the Living Newspaper's realist documentation of events. Nowhere in *Ethiopia*, the earliest incarnation of the Living Newspaper, is there a sustained character who serves as the audience's "bridge," and the human beings are particularly abstracted in this final scene. However, he also claims that abstraction is "the essence of the Living Newspaper"—that is, *"the business of unrolling ten feet of grass carpet on a stage and saying 'This is five acres of land'—and what's more, making your audience believe it."*[94] Perhaps the aspect of *Ethiopia* that comes closest to satisfying both requirements—the need for abstraction and the human element—was, oddly enough, its casting. The play's Ethiopians were portrayed by an African opera troupe, serendipitously stranded in the United States. Isaac writes that the presence of these unemployed performers determined in part the Federal Theater's choice of subject: "This noble company of performers could speak no English, creating an interesting crux that was finally solved by casting them as native citizens of Ethiopia."[95] Audiences, faced with a small group of "authentic" Africans, would be prompted to imagine an actual Walwal encampment onstage:

> *It is the mid-day rest, and soldiers in their white shammas are sprawled on the ground, eating, drinking, etc. A few musical instruments are seen on the ground.*

> *Soon the first few notes of a native song are heard, vague at first, then growing clearer as one instrument after another takes it up. It is a sad, keening sort of air. The song mounts and soon a single plaintive voice is heard. The harmony is picked up by all, pianissimo. Sharply the song ends, and without pause the players start a livelier tune. A soldier starts to dance. The song rises, the tumult increases.*[96]

Rather than giving sentimental lines to a plainspoken character, Arent allows the human element to emerge in small, individualized, and expressive acts: "*a single plaintive voice is heard,*" "*A soldier starts to dance.*" If we compare this organic development of an expressive scene to that other theatrical scene of Ethiopian soldiers dancing—Sam, Ted, and Ray's performance in *Scandals* as restaged for *You Can't Have Everything*—Arent's desire to present the Ethiopian Crisis authentically becomes more apparent.

Arent's play, unfortunately, was censored before it could be staged. Its only performance was a largely uncostumed and Spartan "dress" rehearsal for a select group of drama critics and others. The play was received fairly well by those present.[97] Although the critic for the *New York Times*, Brooks Atkinson, remarked that it was "no masterpiece," he confirmed Rice's assessment that the play was presented "after the manner of a newsreel, showing as factually as possible how an isolated war stirs up repercussions everywhere."[98] An assistant to Harry Hopkins at the WPA, Jacob Baker, was apparently present at the play's rehearsal and, fearing geopolitical ramifications, declared that "no one impersonating a ruler or cabinet shall actually appear on the stage."[99] Hallie Flanagan wrote to Hopkins to insist that all characters "are characterized with great respect and with no attempt at cartooning. This is particularly true of Mussolini, who is presented sympathetically and with power."[100] Her appeal was unsuccessful.

As Arent adapted scripts from actual quotations found in the news, it is difficult to argue that the representation of Mussolini is exaggerated. Atkinson noted that, while the play did depict "Italy as the aggressor," this view corresponds to the League of Nations' assessment and as such the play was an "unbiased dramatic account" that "has suppressed none of the essential news."[101] However, given that *Ethiopia* was a government-sponsored production, Baker's overly circumspect response is not a surprise. The Federal Theater, to quote Isaac, learned that "governments, when they become the sponsoring agents of a play, cannot stand too much reality."[102] Ironically, the aforementioned *Scandals* version of Selassie, along with a lampooned Mussolini, entered the public sphere at precisely the same time. *Scandals*, of course, was privately funded, but it is remarkable that faithful depictions of the leaders were not permitted while a tap-dancing Selassie and a Mussolini singing of "darkies" were perfectly acceptable for public consumption. This interpretation of Selassie as "minstrel clown," to cite again a review mentioned earlier, was a far cry from the sober representation we find in 1930s poetry published in the black press. These poems sought to take the emperor and other representatives of Ethiopian imperial culture out of the realm of popular entertainment entirely—where the caricature of the Savage Statesman dramatized a perceived paradox in imperial Ethiopia's attempts to modernize—and into that of the lyric, as we will see in the following chapter.

CHAPTER SIX

Martial Ethiopianism in Verse

A king has fallen on the field—
The field of war, but not by shot,
Nor even through a broken shield:
He died in exile—awful lot!

—MARCUS GARVEY, "RAS NASIBU OF OGADEN"

WITH A CLAIM to the throne that rested upon an alleged direct line of ancestry reaching back to King Solomon, Emperor Haile Selassie was exhibited and lionized as the visible incarnation of the country's antiquity and permanence. To honor a black king, as Wilson Jeremiah Moses argues, proves troublesome from a democratic pan-African perspective: in discussing Ethiopianism's cousin, which he terms "Egyptomorphic Afrocentrism," he writes that "Black nationalists who cherish proletarian traditions are uncomfortable with the idea of tracing one's descent to an effete pharaoh with ceremonial flail, mascaraed eyes, and 'sneer of cold command,' compelling faceless hordes to drag blocks of sandstone up the side of a pyramid."[1] And yet there is a persistent tension between the desire to celebrate the grandiosity of a historic black empire on the one hand and the commitment to democratic ideals on the other. We see the celebration of pharaohs, for example, in the work of Meta Warrick Fuller, in her pre–Harlem Renaissance sculpture *Ethiopia Awakening*, and later in her protégée Lois Mailou Jones's painting *Ascent of Ethiopia*, with both visual artists conflating Ethiopia and Egypt in order to articulate diaspora through the glorification of royalty. The pomp of Haile Selassie's 1930 coronation was marked by the first of two *Time* magazine cover photos of the emperor, and this cover arguably heralded the start of American, and especially African American, fascination with the figure.

The paradox of imperial Ethiopianism—that is, a reverential attitude toward the Ethiopian regal line existing side by side but at odds with a democratic and collective approach to black solidarity—runs throughout African American literature of the 1930s dealing with Ethiopia. Poets as varied as J. Harvey L. Baxter, Melvin B. Tolson, Langston Hughes, and countless others wrote verse intended as calls to action, encouraging readers to rally in support of the Ethiopian cause, but they often did so through the praising of exemplary regal icons despite ostensibly fighting for justice and equality. In many cases, these regal icons of the 1930s were depicted, as Tewodros was in E. Davidson's poem dedicated to him, in their roles as soldiers. The title of this chapter gestures toward this ideological perspective: a pan-African/black nationalist perspective filtered through the bifocal lenses of militarism and imperialism.

Poets harnessed the collective voices calling for racial solidarity in support of the Ethiopian cause for distillation and expression into the individualized lyric voice of the Ethiopian imperial military hero. The romantic views in these lyric utterances, however, only succeed in emphasizing the challenges that the Ethiopian cause presented to the very racial solidarity marshaled to support it. The anti-democratic nature of the defense of Ethiopian imperialism and the disruptive figure of the Askari soldier, fighting on the side of European imperialist powers, illustrate the impediments to intraracial collaborative action highlighted by the Italo-Ethiopian War.

A Versified Call to Action

When the headlines announced that Italy had invaded Ethiopia in 1935, African Americans called upon historical reserves of sympathy for the nation—reserves drawing from both its ancient symbolism and its modern signification, echoing in this duality the contemporaneous journalistic discourse—and held mass meetings, protests, parades, and boycotts in its support. Viewed not only through the lens of racial solidarity but also through a familiar ideology of Ethiopianism, Mussolini's attempt to colonize Ethiopia was met with a remarkably unified African American response. As Harold Preece (identified by the *Crisis* as a "white Texan") wrote in a November 1935 article titled "War and the Negro," "The rape of Ethiopia is the rape of the Negro race" and "to support any combination of imperialists is to invite destruction of all the hopes now entertained from Harlem to Kenya."[2] As Preece put it, and as many African Americans believed, "Ethiopia can well become a pivotal point in the struggle for the complete emancipation of the black peoples."[3] In other words, it would be reductive to view aid for Ethiopia as simply altruistic, although it was; it was also believed to be an act of self-preservation. Giving support and sympathy, black communities across the United States (and in fact around the world) condemned Italy and demanded action. Many African Americans who desired to fight alongside the Ethiopian army, thwarted by U.S. laws prohibiting fighting in the militaries of foreign nations, approached the Spanish Civil War as a sort of substitute war, as illustrated in the subtitle of a published project of the Abraham Lincoln Brigade Archives: *"This Ain't Ethiopia, but It'll Do."*[4] Still, the speaker of a poem by J. Harvey L. Baxter, "To the Barefoot Lads," yearns to fight in Ethiopia, romantically and patriotically comparing the shoeless and under-armed Ethiopian troops to those led by Washington at Valley Forge, saying, "Oh, how I wish that I could be with the barefoot lads across the sea; / And with some Ras could take my stand, / To fight or die for the Fatherland."[5]

As leaders of the Abyssinian Baptist Church—a church in fact named for Ethiopia—Adam Clayton Powell Sr. (minister from 1908 to 1937), and later Powell Jr. (minister from 1937 to 1971), led efforts to increase awareness of the crisis, the latter involved in the Committee for Ethiopia. But the Abyssinian Baptist Church was only one spoke in the crucial fundraising hub that was Harlem. Important organizations based in Harlem that were active in soliciting support for Ethiopia included the Universal Ethiopian Students' Organization, the United Aid for Ethiopia, the Provisional Committee for the Defense of Ethiopia (PCDE; a group composed of members of the Communist Party and Garvey's Universal Negro Improvement Association, among others), and the Friends of Ethiopia in America, started by historian Willis N. Huggins. In August 1935, on behalf of the International Council of Friends of Ethiopia and sponsored by the PCDE and other groups, Huggins submitted a memorandum to the League of Nations, which failed to intervene in preventing the aggression of one member nation toward another, that expressed the "righteous indignation by the blacks in the western world who are bound by racial kinship to the ancient and illustrious Ethiopian people."[6] Huggins's interest in Ethiopia predates the 1935 crisis; he traces his group's founding to 1919, when an Ethiopian delegation visited Harlem at the invitation of Huggins and other important Harlem luminaries who "welcomed them, not only in the name of Harlem but in the name of black folk throughout America."[7] Eight years later, another Ethiopian dignitary, in the United States for a diplomatic visit, met with Arthur Schomburg, who held the title of curator of the African History Section of the library that now bears his name (then simply the 135th Street Library). In the years following this visit, according to Huggins, Schomburg, "by lecture and by writings, [strove] to keep up a lively interest in Ethiopia."[8] Huggins himself offered classes in African civilization at the 135th Street YMCA starting in 1932.

In addition, representing the marriage of Ethiopian and African American interests literally, a prominent couple, Malaku and Dorothy Bayen, promoted the Ethiopian cause. In 1931, Malaku Bayen, nephew of Haile Selassie, married Dorothy Hadley, an African American woman from Evanston, Illinois, and the couple appears to have seen their marriage not only as a personal love story but also as a performance of black solidarity. Malaku claimed, "My belief in Race Solidarity caused me to select Howard University for my studies, in order that I might have a closer contact with my people. It was this idea that helped me to break my engagement to the daughter of our Minister of Foreign Affairs and to be married to an American girl of the Black Race."[9] The 1939 book from which this quotation comes, with the provocative title *The March of Black Men—Ethiopia Leads*, develops its argument for the military defense of Ethiopia around racial kinship.

Dorothy, for her part, moved to Ethiopia with her husband during the war. Her personal correspondence tells stories of the difficulties they faced, including a bomb scare. When they lived in the United States, she also assisted her husband in running a foundation called the Haile Selassie Fund, which raised money through lectures. In a letter to her sister, she said that they based their operations downtown "to give the nordics a chance to aid us if they wished":

> We didn't want them to say "you went up to Harlem to the blacks to get help from them—not us." . . . In the five weeks there, we got $7 from whites and around $1700 from blacks so we decided that they do not intend to help. It is my belief that the redemption of Ethiopia lies within the hands of the black peoples of the world and that the *unity* of all the black peoples and the redemption of Ethiopia are convergent (?) problems. As you know, our fault and our weakness has been in the fact that we will not unite.[10]

The Bayens, in other words, aimed to marry Ethiopians and African Americans in the 1930s, pointing them toward their common goal of restoring Ethiopia's sovereignty.

Although Hughes and other major authors we associate with the Harlem Renaissance engaged with the Italo-Ethiopian War and its implications in their writing, even more lesser-known and amateur writers took up their pens to join the call to action. One of those minor authors inspired by the war in Ethiopia was J. Harvey L. Baxter. His *Sonnets for the Ethiopians* was published in 1936 in Roanoke, Virginia.[11] In his preface, he confronts the crisis directly and makes his political aims clear: "The world has currently observed the most wanton of the tragedies of the century, the gobbling up of Ethiopia by Italy." A veteran of World War I, and thus framing the defense of Ethiopia as a similarly moral imperative, Baxter claims that the poems in this book "that have been woven around this unholy episode portray the heart and spirit of one eternally and unalterably averse to wars of aggression in any form." Although he acknowledges the seeming hopelessness of the cause, he writes, "let no true votary of freedom despair," because the "League of Nations can be redeemed, and Ethiopia's cause can be saved, if or whenever the spirit, or soul of collective security is recast, or reborn through the personalities of militant men."[12] Presumably, Baxter is one of those militant men, as he hopes his readers are, dedicating his book "to the Votaries of Liberty, Justice and Humanity Everywhere." He hopes to effect real change and to inspire action through his verse—to serve as a "champion," as he calls himself in his sonnet "Africa."

Like other literary treatments of the war from this period, *Sonnets for the Ethiopians* presents both abstract and concrete visions of Ethiopia—a modern-day nation threatened by Mussolini grafted onto an ancestral home shrouded in obscurity. Poems like "Well May I Sing of the Proud Ethiope" and "To Ethiopia" refer to ancient history and invoke the well-worn biblical verse, respectively, the former poem glorifying the country's "primeval speech" and "obfuscated past."[13] Baxter ultimately finds his most effective approach in attempting to synthesize the abstract and concrete visions, a synthesis facilitated by the legendary imperial histories of the two nations in question. In a pair of poems, "Italy to Ethiopia" and "Ethiopia to Italy," two empires speak to one another. The first views the "rape" of the country from Mussolini's point of view as a perverse seduction: as if channeling Marlowe's Passionate Shepherd, he pleads, "Come forth and close embrace me Ethiope."[14] The poem in response takes a long view of the current moment as just one clash in a centuries-long struggle between empires. History repeats itself as, Ethiopia says, "age on age I dealt them blow for blow." Baxter's Ethiopianist perspective allows for a cyclical rather than progressive narrative of time in order to imagine a successful end for Ethiopia, regardless of technological advancements: "Not then I bowed to ancient spear and bow, / Not now I yield to modern shot and shell."[15]

As with many other African American poets of the period, the depth of Baxter's zeal for the Ethiopian cause derives from his sense of a profound diasporic connection. In "Latin or Greek," he discusses the difference between the identifiers "Negro" and "Ethiope," coming down—as did the Star Order of Ethiopia—on the side of the latter.[16] The men with whom he chooses to identify are "old as the ages, as sacred as time: / Burnt-faced features, raven skin, / One and together, ebony men." By the last line, he has merged with the timeless men and stands alongside them. But while Baxter longs for a return to his ancestral identity, he also argues that the hope of linking Africans and African Americans necessarily lies in a bilateral movement. He urges Ethiopia to inch toward Westernization in the poem "King of Kings," encouraging Selassie to "civilize" his "barbarous men" and "have them march before your eyes, / In teguments of mind and dress, / The equals of the East and West."[17] In short, unless they "civilize," he cannot see them as his equals.

"King of Kings" is only one of several poems in the book featuring Selassie. The poem "Haile Selassie" nearly sanctifies the emperor, first comparing him to L'Ouverture, Cromwell, and Washington before descending much further into the annals of time to compare him to "the great / Of Israel" and giving him the ancient-sounding epithet "Haile of the Ethiopes."[18] At times Baxter appears eager to usher Selassie and the Ethiopians into the "modern" age, while at other times he seems to demand that they remain in a perpetual past, much like the Ethiopians in *Of One Blood*, whose frozen-in-time lost civilization of Meroe draws Reuel back, through New World generations, to his rightful place on the ancient Ethiopian throne.

The Imperial Lyric Voice

Poems about Selassie appear frequently in African American periodicals throughout the late 1930s, with several focusing upon his eloquent appeal for help from the League of Nations, a speech even paraphrased by Baxter in "Oh, Hang Your Heads, a Voice Accusing Cries (*A King of Kings before the League*)." Although he writes in his preface that "the League of Nations can be redeemed," Baxter does not shy away from expressing his anger and frustration with the institution. He opens the sestet of his Petrarchan sonnet "The World" with a scathing indictment: "No more the parliaments of justice work!" An even more passionate invective can be found in "To the League of Nations," where he exclaims, "Be dead, Oh, foul instrument! / Today I bid you, League, farewell, / And carve upon your monument, / The fury epitaph of Hell."[19]

Selassie's powerful and persuasive "accusing" voice addressing the League of Nations, for many, proved the dignity of his cause and of his perspective. It is the focus of Baxter's "The Emperor's Voice," which claims that Selassie's "Thor-like voice shook chancelleries" with a godlike violence. Although his public image frequently exhibited him in military uniform, the voice of the diminutive king was seen as his true weapon. Just as Baxter hopes to move readers to action, he himself is moved to action upon hearing the "the thunder of the NEGUS-VOICE," an echo of the "NEGUS-CRY" he hears in "Ethiopia, Ethiopia."[20] Similarly, Rufus Gibson's "The Voice of Ethiopia," published in the January 1936 issue of the *Crisis*, takes the power of voice as its subject—in this case, that of Ethiopia personified. Ethiopia's voice functions as a hypnotic beacon or homing device, summoning the diaspora back to fight:

> What voice this be
> That strangely calls to me
> From out the maze of dreams my slumbers bring?
> Ah! no this seems no captive's cry to be;
> For yesternight I heard its clarion ring
> Within my thoughts dense wilderness, when sleep
> Her somniferous breath upon my eyes
> Had blown, bidding my soul its tryst to keep.

In the haze of this trance, Gibson's speaker heeds Ethiopia's call to plunder the corners of the world in which the diasporic subjects find themselves dispersed. In a strange reversal of the rape of resources suffered by the colonial world, Ethiopia compels her children to avenge her for all that has been stolen from her since "ravenous hordes despoiled our land":

> Now gather to me out of every land
> To which the four-winds bore you long ago,—
> Come you to me again, a motley band,
> Come children all that from my loins did grow,
> Bring borrowed jewels from the strangers' camps
> Yet while in sleep upon their beds they lie,
> Bring to your Motherland oil for her lamps
> To light the path on which your brethren ply
> Through centuries of deep and dark content.[21]

Encouraging the charitable giving of cash and material goods was the goal of fundraising efforts during the Ethiopian crisis, but in this poem charity is not enough. As Baxter did in "To the Barefoot Lads," Gibson yields to a martial fantasy. Ethiopia commands him, "Gird well your loins, take up both sword and shield / And forthwith march. As warriors, meet the foe / As did your sires who ne'er to tyrants yield." Although African Americans were not permitted to fight alongside Ethiopian forces, Gibson and others could not help imagining themselves doing so.

Unsurprisingly, the occasional verse written for periodicals during the war often depicted military scenes, immortalizing Ethiopian military heroes in verse. In July 1937, the *Crisis* published a poem by Jay N. Hill titled "An Ethiope in Spain," inspired by a son of Ras Imru fighting in the Spanish Civil War. Although the Ethiopian soldier fights alongside Americans and Europeans, Hill cannot conceive of him as a truly modern equal, viewing him instead through a romantic and atavistic lens:

> Silent man of the past, he seemed heroic,
> Through disillusion and forced exile,
> Through faded visions of Adowa,
> Of ancient streets in Addis Ababa,
> Of mountains and muddy roads in Abyssinia,
> Where barefoot men
> Trudged their way through centuries
> Of peace, and calmly roamed the hills.[22]

Not only is the soldier trapped in a nebulous fantasy of the past, he is a literary fiction before he even enters Hill's poem, as he is measured against a Shakespearean invention: the poem begins with the declaration that "no jewel shone in this Ethiope's ear." Unlike Selassie, in the poems commemorating the League of Nations speech, this soldier is voiceless, unable to communicate with his fellow soldiers in Italian, Spanish, French, or English. Not even Amharic is flexible enough to express the inscrutable depths of the soldier, as "language could not match / The eloquence of his silence." The exotic prince is not a fellow soldier but a mute and timeless symbol of what they are fighting for.

The Ethiopian language does, however, make its way into Melvin Tolson's "The Bard of Addis Ababa," which, as John Cullen Gruesser points out, "evince[s] an impressive familiarity with Ethiopian history, culture, and geography."[23] Tolson has clearly done his research, integrating esoteric Amharic words into his poem. Discussions of Tolson's manipulations of modernist techniques and strategies, particularly the use of scholarly apparatuses reminiscent of T. S. Eliot's endnotes in *The Waste Land*, abound in scholarship about his work. Unlike his "Harlem Gallery," however, "The Bard of Addis Ababa" is not accompanied by notes. "The Bard of Addis Ababa" is included in *Rendezvous with America*, a collection of poems that, according to Raymond Nelson's "Editorial Statement" to Tolson's

"Harlem Gallery" and Other Poems of Melvin B. Tolson, are "genuinely straightforward; they can and should be read without supplements."[24] Without knowledge of Amharic, however, the poem remains inaccessible. By integrating Amharic words and concepts into his poem rather than, for instance, Greek or Latin, Tolson dignifies African systems of knowledge, granting these references the same authority typically given to classical ones, and in the process obscures the poem for Eurocentric readers.[25] In fact, in Tolson's poem, the Italian soldiers, effectively descended from a Latinate tradition, literally pale in comparison to the vitality of the African traditions embodied in the Bard of Addis Ababa. In contrast to the dull, pedestrian, "granite-eyed" Italians, the Ethiopian Bard has eyes that are "glowing like anthracite."[26]

Carrying with him "the lore of six thousand years," the Bard's gravitas is rooted in his timelessness. If he seems immortal, he is also, paradoxically, eternally dead; Tolson introduces the Bard as "cadaverous." But the Bard's Lazarus-like quality is, of course, in keeping with the Ethiopianist ideology that prophesies the revitalization of a dormant Ethiopia. The poem in fact concludes with the Ethiopian soldiers' call to those long-slumbering descendants, as the Bard (accompanied by a dog) walks into the future: "A great dog and a graybeard ahead. / 'O Bard of Addis Ababa!' / Cry the heroes to wake up the dead." The dog by the Bard's side here is the very dog with which the poem opens, apparently stray and vicious, a foreboding omen of the fight between Italy and Ethiopia: "His growl presaging a menace / Like a fog-horn in a fog." Along with a hyena and a boa, the dog "rips the . . . jackal / With scimitar tooth and claw." Since the jackal is a symbol of Italy and Mussolini, used again later in the poem, the dog comes to represent not just the general harbinger of war but Ethiopia's role in the war specifically; the destruction of the jackal is Tolson's prophesy that Ethiopia will ultimately triumph over Italy.

Not only does the Bard "chan[t] of men fleshed in epic," but he holds a unifying and tremendous power in every community through which he travels, a "hero of *grazmatch* and vendor, / Of *hakim* and beggar and wag" (emphasis in original).[27] Although he is primarily a "blooded Amharic scholar," he is literally an acknowledged legislator whose "name is the emblem of justice": "outdoor courts invoke him / To sentence man or beast; / And debtors chained to their masters / Appeal to the Bard for release." In affording this level of authority to another poet, Tolson imagines an active role for the poet in the world—as one, for example, who would and could influence the carrying out of justice by inspiring a change of course in the Italo-Ethiopian War, just as Baxter hoped to accomplish. (Lorenzo Thomas in fact claims that the Bard's influence as "both the bearer of tradition and the people's inspiration" is "a role that Tolson coveted for himself.")[28] Faced with the injustice of the Italian occupation, the Bard embodies a populist heroism, as he "chants . . . / Of the freedoms that keep men free." He serves as a human repository of patriotic and democratic national history and a warrior besides, complete with dagger, wandering "under his forefathers' flag" as if marching under a guidon. As a versifier, he can inspire others to action—particularly military action—through the "battle-cry of his ballads, / The meters' blood-spurring pace, / The star-reach of his spearing finger." He and his military mission even appear to be sanctioned by God, with a halo-like "Diadem of Light":

> Princes and bishops and scholars
> Pyramid to left and right
> Of the Conquering Lion of Judah
> And the Diadem of Light,
> And the red-and-gold pavilion
> Glitters with vassal and knight.

The Bard appears to have merged with the emperor ("Conquering Lion of Judah"). Just as the Ethiopian royal family claimed a line of descent that linked them to a Solomonic dynasty, the Bard's fight appears to fulfill biblical destiny. He mobilizes the Ethiopian peoples by pointing them toward their religiously determined fate. However, the Bard's inspiration relies upon the usual fantasy of universal regalization. In his chant, which constitutes section II of the poem, he suggests that, with the Ethiopian warriors' defeat of the Italians, "a *ras*, a *dejazmatch*, a king—yoho!—/ Each father's son shall be." Crowns are, in fact, everywhere in this poem: the "Palaver House shall . . . crown / The kith and kin of man"; the Bard himself wears a "bejeweled corona befitting / a *ras* or a chamberlain" as "barbaric splendor crowns him"; even the aforementioned "Diadem of Light" may be grouped with them. That Tolson cannot resist the proliferation of crowns here signals the presence of the fantasy of universal regalization at work.

The Askari Soldier

Even those critical of the emperor, such as Garvey, whose growing disdain for Selassie's imperiousness was compounded by a personal slight—he was snubbed when he attempted to meet with Selassie in England[29]—refuse to give up an Ethiopianism founded upon empire. In 1937, Garvey published in his own periodical, *Black Man*, at least two elegies dedicated to Ethiopian military heroes, "Ras Nasibu of Ogaden" and "Ras Desta" (*ras* being the titular equivalent of a duke), and both notably praise a military strength shaped and informed by imperial culture. For the thoroughly imperial Garvey, the crucial difference between Selassie on the one hand and Nasibu and Desta on the other lies in the latters' military sacrifice, rendering them exemplars of martial Ethiopianism.

The nature of Garvey's veneration of Nasibu as a military hero of the Ethiopian resistance is unmistakably monarchic: he begins "Ras Nasibu" with the line, "A king has fallen on the field."[30] While he criticizes Selassie for fleeing to England—for being, as he puts it, "a great coward who ran away from his country to save his skin and left the millions of his countrymen to struggle through a terrible war"—Garvey instead pities Nasibu for the "awful lot" of "d[ying] in exile." Unlike Selassie, Nasibu is "a king [who] los[t] his part / In building glory with his bricks."[31] Although he refers to Nasibu as a king twice, he also implies that he is a model of collective participation—thwarted or snuffed out—who wanted ardently and democratically to do his part (in fact, Garvey reinforces the word "part" by rhyming it *with itself* here in the poem). Nasibu was not just defending an existing nation but "build[ing]" one.

So, rather than abandoning his nation and willfully separating himself from his people, as Selassie did, Nasibu (in Garvey's eyes) suffers from a longing common to conceptions of diaspora: the desire for return. In fact, Garvey claims that "a king has fallen on the field," despite his acknowledgment three lines later that he did *not*: he died in exile. As Brent Hayes Edwards reminds us, the term "diaspora" looks to the future as well as the past and contains within it "a dialectical tension between dispersal and return, loss and restoration."[32] The anticipatory restoration is expressed in Garvey's poem as not just an Ethiopian one but a pan-African one. After mourning the loss of Nasibu, Garvey writes, "The Negroes of the world shall wait / To take their stand against the foe, / And when they fight to win their State / They'll make Italians drink their woe."

This diasporic dialectic of dispersal and return haunts another poem dedicated to Nasibu, written by the Baroness Maria Atzel. Like Garvey, she mourns his death in the "awful lot" of exile, the reverberations of which are felt in his "dear native land" where "flowers of the Ogaden in sorrow sway; / In distant Ethiopia sounds Thy dirge."[33] The thread connecting him, in absentia, to his homeland is so strong and vital that it persists despite the violence of the separation, which is also hinted at in Garvey's line break: "And tanks that ploughed and also rent / the land." Even the cause of Nasibu's death speaks to how his lived experience in Ethiopia survives exile: he died of delayed aftereffects of his exposure to mustard gas during the war (notably the famous Battle of the Ogaden in 1936), described in Garvey's poem as Mussolini's "liquid flames of steady death."

There is no question that the Italians' use of mustard gas made for what Garvey calls, in his poem "Ras Desta," "history's most unequal fight."[34] However, despite the dramatic mismatch of military technologies of the countries involved, the deciding factor in the failure of the Ethiopians to defend their country, according to Garvey, is in fact the Askari soldiers—"black men fighting black men"—whom he blames for "every battle that the Italians won in Abyssinia." The black colonial soldier, enlisted by European powers in various military campaigns, was the inverse of the figure of martial Ethiopianism exemplified by Ras Nasibu. Where the figure of martial Ethiopianism marries militarism to black empire, serving as an aristocratic symbol on which to project and tether the connections among the black peoples of the world, the Askari soldier fights to uphold European colonial interests, undermining the connections of black diaspora. Both are "exiled," so to speak, but the figure of martial Ethiopianism maintains a clarity of purpose and strength of connection lacking in the Askari soldier, who confounds and frustrates the possibilities of black empire.

Photographs and illustrations depicting these soldiers—especially those from neighboring Eritrea and Somalia, two pillars of the Italian East African empire—survive in archival collections of Italian Fascist propaganda and memorabilia.[35] The representation of black loyalty and commitment to the colonial project was an important facet of colonialist propaganda. The idea that these black soldiers saw themselves as constituents (and beneficiaries) and not simply military tools of the Italian empire was a necessary part of the moral defense of the incursion into the colonies. At the same time, however, the propaganda cannot help but visually assert racial difference. Ethnic and cultural characteristics are represented in the thorny and contradictory use of animal imagery that does triple duty here: (1) the choice of animal (lions, tigers, cheetahs) points to the fierceness and strength of the soldiers; (2) in addition, in some cases, it serves as a legitimate and authentic link preserving the soldier's ethnic identity—the lion, for example, symbolizing the Lion of Judah; and, finally, (3) it is a reminder to the propagandistic image's original audience of the animalistic and dehumanized nature of the African soldier.

There are several images that accomplish all three of these at once. In one postcard, titled "XI Battaglione Arabo-Somalo 'Ferrante,'" the soldier mimics the cheetah's pose. In another, "Artiglieria Camellata Della

FIGURE 6.1. "XI Battaglione Arabo-Somalo 'Ferrante.'" Postcards and printed ephemera documenting the Italian occupation of Ethiopia (MS 1898). Manuscripts and Archives, Yale University Library, New Haven, CT.

Somalia Italiana," the color scheme attempts to draw a parallel between the soldiers, the landscape, and the camels (the soldier in the foreground even appears to have a camel-like hump). In yet another, "V Battaglione Arabo Somalo," the stripes of the lion's flag match the soldier's sash. These parallels are no accident, and they are pervasive. In attempting to overcome racial difference and insist upon the loyalty of these soldiers to the colonial power, the visual argument of the Italian postcards cannot resist dehumanization of the African.

The racism driving this dehumanization inhibits the presumed efforts to make the military forces seem human and heroic, as opposed to the picture of mechanized warfare celebrated, for example, by the Futurist F. T. Marinetti. Specifically about this war, Marinetti wrote, "War is beautiful because—thanks to its gas masks, its terrifying megaphones, its flame throwers, and light tanks—it establishes man's dominion over the subjugated machine. War is beautiful because it inaugurates the dreamed-of metallization of the human body."[36] Marinetti's language returns us to the one-sided, unequal war depicted by Garvey, with distant Italians

FIGURE 6.2. "Artiglieria Camellata Della Somalia Italiana." Postcards and printed ephemera documenting the Italian occupation of Ethiopia (MS 1898). Manuscripts and Archives, Yale University Library, New Haven, CT.

dropping liquid fire on Ethiopian soldiers below. The attempt to mechanize the Askari body is suggested by its placement as the conclusion of a litany of terrors facing the Ethiopians in the following quotation from historian Angelo Del Boca: "The bombs from the air. The shelling from the long-range howitzers. The deadly sputter of machine guns. The tanks. The

FIGURE 6.3. "V Battaglione Arabo Somalo." Postcards and printed ephemera documenting the Italian occupation of Ethiopia (MS 1898). Manuscripts and Archives, Yale University Library, New Haven, CT.

Askaris."[37] However, the visual propaganda insists upon the picture not of cyborgs fighting men but of Black "Italians" fighting Black Africans on the ground: "black men fighting black men," to quote Garvey. Visually, the Italian propaganda attempts to make it seem a fair (and intraracial) fight.

Puncturing this fantasy of noble—albeit brutalized—African Italian soldiers, Baxter's "To the Askaris," for example, accuses them of treachery.

If they are the picture of military bravery, as the Italians would have it, Baxter declares he would "rather dodge, be yellow, dally, shirk."[38] Garvey's 1935 poem "The Brutal Crime" mocks them as "grinning . . . April fools at summer play."[39] Although Garvey's attack is mainly generalized, he singles out one target of his vitriol by name: the Ethiopian Ras Haile Selassie Gugsa, the traitorous son-in-law of Selassie (caricatured in George S. Schuyler's *Revolt in Ethiopia*, which I discuss in the next chapter), whom Garvey castigates as "ignoble of fame." Gugsa is the "cursed fool who fell for Rome / And marched against the Motherland"; in falling for Rome, Garvey suggests, Gugsa reverses the historical fall of the Roman Empire and hastens the rebuilding of it, supporting Mussolini's dream. The polar opposite of Rases Nasibu and Desta, Ras Gugsa, Garvey warns, disrupts and counters the natural order of racial solidarity necessary to black nationalism, the righteousness of which approaches an almost ineffable holiness: "the cause that is sublime."

The Challenges of Décalage

In *The Practice of Diaspora: Literature, Translation and the Rise of Black Internationalism*, Brent Hayes Edwards uses the term *décalage* to describe a spatial and temporal "lag" embedded in the idea of diaspora that both links and divides black peoples of different ethnic-cultural identities. There are impediments to intraracial sympathy that are intrinsic to diasporic *décalage*—the "trace or residue . . . of what resists or escapes translation."[40] Langston Hughes's "Letter from Spain" is a pessimistic expression of this phenomenon. In the poem, an African American soldier fighting in the Spanish Civil War encounters another black man fighting for Franco's army. As Edwards points out in his reading of the poem, "the exchange between the African American and the North African fails to result in any sort of internationalist collaboration":[41]

Addressed to Alabama
    Lincoln Battalion,
    International Brigades,
    November Something, 1937.

Dear Brother at home:

We captured a wounded Moor today.
He was just as dark as me.
I said, Boy, what you been doin' here
Fightin' against the free?

He answered something in a language
I couldn't understand.
But somebody told me he was sayin'
They nabbed him in his land

And made him join the fascist army
And come across to Spain.
And he said he had a feelin'
He'd never get back home again.

He said he had a feelin'
This whole thing wasn't right.
He said he didn't know
The folks he had to fight.

And as he lay there dying
In a village we had taken,
I looked across to Africa
And seed foundations shakin'.

Cause if a free Spain wins this war,
The colonies, too, are free—
Then something wonderful'll happen
To them Moors as dark as me.

I said, I guess that's why old England
And I reckon Italy, too,
Is afraid to let a workers' Spain
Be too good to me and you—

Cause they got slaves in Africa—
And they don't want 'em to be free.
Listen, Moorish prisoner, hell!
Here, shake hands with me!

I knelt down there beside him,
And I took his hand—
But the wounded Moor was dyin'
And he didn't understand.

Salud,

Johnny[42]

The racial solidarity called for by an idealistic pan-Africanism is of course disrupted and short-circuited here, not only because the two black soldiers fight for opposing armies but because they speak mutually incomprehensible languages. The speaker is only able to understand the prisoner through a translator. As Edwards puts it, "If this encounter marks a diasporic instance, it implies that a diaspora is necessarily translated and mediated."[43] The American soldier certainly makes an effort to connect: he explicitly links both his fate and that of the "dying Moor" to the outcome of the Spanish Civil War. In addition, the poem ends with the speaker's effort to transcend this language barrier and reassert racial solidarity through grasping the other soldier's hand, but the effort ultimately falls short. Even in the end, "the wounded Moor was dyin' / And he didn't understand." Nevertheless, Hughes's speaker sees beyond the individual, to the larger collective picture. He "looked across to Africa / And seed foundations shakin' "—the death blow to European colonial power. Hughes's depiction of the colonial soldier's despair, sent to fight in a country he has never seen, stands in stark contrast to the image put forth in the Italian Askari propaganda.

The poem's composition, according to Hughes's autobiography *I Wonder as I Wander*, was prompted by his encounters with Moroccan soldiers fighting for the Fascists—encounters, notably, shaped by various degrees of alienation. He describes a scene similar to the one in the poem, in which he tries to communicate but finds that it is "almost impossible . . . to carry on any sort of conversation" with the wounded Moroccan soldiers captured by the Republicans because "they spoke little or no Spanish and [he] had no interpreter."[44] An earlier encounter he describes, however, is one of even more profound shock and estrangement. While visiting the hospital, Hughes turns a corner to run into "one of the darkest, tallest men I have ever seen in my life":

> His blackness was accentuated by a white hospital gown flopping about his bare legs, and a white bandage around his head. Not having seen a Negro since I'd been in Madrid, the sudden sight of this very dark face almost startled me out of my wits. There at the corner of the corridor the man and I would have collided, had I not stopped in my tracks as he passed me without a word, silently like a black ghost.
>
> I was a bit ashamed of myself for having been startled at the unexpected sight of a dark face in a hospital I had thought filled only with white prisoners. . . . [H]ere I was—a Negro myself—suddenly frightened by another dark face![45]

Here, Hughes finds himself on the other end of the intraracial dialogue: rather than recognizing, as Johnny does, another face "as dark as me" and attempting to foster a racial solidarity that would bridge the cultural divide, Hughes, upon facing the real-life Moorish soldier, enacts the bewilderment of the poem's Moorish soldier. Not only does Hughes fail to recognize the Moroccan man as a racial brother, he dehumanizes him to the point of ghostliness and scolds himself for doing so. The cultural divide allows no handshake; they are two ships passing in the night.

And yet, Hughes mentions two pages later that African Americans fighting in the International Brigades were in constant danger—"amusingly enough," as he curiously puts it—of being mistaken for Moroccan soldiers. He cites the case of Walter Cobb, who is saved only by his ability to speak Spanish and French: when Cobb captures a Fascist truck and returns to the Loyalist front lines with his prize, he is forced to explain at gunpoint that he is an American fighting on their side. Cobb, unlike the linguistically impoverished soldiers on both sides in Hughes's poem, uses his ability to translate in order to avoid misidentification—that is, to assert his difference from those who appear to be his racial brothers.[46]

These two incidences—the first featuring two black men who do not recognize a connection between them, and the second featuring a black man refusing to be recognized as a member of another faction of black men—are even more hopeless examples of the failure of black solidarity than the one in Hughes's poem. However, there is a cross-cultural encounter described in this chapter of *I Wonder as I Wander* that promises, at first, to be a productive one. Hughes meets a thirteen-year-old Moroccan boy who speaks Spanish and has a brief conversation with him, during which he learns that the boy had come to Spain with his mother, who was presumably recruited to wash and cook for the troops and is now deceased.[47] Communication, as Hughes discovers, is predictably not enough; although he learns from this brief exchange, the boy's experience is so alien to Hughes that the dialogue breaks off after the boy's expression of loss.

The poem inspired by these encounters turned out to be an effective propagandistic tool for the Ethiopian cause, with the anecdote of the Moroccan soldier serving as a cautionary tale regarding the dissolution of racial sympathy. "Letter from Spain" was originally published in an English-language periodical for the International Brigades in Spain, but the poem was reprinted in 1937 in the *New Times and Ethiopia News*, a newspaper that claimed to be "doing the biggest thing done for Ethiopia, save only the deathless struggle of the brave people in Ethiopia herself." Initially published in England by suffragist and anti-Fascist Sylvia Pankhurst, and quickly reaching an international circulation of ten thousand, the *New Times and Ethiopia News* strengthened and facilitated the networks of black diaspora. A letter to the editor, for example, from the chairman of the "Negro Co-operative" of the "Dock Workers' Union" of Suriname (then Dutch Guiana) wrote to cheer on the newspaper's efforts, claiming that "the Ethiopia News is reaching many people here, even in the hinterland."[48] Another letter from Nigeria urged them to "keep on, for truth wins."[49] The newspaper was "widely quoted in the emerging African nationalist press—which reproduced many articles from it, often without attribution of the source."[50] In the United States, *Phylon*, edited by W. E. B. Du Bois, expressed interest in the newspaper's project. A 1942 letter from Du Bois to Pankhurst congratulated her on her "very find [*sic*] work for Africa"; after "reading with great interest and using abstracts from your NEW TIMES AND ETHIOPIA NEWS," Du Bois asks for original photographs from the newspaper that he may reprint in *Phylon*.[51] A truly international endeavor, the newspaper printed letters to the editor from all over Africa, the Caribbean, and Europe, and a small section titled "IN THE U.S.A" informed readers where they could obtain the newspaper in America.

The *New Times and Ethiopia News* recognized that this international audience was engaged in critical marketing and publicity for the newspaper, resulting in a mutually enriching relationship. In a column titled "To One and All," thanks went to an "increasing effort, unadvertised, but none the less potent and far reaching, [that] continues among the readers" in securing local library subscriptions and demanding them at newsstands. Readers even bought one-dollar posters to display "on their garden walls or front windows," an effort identified by the paper as "a valuable means of advertisement." The newspaper made no secret of its propagandistic mission: "Our object is to mould opinion and we have evidence that opinion is being moulded by the information given in our paper week by week."[52]

Reprinting Hughes's poem in Pankhurst's newspaper was a clear message. As the newspaper's content in general functioned largely as anti-Fascist propaganda for the Ethiopian cause, and worked to lionize the figure of martial Ethiopianism, who was engaged in the so-called "deathless struggle of the brave people in Ethiopia herself," a reader could not help but read the poem through that lens. As such, the seeming throwaway line in Hughes's poem "And I reckon Italy, too"—that is, Italy is one of the countries "afraid to let a workers' Spain / Be too good to me and you"—gains tremendous significance in this context.

Readers of the *New Times and Ethiopia News* are likely to have seen Hughes's "dying Moor" (like his cousin, the Askari soldier serving in the Italian armed forces in Ethiopia) as a mirror image of the model of martial Ethiopianism represented by figures like Ras Nasibu. The challenges of intraracial filiation acknowledged by Hughes's poem make the bond between Garvey and Nasibu all the more stunning in contrast. Whereas Hughes and the Moroccan cannot understand one another, Garvey implicitly understands his subject who, as he says, "shall live through pen of Negro scribe." Not, notably, "Abyssinian scribe" but more broadly "*Negro* scribe," indicating that there is no issue of translation-as-obstacle here.

Similarly, while Hughes's "dying Moor" and his American soldier cannot understand each other, black readers of the *New Times and Ethiopia News* do understand the Ethiopians' plight and find in it a point of connection. In the *New Times and Ethiopia News*, we see the networks of black diaspora developing and deepening as a result of the uneven Italo-Ethiopian War, in contrast to the Italian Askari propaganda, which promoted imagery that attempted to depict the war between Italy and Ethiopia as an equal fight. The aggrandizement of the figure of martial Ethiopianism stimulated visions of black empire, and black readers of the *New Times and Ethiopia News* utilized the newspaper as a medium to foster a black diasporic network. From the so-called "hinterland" of Suriname, for example, the newspaper's readers could participate in its project of anti-Fascism with a slant of racial solidarity. Although Garvey's poem for Nasibu was published in his own magazine, Baroness Atzel's elegy did appear in the *New Times and Ethiopia News*. In other words, readers could turn directly from Atzel's elegy to Hughes's "Letter from Spain" a few pages later in the same issue of the newspaper. Particularly for those readers at the "edges" of the black world, the newspaper's literary presentations of Nasibu and the Askari soldier as oppositional figures helped shape its role as a point or locus of connection for racial solidarity. The African soldier fighting for European imperial interests, when read in the context of the Italo-Ethiopian War, is a tragic warning; Nasibu, on the other hand, serves as a vector through which racial sympathy could express itself.

War as Prizefight

The poems discussed in this chapter rarely display a vexed view of the fantasy of imperial Ethiopianism, but, of course, many were critical of (to quote Marcus Garvey) "a feudal Monarch who looks down upon his slaves and serfs with contempt" or (to quote George Padmore) Ethiopia's "reactionary religious hierarchy and the feudal system," exploiting the masses under both chattel and wage slavery.[53] African American participation in the Spanish Civil War, Robin D. G. Kelley points out, was therefore not always viewed simply as a substitute for fighting in Ethiopia; the political goals and ideals for which they fought were believed by most soldiers to be absolutely noble and unsullied, whereas the presumed end result of a Selassie victory would be more fraught.[54] Fighting to preserve a centralized Ethiopian empire under an imperial monarchy would in fact run counter to idealized networks of black internationalism.

One of Hughes's many Ethiopia-inspired poems, "Ballad of Ethiopia," published in 1935,[55] demonstrates clearly how Ethiopianism became a paradoxical ideology when used in service of anti-imperialism. There was a profound irony in the fact that, as Etsuko Taketani writes, "in campaigning against empire . . . , the African American public lent support to a black empire and its ruler."[56] Michelle Ann Stephens, in a book on the model of Black Empire and Caribbean American public figures who "attempted to chart a course for the race somewhere in the interstices between empire, nation, and state," suggests something similar when she points to "the tension of a cultural politics constituted by both radical and reactionary impulses—impulses toward racial revolution, movement, and freedom and impulses toward militarism, statehood, and empire."[57] These tensions are manifested in Hughes's representations of Ethiopia in the 1930s and expose the ideological instability embedded in Ethiopianism generally during this period. Many African American writers (like Hughes) viewed Ethiopia, an imperial state that had doubled in size during Emperor Menelik's reign, through both imperial and anti-imperialist lenses.

Hughes's vexed attempt to democratically unify Africans and African Americans while at the same time slipping into an imperial transnationalism is most clearly reflected in the instability of the pronouns in "Ballad of Ethiopia." The first stanza begins with an imperative: "Bow *your* head in prayer / Lift *your* soul in song" (emphasis added), with the second-person plural referring at once to Ethiopia and/or its people on the one hand, and the African American reader on the other, a conflation designed to strengthen the sense of affiliation. Of course, Ethiopia would pray that the war be short, but the poem intends to inspire African Americans to pray for the same, in the spirit of racial solidarity. After all, this is where, we are told later in the poem, the "black man's flag"—not just the Ethiopian flag—"flies." By the second stanza, the focus shifts to the first-person singular: "I have been a slave." For readers of Hughes's poetry, this might sound like the generalized, historical African American voice found often in his work, but it is also a transnational black voice that bridges Africa and America like the one in "The Negro Speaks of Rivers" (especially if "slavery" is abstracted to include oppression and colonialism). In any case, it does not appear to be a personal voice. As in the first stanza, we have a second-person address, but here the "you" refers to Mussolini. At first, this appears to be a momentary lapse, because the "you" later reverts back to "Ethiopian warriors," "Ethiopian women," and "All you colored peoples / No matter where you be," again in an effort to link black people around the world. But then the poem ends with the address to Mussolini again. And, strangely, the collective effort seen in lines like "Let us tell the world / Fascism must end" is compromised by the interjections of the first-person singular throughout, especially in the final lines, "Mussolini, / Don't you mess with me." These lines appear to frame the struggle as a mano-a-mano boxing challenge rather than a war between armies. In other words, unlike the first person of "I have been a slave," the first person in the lines invoking the boxing metaphor must be a personal, singular voice in order for the metaphor to work.

My reading of Hughes's use of the boxing metaphor here is inflected by the stanza about Joe Louis (who would, only a few years later, represent America in a fight against Max Schmeling): "Carnera thought that / He would have his way—/ But the big Brown Bomber / Just said hey . . . hey!" The fight between Louis and the Italian Primo Carnera was frequently depicted, as Ivy G. Wilson and others have pointed out, as a personification of the concurrent struggle between Ethiopia and Italy, or even an indirect representation of Selassie v. Mussolini. Only a few months after knocking out Carnera, Louis would knock out Max Baer, and the issue of the *Baltimore Afro-American* in which Hughes's poem appears features in-depth coverage and several large photos of Louis's fight with Baer, taking up most of the front page and perhaps even most of the issue. There is even a children's laxative advertisement featuring Louis right next to Hughes's poem. This page is a perfect example of the productive juxtapositions pointed out by Theresa E. Runstedtler: "In the major black weeklies, stories and photos of Louis's training regimen, his victory, and the subsequent celebrations ran side-by-side with reports of the Abyssinian crisis and pictures of the Ethiopian emperor. Arguably, even African Americans who did not read the papers must have picked up on the obvious analogy."[58] One of those who picked up on the analogy was an enthusiastic supporter of the Ethiopian resistance quoted in a 1935 *New York Times* article ("a soap-box orator," the reporter calls him), who shouts, "'If Joe Louis could knock that giant Carnera on his ear, . . . then Ethiopia's army could march into Rome and lick those Italians with their natural fists.'"[59]

In a sense, the logic of the soap-box orator's conditional (if Louis beats Carnera, then Ethiopian army beats Italian army) is what drives Hughes's poem. The "Ethiopian warriors," "Ethiopian women," "colored peoples," "Harlem"—all will fight and beat "Mussolini's men." But instead of going from the individual prizefight to the collective fight, Hughes returns to the prizefight at the end. In retrospect, the Joe Louis stanza sheds new light on the poem's second stanza, in which the speaker says, "I've been beaten down. / But you cannot keep me, / Keep me on the ground." Like Louis v. Carnera, Hughes v. Mussolini is another manifestation of the battle between Selassie and Mussolini. Hughes is simply Selassie's stand-in. In other words, Hughes is both poet and boxer, writing and fighting for empire in a way that recalls George Bernard Shaw's very condescending remark to Claude McKay: "You might have developed into a successful boxer with training. Poets remain poor, unless they have an empire to glorify and popularize like Kipling."[60] Hughes chooses not to choose: he glorifies Ethiopian empire through both his poetry and his (imaginary) boxing. In this way, individualism intrudes in a poem about collective action and is symptomatic of Hughes's identification with Selassie and the imperial center. The "Ethiopian women" and "Ethiopian warriors" fall out of the picture in favor of the individual, represented by Hughes or Selassie. Martial Ethiopianism succumbs to its imperial roots.

By aligning himself with the emperor, Hughes reveals—despite his ostensible desire to promote collectivity—a reverence for an imperial center that is not at all unusual in African American poetry about Ethiopia in the 1930s. The weight of the "Ethiopian" tradition in African American letters, as Moses calls it, bore down upon and inevitably shaped modern lyric representations of the nation, infusing those representations with a romanticism that made criticism of the monarchy unwelcome and difficult. In fact, because Ethiopianism historically drew its power from the dignity and grandeur offered by the idea of an ancient black empire, anti-monarchical views could be seen as undermining the essence of the Ethiopianist perspective upon which the poetry about the war depended. Although criticism of Selassie increased during World War II (particularly during his exile in England), his iconic signification still bolsters Ethiopianist ideologies today. Despite the challenges to racial solidarity posed by the figure of the Askari soldier, the celebration of Ethiopian imperial culture, particularly through the figure of martial Ethiopianism, remained a powerful propagandistic tool throughout the Italo-Ethiopian War.

Because the dramatic events taking place in Ethiopia in the 1930s were filtered for many African Americans through the country's longstanding and profound symbolism, Ethiopia was simultaneously a topical and deep-rooted subject for Harlem Renaissance poetry. These poems often constituted calls for action—particularly military action—entreating the diaspora to summon a consanguineous sympathy and to come to the aid of what was both an ancestral home and the seat of a historic black empire. Ethiopia was no longer, as Gibbon called it, forgotten and sleeping, and African America dedicated verse to the nation as it fought for its sovereignty on the world stage.

CHAPTER SEVEN

George S. Schuyler and the Appeal of Imperial Ethiopia

Even when my good friend J. A. Rogers turned tail and scooted home, leaving the Ethiopians to face their fate, his accounts were still bubbling with optimism. He got out of Addis Ababa two jumps ahead of the Italian posse, but said that's my story and I'm going to stick to it.

. . . [O]ld Haile should have been sport enough to help the paper boys out of their crack by dying with his boots on, but nope. He tricked us up to the last and would neither save the face of the colored press nor his own.

—RALPH MATTHEWS, "MANHATTAN MERRY-GO-ROUND: HARLEM AND ETHIOPIA"

IT WAS IN 1935 that, according to *Time*, Emperor Selassie's name truly "entered the U.S. vocabulary in such homely exclamations as, 'Well! If that's so, then I'm Haile Selassie!'"[1] This example of idiomatic incorporation illustrates just how thoroughly and pervasively the exploits of *Time*'s choice for Man of the Year had impressed themselves upon Americans, even to the point of landing on everyone's lips. But the structure of the expression—reminiscent of the familiar expression ending "then I'm the Queen of Sheba"—serves to highlight what would be among the most unlikely and strenuous identifications one could make.[2] There is hardly anything more implausible than the prospect that you *could* be Haile Selassie.

Despite our absolute inability to truly and empathetically imagine ourselves in his place, the *Time* journalist writes that Selassie "has created a general, warm and blind sympathy for uncivilized Ethiopia throughout civilized Christendom."[3] Although the Ethiopian crisis was treated extensively by mainstream periodicals like *Time* in the 1930s, it was in the African American press that the crisis was covered most extensively. It was, as John Munro points out, "the story of the year in the black press in 1935," and "although the major publications of the African American press had varying editorial positions on the issues of the day, they were uniform in their continued sympathetic coverage of the Ethiopian story."[4] In October 1935—the month that marked the Italian invasion of Ethiopia—George S. Schuyler began publishing installments of his first Ethiopian story in the *Pittsburgh Courier*, an important African American newspaper for which he regularly wrote editorials, articles, and fiction.[5] As Robert A. Hill writes, "The *Courier* began to promote Schuyler, along with J. A. Rogers, as the 'Two Best Informed Men on Ethiopia in U.S.A.!' "[6] Schuyler's fictional contributions to the newspaper worked in concert with journalistic contributions by both Schuyler and Rogers, who was sent to Ethiopia in 1935 to cover the war writing articles and conducting interviews that served as propaganda in the defense of Ethiopia. Although Selassie, in an interview with Rogers, casts African American support for the cause as sympathy for the nation's predicament—"I know well of America's sympathetic attitude towards Ethiopia and I am very grateful for it"—most of Rogers's and Schuyler's writing for the *Courier* surprisingly attempted to stimulate sympathy among the newspaper's readers not around the Ethiopian cause generally but around Selassie himself.[7]

Of course, we should not be surprised, given present-day tabloid coverage of the British royal family, by the prospect that royalty sells, and ironically seems to sell best in the United States. Both of Schuyler's *Ethiopian Stories*, as they were called when they were published together in book form in 1994, are mysteries involving princes and princesses, and I argue that this focus on royalty was designed first to exploit American (and especially African American) fascination with the Ethiopian monarchy. Schuyler had a rapt audience among his *Courier* readers: for example, the newspaper's printing of an advertisement for a Selassie pin, offered by the Moss Studio in Pittsburgh and selling for ten cents individually or "in lots from 100 to 500 for clubs, societies, organizations, etc.," sought to capitalize upon readers' desire to align themselves with the monarch. The advertisement asks, "*Do You Believe in Justice?* Then wear a Picture-Button of HAILE SELASSIE, KING OF KINGS, EMPEROR OF ABYSSINIA." The wearing of the pin would clearly express and perform a consumer's solidarity with the emperor, reminiscent of the type of "commodity spectacle" that, according to Michelle Ann Stephens, citing Anne McClintock's use of the term, includes "the myriad fetish objects of modern nationalism such as flags and uniforms, organized in various events of collective display such as military displays and mass rallies."[8]

Robert A. Hill claims that Schuyler "emerged in 1935–36 as one of the most outspoken voices in African American circles in defending the ideal of racial solidarity in support of Ethiopia."[9] This is certainly true. In the end, however, I argue that Schuyler complicates the propagandistic messages of his *Ethiopian Stories* with anti-monarchist views, in essence undermining the construction of the newspaper's sympathetic position. Publishing stories that pass themselves off as news and editorials, thereby lending support to Ethiopia in multiple genres but also infiltrating and modifying the newspaper's official stance, Schuyler makes an argument through his fiction that was more nuanced than that in his nonfiction. In an article about Schuyler's *Black Empire*, Etsuko Taketani rightly questions those "historical narratives of the Italo-Ethiopian War . . . that have equated black internationalism with anti-imperialism."[10] The tensions between the anti-imperialist impulse that led to African American concern for Ethiopia's plight on the one hand and the general fascination with Ethiopia's imperial history on the other led Schuyler to expose that contradiction in his *Ethiopian Stories*.

"What Are the Deaths of a Few Men?"

The first Ethiopian story published serially in the *Courier*, *The Ethiopian Murder Mystery: A Story of Love and International Intrigue*, opens with the murder of Prince Haile Destu, a friend and possible lover of Crissina Van Dyke, the wealthy African American woman who is the prime suspect in the murder. Van Dyke's long-time friend and admirer, Roger Bates, is convinced of her innocence and determined to clear her name by solving the murder himself. This leads him down a rabbit hole into the sort of international intrigue promised us in the novel's subtitle, peopled by exotic and mysterious figures of various nationalities: an Eritrean named Ali Sibra (whose room, the maid tells Roger, smells of reefer), a glamorous and veiled British woman (who is also probably a lover of Destu's and Sibra's), a possible Spaniard, and many Italians. One by one, suspects turn up murdered just as Roger is pursuing them, and, when he uncovers the source of it all, he finds himself ensnared in a plot involving high-level Ethiopian spies.

In a wish-fulfillment type of plot twist that could have excited *Courier* readers rooting for Ethiopia, Sadiu Mattchu, the spy at the head of the operation, reveals to Roger that they are in the midst of developing a "death ray which will annihilate the Italians who have invaded our country," a sci-fi technological advancement anticipating those in *Black Empire*.[11] However, the unsympathetic coolness with which the characters are dispatched—both Ethiopian and Italian, if they find themselves in the way of the Ethiopian government's goals—angers Roger. When the spy notices "with amusement" the "outraged expression which the callous recital had induced," he replies, "'This is war, my friend, . . . Ethiopia is fighting for her life. We cannot be squeamish. Italian bombs have killed thousands of defenseless women and children. What are the deaths of a few men like Sibra, Morona, Donatelli and Bostoni compared to them?'" (*EMM* 122). Although he is not named, we might add Destu himself to this list, who is murdered by the Ethiopian spies because he is a "sensualist" with a weakness for drugs and sex whom the Italian spies have used in order to "disgrace Ethiopian royalty" (121, 120). So, even though the progress of the novel depends upon our investment and interest in the murders of these characters—in solving the mystery named in the novel's title—the wizard behind the curtain attempts to convince us that, in fact, these deaths do not matter. Our "warm and blind sympathy" has been invested in the wrong place.

This surprise is only revealed at the end; before reaching this point, Schuyler guides his reader to support the cause in large part because we care about and are interested in what has happened to a royal and to those pursuing him. Throughout the novel, Roger's primary goal in his investigation of Destu's murder is to clear Crissina Van Dyke's name, but a secondary and indirect goal appears to be the defense of Ethiopia through the imperial line. Haile Destu may be his rival in love, but he is also a meaningful regal symbol of an imperiled black nation in the same manner that, looking elsewhere in the *Courier*, we see clearly that Selassie was a meaningful regal symbol. Roger might have been driven to solve Destu's murder even if Crissina hadn't been involved; he is, after all, not just a "newspaper man" but a "race man," which is how he introduces himself to the chairman of the fictionalized Help Ethiopia League (*EMM* 114). Even Crissina, it turns out, keeps a surprising secret about her role in Ethiopian espionage, a role that is explained to Roger (but cryptically kept from the reader), leaving him with "a new respect for her." In order to legitimate the choices that led to her becoming embroiled in this murder investigation, Roger tells her, "I know you did it for the love of the race" (89). Crissina's identification as a spy and therefore an "honorary" Ethiopian marks her, like Destu, as yet another symbol of the country. This is made clear by a nightmare Roger has later, in which "he was struggling with a thousand blood-thirsty Italians who held Crissina van Dyke captive" (103). The terrifying scene is played out for Roger as simultaneously the literalized rape of his beloved and the abstract rape of Ethiopia. Just as he would fight to protect Crissina, he would fight to protect Ethiopia.

Like Princess Ettara's desperate appeal in *Revolt in Ethiopia: A Tale of Black Insurrection against Italian Imperialism* (Schuyler's other Ethiopian story, published in 1938–39 during the Italian occupation), the representation of Crissina's victimization resembles that of Ethiopia's actual Princess Tsehai, profiled in a *Courier* article titled "Protect Us from Poison Gases! Beseeches Ethiopian Princess." (It is worth noting, too, that Crissina is said to have the "poise of a princess" [*EMM* 65].) President of the Ethiopian Women's Work Association, Princess Tsehai originally published her plea in the *London Telegraph*, which was reprinted in the *Courier*: "For seven days without break the enemy has been bombing the armies and people of my country, including women and children, with terrible gases. . . . Many, many of them are unrecognizable since the skin has been burned off their faces. These are facts."[12] Similar to Selassie's own appeal to the League of Nations in June 1936, during which he bore witness to the Italian forces' use of mustard gas to kill civilians, Princess Tsehai's appeal directs readers to view it as an entreaty for the defense of the "people," indiscriminately slaughtered. But it was an appeal made more audible by its voicing by the Ethiopian aristocracy.

These appeals were effective, ironically using the exclusive sphere of the royal family to broaden the Ethiopian cause to one of relevance to a general black international public. This is made clear in a *Courier* interview with Selassie conducted by Rogers in which he expresses African American interest in Ethiopia as "deep devotion" to the emperor. Rogers asserts:

> Your Majesty, among the many millions of your warm friends in America are twelve million peoples of African descent. I wish I had the power to express to you, Sire, how deeply devoted they are to you. . . . At this time, when Ethiopia is struggling so gallantly to maintain her seven thousand years of unbroken independence, these children of the African motherland are eager to know in what way they can serve, because they feel that Ethiopia's fight is their fight also.[13]

Can it be an accident that Schuyler's protagonist almost shares a name with this other "best informed m[a]n on Ethiopia in U.S.A.," his friend and colleague? Like the many African Americans who sought to serve with the Ethiopian army, Roger, driven by a spirit of fraternity, has assumed

Ethiopia's fight as his own. *The Ethiopian Murder Mystery* begins with an assertion of extreme localism: "New Yorkers mind their business because they have so much business to mind. What goes on in the next apartment is the concern of its occupants—if they are not too loud" (*EMM* 53). But, in drawing African Americans such as Crissina and Roger into the murder mystery, Schuyler challenges these isolationist attitudes, making it our business.

In one of his columns in the *Courier*, Schuyler writes of the Italo-Ethiopian conflict, "*As an old soldier, I would certainly like to participate in such an adventure and press a machine-gun trigger on the Italian hordes as they toiled over the Ethiopian terrain. It is one of the few wars in which I could participate with enthusiasm*."[14] The chance to destroy "Italian hordes," illimitable masses of enemy forces upon whom he would rain machine-gun bullets (a weapon-of-mass-destruction technology that allowed for many victims to be killed at once), would permit a sympathetic Schuyler to live out Roger's nightmare fantasy of killing the thousand Italians who threaten Crissina and to avenge the deaths of the thousands of Ethiopians cited by Sadiu. Although the naming of particular officers on the Italian side in both *Ethiopian Stories* could lead one to believe that the stories are concerned with the deaths of "a few men," the final assault upon the Italians in *Revolt in Ethiopia* reverses the dehumanization behind the mass-destruction military attacks upon Ethiopian civilians: "a thousand [Ethiopians] were gathered outside the town. Most of them were carrying some article of Italian equipment or uniform, evidence enough that the Italians had been wiped out."[15] No bodies are left. These are the "horrible features of imperialistic warfare" Walter Benjamin considers in the epilogue of "The Work of Art in the Age of Mechanical Reproduction," after quoting F. T. Marinetti's previously cited manifesto about the Italo-Ethiopian conflict in which he advocates the aestheticization of war: "War is beautiful because it enriches a flowering meadow with the fiery orchids of machine guns. War is beautiful because it combines the gunfire, the cannonades, the cease-fire, the scents, and the stench of putrefaction into a symphony."[16] Marinetti of course views the exacting of war as beautiful when its primary victims are the colonized, lacking the technological power of the aggressor; Schuyler instead directs the modern technologies of machine guns and bombers against the colonizer.

It is thus in *Revolt in Ethiopia* that Schuyler most emphatically breathes life into the fantasy he and his readers shared. Mark Christian Thompson makes this claim in relation to *Black Empire*—"Unable to write columns containing factual accounts of African American valor on the battlefields of Ethiopia, Schuyler manifests in fantasy what African Americans had been barred from doing"—but the pro-Ethiopia fantasy is in fact more explicitly enacted in *Revolt in Ethiopia*.[17] Roger's (and Schuyler's) sympathetic impulse can be understood in light of what Stephens recognizes as the "profound desire" associated with the "diasporic condition," comparable to "what David Lloyd has described (in the context of discussions of Ireland as colony) as 'the desire of nationalism for the state' which occurs precisely in those colonial contexts in which the state seems furthest out of reach."[18] In the case of the Italo-Ethiopian War, however, the suddenly clear and insistent media focus on this once inenubilable country meant that a seemingly viable model of black empire was not out of reach, and its spiritual proximity deepened readers' sympathetic impulse. Furthermore, in his didactic function for Schuyler, Roger in *The Ethiopian Murder Mystery* encourages readers of the *Courier* to see the defense of Ethiopia not only as something one should do "for the [abstract] love of the race" but also as a personal issue that is literally happening next door and that threatens to invade one's quotidian life with the arrival of the weekly newspaper.

Ethiopia in the Headlines

The bizarre generic ambiguity of *The Ethiopian Murder Mystery* as it was printed in the *Courier* contributes to the story's propagandistic effect. Many of the titles of Schuyler's chapters (omitted from the reprinted book edition)—for example, "Sensational Murder of Ethiopian Prince Stirs, Puzzles NY"—are clearly designed to evoke the elliptical language found in the headlines of news articles. We might view this ambiguity as a demonstration of "an *international longing for form* that links the styles of black radicalism to the energies of literary modernism," as Alexander M. Bain writes of Schuyler's *Courier* fiction during this period, one participating in a larger trend including texts by Rogers, W. E. B. Du Bois, Claude McKay, and others that "use formal strategies like generic mixture, juxtaposition and montage, and nonlinear narratives to frame the geography and consequences of 'black globality.' "[19] A. B. Christa Schwarz has argued that Schuyler's melodramatic plots may have been inspired in part by the *Courier*'s news headlines, which "next to announcing news on the Italo-Ethiopian conflict, highlighted espionage cases and screamed murder": for example, an article by Rogers titled "Shrewd Ethiopian Secret Police Trap Spies: Greek Is Trapped in Net and Deported." Schwarz claims that Schuyler's "references to the conflict are usually brief" because his story, printed in the context of the newspaper's extensive war coverage, "presents an additional 'lighter,' more entertaining narrative."[20] But this distinction between "light" detective fiction and "heavy" news coverage in actuality breaks down in the juxtaposition, as her own example of the Rogers article illustrates; Rogers's title is not so different from "Tapped Wires Reveal New Leads in Strange Murder of Ali Sibra," one of Schuyler's titles. Schuyler's fiction is interwoven so tightly with the rest of the *Courier*'s Ethiopia coverage that readers move from one to the other seamlessly.

In fact, in addition to Schuyler's chapter titles, newspaper headlines appear throughout the novel. For example, the fifth chapter opens with a floating string of headlines: "'Harlem Society Woman Charged with African Prince's Murder' . . . 'Police Arrest Harlem Negress in Prince's Murder' . . . 'Pretty Octaroon Charged with Ethiopian Death' . . . 'Police say Harlem Girl Killed African Prince'" (*EMM* 69). The eleventh chapter even embeds an entire article similar to the Rogers article mentioned by Schwarz, titled "Negro Found Murdered in 'Little Italy.'" What makes these intrusions of journalistic discourse different from, for example, those found in *Native Son* published a few years later is the obvious fact that the reader encounters them *in a newspaper*, where they can be mistaken for "real" news. (In fact, as Thompson points out, in the case of *Black Empire*, many *Courier* readers somehow mistook the fiction for a true story.)[21] Moreover, the "newspaper man" at the center of the novel does not work for just any newspaper: he is a reporter for the *Courier*. This self-reflexivity, besides being self-promotional for both Schuyler as a journalist and the *Courier* as the premier newspaper for news related to the conflict, moves the story we are reading away from fiction and toward "story" in the journalistic sense for the simple reason that the plot is being generated by a reporter. This blurring of generic boundaries, again, encourages readers not to think of the novel simply as escapist, thrilling fiction—even the story of a murder mystery should not allow the Ethiopian crisis to be pushed from the forefront of their minds. And, not only does Schuyler's fiction encourage readers to inform themselves about the Ethiopian crisis, it encourages readers to do so specifically by reading the *Courier*. In *Revolt in Ethiopia*, the protagonist is *twice* scolded and mocked for picking up misinformation about the crisis by "reading the white press" (130).

Nor does J. A. Rogers's war coverage use an approach we would associate with "hard news." It does not pretend to be objective, and it reveals emotional investment and bold opinion, linking it even more strongly to the views of the crisis reflected in Schuyler's fiction. For example, a typical front-page article, curiously published only two days before *Time*'s

Man-of-the-Year issue, begins with the following bombastic rhetoric: "Ethiopia's triumphant God, hurling his thunderbolts from sky-tipped mountain peaks[,] and her dauntless warriors, fighting for home and country, have thrust the legions of Rome's modern Caesar back toward the sun-parched deserts of Eritrea."[22] This is not to say that Rogers's coverage was not treated by readers as honest, a proper and appropriate counter-offensive against what they would find in the white press. In fact, an article announcing the sending of Rogers to Ethiopia was subtitled "Hundreds Awaiting Truthful Reports." A letter to the editor written by one of these hundreds complains about the "prejudiced stuff" in the mainstream media and states that he is "confident that we will read the truth now."[23] Another letter writer "feel[s] sure that we are getting the correct news from the battlefront from our correspondent."[24] These were only two among many letters to the editor on the subject; as Munro points out, "In the 27 July 'What the People Think' section of the *Courier*, for example, thirty letters about Ethiopia crowded the page."[25]

The spirit of generic amalgamation binding Schuyler's fiction to the *Courier*'s news coverage also ties both to an illustrated piece published alongside the initial installment of Schuyler's novel, part of a series written by Rogers and illustrated by George L. Lee. Titled "Your History" and prefaced by a note reading, "Your history dates back beyond the cotton fields of the South; back thousands of years before Christ," Rogers's series profiles important historical personages of African descent. Here, coincidentally—or perhaps not—two of the three are Ethiopian. Ivan Hannibal, ancestor of Pushkin, descends from Abram Petrovich Gannibal, better known as the Moor of Peter the Great. Although his ancestry is not definitively known, many believed that he was born in Ethiopia, a subtextual element not explicitly mentioned by Rogers. The other figure, Bahir Aghasi, even manages to combine the mythologies of Selassie and Abram Gannibal (and prefigures that of Emperor Menelik, as we will see later), as leader of an empire rising from the position of enslaved person. Compared to Rogers's multigeneric treatments of the Ethiopian crisis, Schuyler's stories reflect what I see as a real ambivalence about Ethiopia's imperial legacy.

Of the three—the "Your History" illustrations, Schuyler's novel, and the *Courier*'s news—"Your History" aims to do the most work to bridge the gap between "civilized" African America and "uncivilized" Ethiopia. Educating his readers about their own ancient history in "Your History," reaching back "thousands of years before Christ," Rogers argues explicitly that antiquity should be celebrated as something more than romantic obsolescence, as something with currency in the modern world, and links Africans and African Americans through a shared, proud ancestry. Schuyler in his *Revolt in Ethiopia* attempts to dramatize this link by featuring a love story between an Ethiopian princess and an African American millionaire who joins her in a dangerous adventure to retrieve an ancient Ethiopian treasure, which they plan to exchange for arms for the Ethiopian military.

That it is an ancient treasure, hidden in a centuries-old secret temple, certainly adds to the romance, but there is more at stake here. Both Italo-Ethiopian wars were stories of mismatched technologies, but with different outcomes: the Battle of Adwa in 1896, during which the Ethiopian military countered the Italians' modern mountain guns with spears and rifles, ended with the defeat of Italy and was a powerful challenge to the progress narrative justifying colonialism. When Schuyler writes that the ancient treasure discovered in *Revolt in Ethiopia* contains jewels that are cut "as good as we can do today," despite the fact that "some of them must be thousands of years old," he demonstrates just how advanced the supposedly uncivilized underdog is (*RE* 225). When he notes that the Bishop (intriguingly dubbed "strange monarch of the mountain") guarding that treasure is joined by a priest who "intone[s] a chant that must have been old when Rome flourished," the mention of Rome here is strategic: if ancient Ethiopia rivals ancient Rome, then modern Ethiopia can legitimately rival modern Italy (182).

Civilization and Black Transnational Affiliation

Ethiopia, being ancient, was paradoxically believed to be both more "civilized" and less "civilized" than African America. As the only nation in Africa to escape colonization (with the unique exception of Liberia), Ethiopia was a source of pride to many African Americans but was also seen as a comparatively primitive civilization. As Thompson writes, "These images of Ethiopia allowed African America to envision itself as both redeemer and redeemed."[26] In the *Courier*, the mythology of a glorious, ancient, and peaceful Ethiopia was always superimposed upon prevailing impressions of the modern country as savage and primitive, and it was this formula that implicitly provided the justification for its defense. Dick Welland, the African American hero of *Revolt in Ethiopia*, is moved to tears and inspired to action by the Bishop's chant for precisely this reason:

> It all moved Dick profoundly and made him feel rewarded for venturing on such a risky undertaking. Here was a Negro civilization older

> than any other except India and China; a civilization that had flourished before Greece and Rome, before Carthage, yes, before Egypt. Here were all the forms, the elaborate ritual, the culture that had made Ethiopia the admiration of the ancient world. Here it survived in spite of Mussolini, in spite of perfidious England, in spite of Ethiopia's desertion by the traitorous League of Nations.
>
> As the weird ancient music finally died and the priests fell back to their places, Dick wept unashamed. What a pity that this civilization should be destroyed by brutal Fascism. No, he resolved anew, it must not die; not if he could prevent it. (*RE* 182)

Dick expresses here a sympathetic urge—even weeping—to fight for Ethiopia, echoing Roger's in *The Ethiopian Murder Mystery*.

However, the localism with which *The Ethiopian Murder Mystery* opens may be supplemented but not supplanted by international sympathies. In pointing out that "'press[ing] a machine-gun trigger on the Italian hordes' is a Belsidus-style fantasy detached from the act of killing and from those being killed," referring here to the protagonist of Schuyler's *Black Empire*, Bain claims that "regardless of their identification with 'dear old Ethiopia,' Schuyler warns his readers that fantasy can only be validated through some correlation to meeting the demands of the home front."[27] One way of solving this domestic dilemma, I argue, is to justify African American sympathy with Ethiopia's plight by not only making African Americans honorary Ethiopians, as Crissina van Dyke was, but making Ethiopians seem American. Dick Welland and Princess Ettara literally meet halfway: their first encounter is on a cruise ship, a liminal space that is neither Ethiopia nor America. Dick has already at this point "left America behind" (*RE* 125). Calling to mind Paul Gilroy's guiding image of "ships in motion across the spaces between Europe, America, Africa, and the Caribbean as a central organising symbol," later taken up by Stephens in the idea of the "Negro ship of state," Dick and Ettara's mutual identification is aided by the transatlantic context of their meeting.[28] However, despite Dick's apparent renunciation of his Americanness, he introduces himself to the princess by emphasizing his national identity: "'My name's Dick Welland,' he announced, 'I'm an American'" (128). We could say, then, of each character that he or she is neither Ethiopian nor American but both.

Dick Welland's spiritual connection to Ethiopia in this story is reinforced in the end by his impending marriage to Princess Ettara, which makes him a member of the royal family. But what is more unusual here is that the naturalization is reciprocal: not only does Dick become Ethiopian, the princess becomes American. Even from the beginning, Dick notices upon meeting her that she sounds like an American, and then he learns that she is actually a Howard University graduate. (It is probable that Schuyler's character follows the example of the aforementioned Malaku Bayen, the first Ethiopian to be educated in the United States, who attended Howard University's medical school "in order that [he] might have a closer contact with [his] people" and also married an American.)[29] The novel ends with the princess declaring, "I'm going to be an American, too"—presumably through marriage, in the same manner that Dick becomes Ethiopian (*RE* 227). In light of this declaration, Bain argues that "Welland's newfound 'interest' in Africa Americanizes the woman who has complexly embodied the appeal and location of radical transnationalism. . . . Being 'an American,' however, not just 'almost American,' or 'free' (145), is the status that is awarded privilege of place at the story's end."[30] Similarly, Ivy G. Wilson argues that Ettara's statement signifies that, "at the close of the story, transnational subjectivity dissolves, producing an asymmetrical relationship between the categories 'American' and 'Ethiopian,' one where the 'Ethiopian' remains subordinate to the primary position of the 'American.'"[31] Although I see more of an attempted reciprocity than asymmetry, I will admit that the princess's performative assumption of citizenship is very strange and unexpected, given her nationalistic fervor throughout: her life is "tied up with Ethiopia," and she refuses to marry until her work for the country is done (207). But, culturally, she is an American, she talks like an American, and her "true" American identity cannot help but come out at the end. This does not necessarily make her any less Ethiopian, however, if we understand her "too" to mean that she will be American as well as Ethiopian, not simply that she will be American like her fiancé.

Princess Ettara's congenital Americanness seems designed to allow the *Courier*'s readers to feel a closer affinity to the character. Likewise, stories about Selassie, despite the sense of exotic and biblical antiquity attached to him, often emphasized—as discussed in chapter 5—his modern and "American" nature seemingly in an effort to elicit readers' sympathy. Like Princess Ettara, who "fairly breathed aristocracy" and whose "neck arched proudly with all the noble blood of twenty centuries," such that "there was something of another age about her, something of the nameless wisdom of the oldest Christian country in the world," the embattled Selassie was described in one article as a "frail, gentle-eyed figure" who "seemed a Judean figure out of the Bible."[32] However, the aforementioned *Time*

Man-of-the-Year profile of Selassie also claims that "until 1935 the country was known . . . as a 'museum of peoples' who remarkably preserve the habits and customs of their various antiquities," borrowing a then familiar and oft-cited trope from Edward Gibbon, who, in his *History of the Decline and Fall of the Roman Empire*, wrote that the Ethiopians "slept near a thousand years, forgetful of the world, by whom they were forgotten."[33] Now, Selassie is credited with "r[ising] out of murky obscurity and carr[ying] his country with him up & up into brilliant focus before a pop-eyed world."[34] Paradoxically, alongside the numerous descriptions that refused to advance him beyond biblical times is the implication that Selassie modernized Ethiopia and freed the country from its "museum" of antiquity.

In fact, Schuyler does make a point of including many modern conveniences throughout the *Ethiopian Stories*. When Dick expresses surprise that there is a telephone in the hidden mountain holding the ancient treasure, Ettara chides him: "They are not as backward as you think" (*RE* 178). In addition, Schuyler saves the day through the presence of airplanes. Historically, the first Ethiopian aircraft was used in 1930—*prior* to the Second Italo-Abyssinian War—in a campaign by Ras Tafari (later Haile Selassie) to tamp down an internal rebellion that challenged his power.[35] Nevertheless, a few years later, the eleven airplanes in the Ethiopian air force—"of which only eight were serviceable, and they were used mainly for transport"—were no match for the Italian air force's four hundred airplanes.[36] Despite Selassie's modernization efforts, "until Mussolini's aircraft spread poison gas and incendiary bombs over Ethiopia's villages and armies in 1936, the airplane was an uncommon sight in isolated Ethiopia."[37] In Schuyler's story, however, Dick Welland and Princess Ettara are surprisingly able to find an Ethiopian in a rural village who can pilot their private jet with skill and derring-do: he had learned to fly in England. In fact, many of the hair's-breadth escapes in *Revolt in Ethiopia* are made possible by airplanes, illustrating that, as Dick says, "airplanes made such a difference" (221).

Instead of the opportunity for connection between Africans and African Americans suggested by the presence of airplanes and Ettara's familiar Americanness, modernity only succeeds in transforming feudal monarchism into something more reminiscent of a modern-era colonialist relationship between the now Franco-American Selassie and his subjects, still Ethiopian and still his inferiors. Although Schuyler's Princess Ettara claims throughout to be fighting for her country, and even says, "titles mean very little these days," she slips at the very end, revealing an attitude less than democratic. After they have escaped with the jewels and saved the country, Dick proposes to the princess. She says, "Well, just wait until this job is over with. . . . The Emperor comes first, you know," to which he responds, "You mean Ethiopia comes first." She backtracks: "Yes, that's what I mean, Ethiopia" (*RE* 223).

This may at first seem to be simply a weird moment of confusion, but I believe that Schuyler, for all of his pro-Ethiopia advocacy, is ultimately bringing his reader's attention to the irony of fighting for the freedom of a monarchy. When Princess Ettara tells Dick about her plans to save her country, she says, "Ethiopia is enslaved. Ethiopia must be freed" (*RE* 129). But later in the novel, when they reach the inner sanctum of the hidden temple, Dick's valet, Bill—who has accompanied them for the entire treacherous journey and whose relationship to Dick was "more like [that of] companions than master and servant" (126)—is not permitted to enter. She tells Dick that "Bill is considered a slave by these people." (Bill decides later that he does not "like these here Africans no more'n them Eyetalians" [187].) At one point, the narrator describes the princess's expression "as haughty[,] as though she were addressing the slaves on her former vast estates" (176). This description comes, strangely enough, during a scene in which Ettara and Dick are being whipped by Italian soldiers. As John Cullen Gruesser and Ivy G. Wilson rightly point out, the scene seems straight out of an American slave narrative. However, what scholars have neglected to note is that this would make her both slave and slave owner. It is difficult to argue then, as Gruesser puts it, that "the morality of the Ethiopian cause is presented without ambiguity" in the novel.[38]

The "Bugaboo of Slavery" and the Picture of Black Sovereignty

The Fascist argument for the occupation of Ethiopia claimed to view it as a liberation on the grounds that it was a slave state. In 1923, Ethiopia had gained international attention for its continuing slave trade when the League of Nations required that the country take action to end slavery as a condition of its admission to the organization. Although slavery was officially abolished in the mid-nineteenth century, no effort was made to enforce its abolition and so slaveholding continued to exist unofficially; Italy therefore justified its aggression to the League of Nations by citing the "alleged violation of the special pledges made by Abyssinia towards the League, especially that regarding the repression of slavery," presenting reports "to show that slavery in Abyssinia is the foundation of the economic system of the country."[39] This was, naturally, a major concern for African American newspaper readers. Rogers broaches the subject gingerly in his interview with the emperor, with the preface that he "felt all Americans [would be] keenly interested" in his addressing Ethiopia's relationship to the "bugaboo of slavery." In response, Selassie attempts to reassure African Americans that Ethiopian slavery "differed greatly from western or plantation slavery. Often a 'slave' was a member of the family and treated as such."[40] Another article in the *Courier*, titled "Pemberton Contends 'Slavery' in Ethiopia Is Superior to U.S.," makes similar claims, comparing it to "the benevolent form seen in old Greece." Schuyler, who wrote a novel criticizing slavery in Liberia, would not have missed the hypocrisy of these apologies. In his foreword to *Slaves Today* (1931), he writes, "Slavery, in the form of forced labor with little or no compensation, exists under various euphemisms today," including "in the Negro-ruled states of Abyssinia [or Ethiopia] and Liberia."[41]

The perception that Ethiopian slavery was less problematic and less virulent than other forms found support among those who believed that enslavement was not a state one need occupy in perpetuity in Ethiopian society and that one could easily transcend that position. In his interview with Rogers, Selassie asserts that "Some of Ethiopia's greatest [chief?] cabinet ministers began as 'slaves.'"[42] In addition, in a 1936 letter, Marcus Garvey mocks a woman who points out that even Menelik's mother was enslaved in her attempt to demonstrate the social mobility of enslaved people in Ethiopian society, to which he responds sardonically, "If you like the kind of slavery that the Abyssinians have been kept in by their Government, why didn't you go there and live under it. Probably you would have been an Empress later on."[43] If it were not so improbable, this unexpected path to the royal court could have allowed many readers to exclaim, "If that's so—that an emperor or a cabinet member might have descended from a slave—then I'm Haile Selassie!"

But what does it mean to sympathize with a monarch? In literary approaches to sympathy, Sara Crosby points out, recent work has tended to accommodate a paradox between "the 'subversive' line," which attempts "to recover sentimental literature's liberatory or even protofeminist functions," and "the 'colonization' angle," which "emphasizes its disciplinary function and its tendency to elide agency and (especially racial) difference and to colonize the subjectivity of its objects."[44] But what happens when readers are implicitly encouraged to sympathize in this paradoxical manner, along racial lines, with an oppressed ruler who is potentially an oppressive colonizer and imperial force himself? The question of whether modern Ethiopian imperialism—dating at least from the reign of Menelik II, who "subjugated a vast range of outlying kingdoms and decentralised polities in regions to the south, east and west of his newly established capital at Addis Ababa"—is comparable to European imperialism has been taken up by many historians. The 1896 Battle of Adwa waged during his reign "preserved independence, revitalised the monarchy and inspired an Ethiopian imperialism."[45] As Cedric J. Robinson writes, while the other independent black nations of "Haiti, Sierra Leone and Liberia lurched towards variants of republican government (in decidedly different ways, paces and degrees)," Ethiopia "sustained its essentially imperial character" and, in fact, "by the end of the nineteenth century, the central imperial authority in Ethiopia was more secure than it had been since the mid-eighteenth century."[46]

Given this legacy, I believe that, although Thompson and others claim that Schuyler "vigorously supported the emperor and the growing Pan-African sentiment in the United States," the two *Ethiopian Stories* reveal Schuyler's ambivalence about supporting Selassie.[47] To read Schuyler's picture of a black imperial leader in *Black Empire* as satiric and by extension critical of Selassie would, however, align one uncomfortably with the perspective of Fascist Italy, as Taketani writes:

> The rhetoric of the Ethiopian empire as "black oppression of black people," as in a parodic reading of *Black Empire*, is the very rhetoric profascist apologists such as Baron Roman Procházka found most serviceable to their cause. In his libelous pamphlet, *Abyssinia: The Powder Barrel* (1936), Procházka contends, "[T]he opponents of Imperialism should bear in mind that the numerous non-Amharic native tribes in Ethiopia, and these constitute by far the greater part of the total population of the empire, are themselves the victims of *Abyssinian imperialism*."[48]

Interestingly, Schuyler's *Ethiopian Stories* included many black characters who were neither Abyssinians nor African Americans, and the resulting plots were emphatically not happy pictures of black imperial solidarity but disruptive scenarios. Ali Sibra, in *The Ethiopian Murder Mystery*, is notably from Eritrea, an Italian colony bordering Ethiopia. Sibra is also, notably, a Muslim. Because the Christians of the imperial family, to quote the *Time* article, "form an island in the Mohammedan and pagan sea of peoples which is Ethiopia," Sibra's Islamic presence gains an especially threatening meaning.[49] Although Destu is said to "talk kind of funny like a foreigner," the attention to Sibra's foreignness is relentless: he is described as "some kind of foreign Negro," and his maid notes his "funny smellin' apa'tment" and books of "funny writin', lack uh chicken done stepped in uh inkpot en walked up en down on de pages," which Roger speculates must be Arabic (*EMM* 53–54, 77, 81–82).

In Harlem, the Muslim Sibra, more than Destu, emerges as the true specter of unassimilable black foreignness. Within Ethiopia's borders, too, Islam's existence has been largely elided historically because of its perceived menace; consider the example of Lij Iyasu, the heir to Menelik who reigned briefly but, in part because he was believed to be a convert to Islam, was deposed and "was practically an 'unperson'" for decades after Selassie took the throne.[50] Promoting the long-standing idea of Ethiopia as a unified Christian nation, Selassie put an end to his predecessor's attempts to "redress the injustices of the past [and make] the Muslims feel at home in their own country" by increasing tolerance of Islam, a religion practiced by a large percentage of Ethiopians.[51] Generally speaking, villains in the *Ethiopian Stories* are enemies of the state because they, in one way or another, threaten its fragile coherence. For example, Ras Resta Gusa, an erstwhile suitor of Princess Ettara's who is also a caricatured antagonist revealed to be collaborating with the Italians, is transparently modeled after Haile Selassie Gugsa, whom *Time* describes in exaggerated language calculated to paint a picture of buffoonish villainy: "Mounted on a prancing ass, and with an embroidered velvet chieftain's robe worn like a chasuble over his Italian army uniform, bug-eyed Haile Selassie Gugsa, traitorous son-in-law of Emperor Haile Selassie, rode in triumph last week into his old capital of Makale."[52] In addition, Askaris, the "black men fighting black men" discussed in chapter 6 whom Marcus Garvey blames for "every battle that the Italians won in Abyssinia," emerge toward the end of *Revolt in Ethiopia* to capture our heroes just when it looks as if they will finally succeed in their quest to save Ethiopia, and they are examples of whom Ettara calls "certain traitors among our own people" (142). One character in *The Ethiopian Murder Mystery* even says of Sibra, "If he hadn't been black I'd have said he was an Italian" (78). The interactions of these disruptive black figures in Ethiopian imperial culture and the black international sphere in general produce what Brent Hayes Edwards calls *décalage*, that which needs to "propped up" (etymologically) in the diasporic connections among Africans and African Americans in Schuyler's fiction.[53] Even characters like Gusa, who is a relative of the emperor's, are forces potentially destructive to imperial coherence, standing in for insurgent ethnic, cultural, and religious identities both internal and external to imperial Ethiopia. However, to draw attention to these disunities—in other words, to call Selassie's Ethiopia imperialist, to call it a slave state—would ally one uncomfortably, as Taketani points out, with existing Italian propagandistic arguments used in the service of colonization.

Although the warmth of African American sympathy for Ethiopia is readily apparent, the "blindness" of that sympathy lies in the fact that, as I have said, it was undemocratically directed toward the throne rather than toward the ordinary Ethiopians who suffered most greatly from the Italian invasion. In fact, as Schuyler was publishing his *Ethiopian Stories*, Selassie was living in exile in Bath. During his exile, Marcus Garvey attacked him for leaving the country and pointed out the irony of his settling in England: "In truth, the Emperor is out of place in democratic England. He wants to be once more in the environment of the feudal Monarch who looks down upon his slaves and serfs with contempt."[54] Without subjects, he is no monarch; geographical distance ironically blunts the power of the necessary social distance between him and those who serve him that constitutes an emperor.

As Peter DeGabriele writes in an essay on Edward Gibbon's *The Decline and Fall of the Roman Empire*, "Gibbon questions the ability of sympathy to bridge the vast social gap between sovereign and subject, and also between Imperial center and colonial periphery." Explaining that recent scholarship has tended to locate a shift, in the 1770s and 1780s, "away from the importance of national sovereignty and sovereign power," DeGabriele writes that Gibbon—whose history, as I have mentioned, includes discussion of the "sleeping" Abyssinians—demonstrates how interactions with others failed to produce sympathy. This failure begins with what "Gibbon describes [as] a fundamental disjunction between the happiness of the sovereign and his subjects, a caesura at the center of political society which disrupts any attempt to make the social field into a representative space in which all interests can be shared and represented," a disjunction that is repeated in the relationship between metropole and colony.[55] A century and a half later, African American sympathetic desire to uphold a model of black sovereignty, one that could even be called imperialist depending upon one's perspective, potentially as a means of integrating and connecting an international black populace, appears especially curious. The strangeness of this sympathy, of course, is modulated by the conviction that the sovereign is himself a victim and a fitting representation of a nation that is "enslaved."

Interestingly, Schuyler's *Black Empire* (serialized from 1936 to 1938) has received greater critical attention as pro-Ethiopia propaganda than his *Ethiopian Stories*. Taketani chooses it for the focus of her article's argument about African American interest in the Italo-Ethiopian War, calling it a "narrative of the liberation of Ethiopia from white colonization," and Thompson argues that *Black Empire*'s black "Mussolini figure," Dr. Henry Belsidus, embodies "the idea of Africa 'liberated' by an African American Übermensch" and "quench[ed] the thirst for revenge blacks felt over the Italian invasion of Ethiopia."[56] A figure such as Belsidus in *Black Empire*, a strong and hypermasculine fascist dictator who centralizes the power of the black imperial world, is missing from the *Ethiopian Stories*, whose figures representing imperial leadership are peripheral—princes and princesses who report to people higher up in the hierarchy. In addition, although Princess Ettara is admittedly a strong figure, Destu is a weak "sensualist" and hardly the picture of authoritarian black masculinity.

In her discussion of Marcus Garvey, Claude McKay, and C. L. R. James, Stephens writes that "these figures drew first on a key element of imperial and national discourse—the belief in the *sovereignty* of both the self and of the state. That investment in sovereignty created the space for highly masculine definitions of racial freedom, embodied in varying male figures and tropes for the black, revolutionary hero." It is easy to see how someone like Garvey satisfied this "vision of the sovereign state figured in the black male sovereign" in the early twentieth century. After World War I, Stephens identifies a "shift away from visions of sovereignty for the race embodied in the figure of the revolutionary male sovereign who leads the racial community in its struggle and claiming of particular state forms toward the crafting of more mobile insurgent forms of black resistance politics emphasizing primarily black subjects' right to (free) movement versus independent statehood."[57] Public interest in Selassie in the 1930s presents a challenge to this view. Clearly, the figure of the black male sovereign still had its appeal.

However, an important difference between the figure of the black male sovereign as represented by someone like Garvey as opposed to Selassie that emerges in media descriptions is that Selassie is not viewed as highly masculine but as frail, small, and effeminate. A photograph accompanying the *Time* profile shows the emperor—"that proud, reserved little Semite"—with a group of "white ladies," sharing some "giggles."[58] The contrast between Garvey and Selassie as diverging paths of potential leadership for the black empire is further complicated by tensions between the two leaders. In 1937, Garvey accused Selassie of being "a great coward who ran away from his country to save his skin and left the millions of his countrymen to struggle through a terrible war."[59]

In *Ethiopian Stories*, Selassie is a shadowy figure driving the plots from behind a curtain. Ettara in *Revolt in Ethiopia* relishes the chance to work as his proxy, and Sadiu in *The Ethiopian Murder Mystery* mentions that he expects the emperor to reward the assassin responsible for killing Destu and the other murder victims in the story, but Selassie himself never appears—not even his voice on a telephone, in a letter, or in a telegram. He "r[u]ns away" from the action, as Garvey might say, standing at a remove from the melodrama. His simultaneous absence and omnipresence make him godlike in Schuyler's fictional universe.

The Business of War

At the conclusion of *The Ethiopian Murder Mystery*, Sadiu, the Ethiopian spy whom Roger encounters, explains his lack of sympathy for his murdered victims with the simple declaration, "This is war, my friend" (122). By the end of *Revolt in Ethiopia*, published when Italy's annexation of the country was a fait accompli, a representative from a German auction house to whom Dick and Ettara sell the Ethiopian jewels that they have managed to transport to Europe responds to Dick's surprise that Germany would indirectly work against Italy's best interests with a parallel declaration: "This is business" (224). When Dick learns that the delivery of arms will be made through the Sudan, he again expresses surprise, because this is British territory. The German tells him that the delivery will be made smoothly and jokes that he and Ettara's father, who has joined the victorious group in Antwerp ("this staid city of merchants and jewelers"), have "done business before" (225–26).

The business of war—the exchange through which the solution to Ethiopia's problems in *Revolt in Ethiopia* must come—provides Schuyler with a new capitalistic path to black internationalist sympathy at the end of the war. It is no accident that his protagonist is a millionaire: he escapes peril on the cruise ship by obtaining a seaplane at great personal expense; he uses his American Express traveler's checks to pay for a private plane; when customs officials uncover heroin planted by his enemies in his suitcase, he protests that he is a "man of independent wealth" and the officials "can easily check on [his] credit rating" (158). Money has the potential to override national or international loyalties; as Dick says when Ettara questions whether their friends Gunsa Hernum and Dedjasmatch Yamrou could have betrayed them, "Money has changed people's allegiance before" (202). But even if money could sway soldiers and civilians to fight alongside their putative enemies, *Revolt in Ethiopia* concludes with the argument that it could also purchase the weapons that are almost all that are needed to win a modern war. As Schuyler wrote in one of his columns,

"Ethiopia does not need men. . . . What Ethiopia needs is money."[60] With the ancient jewels, Dick and Ettara are able to buy from the Germans "one hundred thousand rifles with one hundred fifty rounds apiece[,] . . . ten bombing planes and twenty fighters[,] . . . five hundred machine guns [with] two thousand rounds apiece[,] . . . field radio sets and medical supplies" (226). Even after these expenditures, half of Ethiopia's credit remains. The story ends with the fantasy that Ethiopia's ultimate victory is imminent, thanks to these purchases. In writing *Revolt in Ethiopia* after *Black Empire*—a text that, as I have said, fetishizes modern and even futuristic weaponry in a manner that is surprisingly reminiscent of the Futurists' fetishization of weaponry—Schuyler turns from science fiction to a more realistic genre, imagining Ethiopia's triumph as a viable and realistic outcome when in actuality the picture was bleak.

Nevertheless, the impediments to sympathy intrinsic to diasporic *décalage*, to return to Edwards's term (itself adapted from Léopold Senghor), were already beginning to show as early as the end of *The Ethiopian Murder Mystery*.[61] Roger is dissatisfied with Sadiu's unsympathetic modus operandi and Sadiu lives by the patriotic assertion that his "only allegiance is to Ethiopia" (122). These two positions cannot be reconciled: if African Americans are invited and even expected to devote transnational sympathetic allegiance to Ethiopia, and Ethiopians are expected to direct their devotion inward toward the crown, then this unilateral relation could be a thorn in the side for an integrated black internationalism. The centripetal imperial pull is surprisingly toward Ethiopia rather than toward the West. In this light, the desire to see Americanness in Selassie starts to look like an attempt to smooth over the disruptions of *décalage*, to give pride of place back to Western cultural hegemony, and to direct attention back toward the putative center rather than periphery. Either there are truly Western qualities adopted by the emperor, with his French physician and Hungarian chef, or those qualities are projected upon him. Either way, he becomes visible and thus sympathetic only as a culturally hybrid figure.

Furthermore, if the business of war could only be conducted with the financial support of African Americans who would buy pins picturing Haile Selassie and donate funds to organizations like the Friends of Ethiopia, then the generosity and charity behind this activity ironically only increase the gap. It is worth noting again that the plot of *Revolt in Ethiopia* revolves entirely around the idea of *helping* Ethiopia. The model of reciprocal and mutual construction of black ethnic identity implied by the relationship between Ettara and Dick—where he helps her and becomes Ethiopian, and then she literally ennobles him through marriage and becomes American—is a fantasy beyond which we are not permitted to see; the story ends there. Ettara's assumed American identity is suspended in the future tense.

In a chapter titled "On Reciprocity: René Maran and Alain Locke," Edwards writes that Locke, in his 1924 essay "Apropos of Africa,"

> call[s] for what he terms "reciprocity" in African diasporic politics. . . . The "spirit" of emerging black *political* internationalism, then, must for Locke be "reciprocal," rather than provincial or condescending (the notion of some "civilizing mission"), because that internationalism is necessarily a politics of difference—a dialogue among blacks placed unevenly in transnational political environments. . . . "We must realize that in some respects we need what Africa has to give us as much as, or even more than, Africa needs what we in turn have to give her," Locke instructs.[62]

The lack of reciprocity in Schuyler's fiction—does marrying someone demonstrate as much sympathy as helping someone win a war?—highlights the challenges to black solidarity that are only compounded in the end by the presence of imperial monarchy.

In concluding this chapter, I would like to turn briefly to a character in *Revolt in Ethiopia* who, at first, might not seem to merit much attention. Dick's valet, Bill, who does not "like these here Africans no more'n them Eyetalians," is treated as comic relief, but Ethiopia's victory would have been entirely impossible without him. It is Bill who ingeniously thinks to hide the gems in a large bar of soap, because he believes that the soap will go unnoticed, as "these Eyetalians an' Ethiopians ain't so strong on bathin'" (216). Significantly, Bill sees no difference between foreign whiteness and foreign blackness. Not only do Gusa and the Askaris fight alongside the Italians, they share certain cultural behaviors and habits in common that Bill recognizes as alien. The soap trick is the plot turn that allows the characters to escape the country.

Throughout the adventure, Bill complains bitterly and wishes to return to the United States. Why would Schuyler allow such a character to be the one who ultimately succeeds in helping Ethiopia? He is arguably the least sympathetic character in the novel, in both senses of the word, resembling no one so much as Sadiu, the cold spy at the end of *The Ethiopian Murder Mystery*. And perhaps this is the reason: because Bill, the "slave," is as removed from royal circles as Ettara and Dick are integrated into them, he can operate outside of those lines of reciprocity that have been corrupted by imperial culture. He does not weep for Ethiopia, as Dick does. To plan their escape, he simply passes a note to "one o' them good-lookin' Ethiopian browns" and repeats the name of his note's intended recipient a few times "'cause Ah don't know her lingo" (215). He never feels a connection to any Ethiopian in the novel. While other well-intentioned characters in Schuyler's *Ethiopian Stories* are driven by a "warm and blind sympathy," Bill's cold indifference, strangely, allows him to see.

CHAPTER EIGHT

Claude McKay and the Display of Aristocracy

Into the streets, Black Brothers,
Into the dust and rain;
. . . .
Up from our knees of prayer,
Up with our voices sing,
Brothers, Black, Brown, Yellow,
Selassie's Emperor and King.

Forward march, Black Brothers,
Break through the barricades.

—ARTHUR N. WRIGHT, "ETHIOPIA'S BLACKS"

NESTLED AMONG THE letters to the editor of the 3 August 1935 issue of the *Baltimore Afro-American* we find the above rousing call to action. To its left, a letter submitted by "Baltimore youth" encouraged a boycott of Italian businesses. To its right, two letters—from Ohio and West Virginia—inquire about enlisting in the Ethiopian army. Other letters supporting the nation during the Second Italo-Abyssinian War of 1935–36 come from as far afield as Chicago; Roxbury, Massachusetts; and Kansas City, Missouri. Above all, Harlem's desire to defend Ethiopia reached a pitch more fevered than in any other American city, with volunteers offering to fight in the Ethiopian military and groups organizing mass meetings, rallies, parades, and boycotts for the cause. It was, however, during the dispirited period in the interim immediately following the Italian occupation that Claude McKay wrote his biting 1941 anti-communist novel, *Amiable with Big Teeth: A Novel of the Love Affair between the Communists and the Poor Black Sheep of Harlem*, unpublished and recently discovered among Samuel Roth's papers in the Rare Books and Manuscripts archives at Columbia University.

The novel looks back at various fervent and often competing Harlem campaigns to raise funds for Ethiopia and parodies the intrigue that developed as a result of this "sudden collective flare-up," to quote McKay, which most often assumed the form of public demonstrations of solidarity in the streets.[1] In light of the subsequent collapse of the pan-Africanist sentiment inspired by the war, McKay's novel explores whether an Ethiopianist conception of an originary Africanness binding black peoples through a shared devotion to imperial culture remains possible. He mocks the persistent equation of Africanness with a feudal anti-modernity using a plot that revolves around the question of what it means to be an "authentic" representation of Ethiopian aristocracy and that, in examining the seductive effects of transformative Ethiopianist self-invention, exposes an emperor who wears no clothes.

In Harlem, the public appearance, as an effort of generating support for the Ethiopian cause, was most effective in the form of a parade or protest, and the authentic protest or parade leader was he who served as the most perfect avatar for his people. He defines his people as his people define him, in a relationship of perfect reciprocity. In other words, as the author of *John Hoy of Ethiopia* wrote of his apparent focus upon the citizenry rather than Haile Selassie himself, "the parade is part of him, and, watching it, I learn of him."[2] McKay, on the other hand, watches the parade not to learn about the man at its center but to learn about the sympathetic networks that mutually define the man and his spectators.

The Spectacular Uniform

McKay opens his novel with a Harlem parade featuring a man in Ethiopian costume who calls himself Professor Koazhy, a spectacular "full-sized ebon-hued man, bedecked in a uniform so rare, so gorgeous, it made the people prance and shout with joy" (4). This elaborate uniform—"a mailed shirt extravagantly covered with golden gleaming arabesques and a wonderfully high shako, white and surmounted by a variegated cluster of ostrich plumes" (4)—is marked by its decorative excess. As Paul Gilroy writes in relation to Garvey's views regarding the fortification of race as an ongoing and deliberate process, "martial technologies of racial becoming—drills, uniforms, medals, titles, rallies—are necessary to standardize a racial outlook that cannot arise spontaneously."[3] The assertiveness and conspicuousness of the uniform's militarism, therefore, serves an emphatically pan-Africanist function. There is no question that Koazhy is modeled after figures like Garvey, whose dress Du Bois described as a "military uniform of the gayest mid-Victorian type, heavy with gold lace, epaulets, plume, and sword."[4]

Du Bois's impression of Victorianism, however, differs distinctly from McKay's description of Garvey's style and uniform: Garvey's lectures, he writes, "could be as decorative as arabesques and his raiment as rich as an Eastern potentate's."[5] Despite the fact that popular images of Garvey find him "clad in a field marshal's uniform of World War I vintage," McKay discerns a pronounced Orientalism both in Garvey's dress and speaking style. It is this Orientalism that McKay appropriates later in his novel's descriptions of Koazhy.[6] Whatever is military about the character's costume, notably, is also antique and Orientalist: in addition to McKay's repetition of the word "arabesques," he compares Koazhy to a "medieval knight," and, rather than firearms, Koazhy carries a sword, which he "brandished at heaven" (5, 4). Dressed as an Ethiopian warrior, he combines antiquity with splendor in order to visually prompt an ecstatic response from the audience.

It is Koazhy's martial Ethiopianism—combining Orientalism and militarism—specifically that resonates with the crowd. Performances of this sort of African American militarism can be traced back, as Gilroy points out, past Garvey to Booker T. Washington and Frederick Douglass in the regimented practices of the Hampton-Tuskegee educational tradition and calls for the establishment of black fraternal orders, respectively. In addition to the thrill of the new that the crowd craves in Koazhy's appearance, they are also drawn to a comfortable familiarity in his brand of martial authoritarianism. As Du Bois had said critically and condescendingly of Garvey's appeal in 1923, it was "the sort of appeal that easily throws ignorant and inexperienced people into orgies of response and generosity."[7] Similarly, in response to McKay's questioning of the "Oriental toggery" worn by the controversial Sufi Abdul Hamid, the mystic replied that "there was so much religion and regalia in the soul of the Negroes one could do nothing with them without some show of it."[8] But Koazhy's finery surpasses even that of Hamid, who makes an appearance in McKay's novel as "a black Buddha in his turban and baroque Oriental costume"; Hamid is "out-dazzled by Professor Koazhy, who sat beside him in his glittering uniform of an Ethiopian Ras with his shako of many-colored plumes" (144). These spectacular costumes not only work as a shorthand or visual cue of consummate showmanship, designed to attract followers through their charisma, they are also calculated to inspire a reciprocal extravagance or immoderation from their viewers.

As a result, Koazhy inspires mass hysteria for the Ethiopian cause among the people of Harlem through his costume in a way that the unassuming prince of Ethiopia present at the same demonstration, wearing a simple red sash, cannot. The mild, appreciative reception given to Lij Tekla Alamaya ("lij" being an Ethiopian regal title) is completely overshadowed by the crowd's "mighty roar" at the sight of Koazhy (4). In fact, because of Koazhy's "richly bedecked apparition," he is even misidentified as the Ethiopian prince, and the newspaper article covering the event, although bearing the headline "Negroes Organize to Aid Ethiopia," instead "was written around Professor Koazhy and his gorgeous uniform" (29). This is despite the fact that there is nothing official about his surprise presence at the parade and that he is an embarrassment to the novel's black bourgeois characters who have planned the event and who view his appearance as an "extravagant injection of himself into the ceremony" (12). In order to avoid becoming upstaged in the future, it is decided that Alamaya should dress in uniform for public appearances.

Aware that the crowd is responding to his striking appearance, Koazhy announces, "I know that the majority are applauding this uniform. That is as it should be" (9). He knows that the spectacle of his supremely individualized costume has the power to mobilize his audience, as he witnesses how "the mass roared in a frenzy" (4). However, he insists that he did not intend for the uniform to serve as "merely a gaudy show"; he wants the crowd "not to see me, but the great warriors of Ethiopia" (9). Garvey's dress had conflated imperial and militaristic elements in fashioning a cult of personality, but Koazhy fashions himself simply as a nameless, unknown soldier in the Ethiopian army. He attempts to present himself not as Selassie or Menelik but as Ethiopianness itself.

Alamaya, for his part, finds it "puzzling that that uniform had made such a powerful appeal to the senses of the crowd," given that it was a "barbaric fantastic costume, which was not symbolic of the new spirit of Ethiopia" (6). It is not, in other words, authentic. To paraphrase Leigh Raiford on Garvey's uniform, Koazhy's too must be read "as an indication of both an atavistic desire for autocratic power but one that imagines—creates in this case, not entirely fictionalizes—an ancient precolonial, prelapsarian African glory."[9] Viewing the crowd as "more like European crowds" than "tribal Ethiopians," Alamaya cannot reconcile their attraction to what he sees as the visual presentation of anachronism. However, in his choice of the word "fantastic" to describe the costume, he hits upon what he will ultimately realize explains the attraction. The image of the Ethiopian warrior attracts the crowd for its fantasy and romanticism, while a modern Ethiopian uniform holds less appeal. The event is organized in order to seek African American support of the Ethiopian cause on the basis of consanguinity, but the crowd relishes and craves cultural difference. According to Alamaya, "All the world loves uniforms. . . . Perhaps the best uniform for this age is the obsolete theatrical kind that was chosen by Professor Koazhy" (17).

That it is specifically "this age"—the modern age—that requires obsolescence in the visual symbol of solidarity is precisely the paradox at the heart of twentieth-century Ethiopianism, as is the ironic requirement of difference as the basis for sympathy. As one of McKay's characters eager to move into an apartment downtown puts it, Harlem, despite all appearances to the contrary, "is no more modernistic than Chinatown" (163). The spectacle of the parade is a perfect example of a surprising celebration of archaism. As Raiford writes of the Universal Negro Improvement Association (UNIA) demonstrations in Harlem, "The showy display of these parades invoked both the modernity of the nation-state and the splendor of an imagined African past"; she cites a *Negro World* reporter who described a UNIA event in 1921 as "a ceremonial that may correctly be regarded as a revival of ancient glory, pomp and splendor of Ethiopia in the days of Queen of Sheba."[10] Hoping for a reprieve in the United States from the incessant demands and strictures of imperial culture, Alamaya expects that, "of all Americans, the Aframericans would be less interested in the formalities of titles and courts" and is surprised to find the opposite (15). Although Alamaya's formal suit is comparatively unimpressive, prompting him to wonder if "perhaps he too should have worn a uniform," he recognizes that, even if he had chosen a modern Ethiopian military uniform, "nothing he might have worn could compare with the resplendent splendor of Professor Koazhy's accoutrement" (5, 6).

The spectacle Koazhy produces directly serves his goal, as his "appeal brought in twice as much money as was previously collected" (11–12). And, in fact, he appears to redirect and funnel the attention he earns through his performance charitably toward Alamaya: "Here in your midst in flesh and blood you have an Ethiopian—a Prince of Africa" (9). Upon closer examination, however, he does not seem to be referring to Alamaya but to *himself*. Immediately following this pronouncement, Koazhy claims a profound and extensive knowledge of African history inaccessible both to the African Americans in his audience and to the Ethiopians themselves, and it is a history that only Koazhy is equipped to teach. In his eyes, he is the true Prince of Africa.

As theatrical as he is—he is described both as a "one-man show" and a "major showman" (18, 10)—he is not ridiculous. We are told that "there was no hint of the spirit of clowning in him" (10). Just as Du Bois says of a UNIA event he attended, "a casual observer might have mistaken it for the dress-rehearsal of a new comic opera, and looked instinctively for Bert Williams and Miller and Lyle," and yet "it was a serious occasion, done on the whole soberly and solemnly."[11] Koazhy combines the roles of educator and entertainer. Although Alamaya is inspired by Koazhy's display of knowledge, another character, Professor Dorsey Flagg, says of Koazhy, "he wants to be a modern scholar as well as an African medicine-man and he gets all tangled up in a crazy jumble of information. . . . He's just a burlesque of an unconvincing pedant" (16). From the start of the novel, however, this synthetic approach—one that combines the didactic and the entertaining, the contemporary and the ancient, the African and the American in a productive incarnation of Du Boisian double consciousness—allows Koazhy to serve as a representative of generic blackness, one therefore best positioned to make the case for Ethiopia as a black transnational cause. He is the authentic Ethiopian.

It is no accident, then, that Koazhy (*né* Matthew Preston) has adopted an African name. McKay characterizes this rechristening as an act of self-invention: "he had turned Quashie into Koazhy and prefaced it with 'Professor'" (13). "Quashie," a term previously used in poems by McKay such as "Quashie to Buccra," is defined by the *Oxford English Dictionary* as "a generic name for: a black person, esp. one considered as credulous or insignificant," with the note, "*Caribbean, chiefly derogatory*." In other words, his renaming is a by-now familiar attempt at reappropriation of a potentially offensive term to transform it into a term of pride: he re-Africanizes it, restores it to its original Akan etymology, making it the translation of a translation.

In contrast, Alamaya is somehow less successfully "African" than Koazhy. His light complexion enables him to cross the color line, and, according to the mother of his initial love interest in the novel, the similarly light-skinned Seraphine Peixota, "he can work both ways between white and black" (63). Alamaya's only public appearance to approach Koazhy's in its frenzy-generating reception is one that asserts his Ethio-American hybridity as well as his unusual ability to foster interracial and intraracial collaboration. When a fundraising meeting threatens to devolve into chaos, Alamaya removes his coat before shaking hands with

Dorsey Flagg, an African American professor accused of Fascism by the White Friends of Ethiopia. The gesture, Pablo Peixota explains to Alamaya, is interpreted by the crowd as "shirt-sleeve diplomacy," as if he were "staging a little exhibition of Americanism for their benefit" (98). As a result, the women in the crowd are inspired to inundate Alamaya with kisses. According to Peixota, they saw him as "a living symbol of Ethiopia," but Peixota's wife disagrees: "You know as well as I that those women were not excited about Lij Alamaya as a symbol, but because he's just plain *it*" (101). This language, along with the fact that Alamaya is said later to have "bright ideas like any American salesman," links him to the public perception of Haile Selassie discussed in chapter 5 as an unexpectedly thrilling but seemingly inauthentic juxtaposition of American modernity and Eastern antiquity (246).

The Authentic Ethiopian

In one of the few critical treatments of the novel thus far, Jean-Christophe Cloutier claims that Koazhy is "likely a hybrid of Dr. Willis N. Huggins and Charles C. Seifert,"[12] but, as I have argued, the resemblance between Garvey and Koazhy—especially in the novel's opening chapter—is uncanny. Cloutier also sees Alamaya as "a composite character that seems largely based on McKay's friend, Dr. Malaku Bayen, an Ethiopian emissary who was director of the Harlem United Aid to Ethiopia organization," but, as he more accurately observes in his recent introduction to the novel (co-written with Brent Hayes Edwards), a significant portion of this composite actually comes from Lij Tasfaye Zaphiro.[13] Bayen's black self-identification and spirit of pan-African solidarity were unquestionable. As McKay writes in *Harlem: Negro Metropolis*, "In Dr. Bayen's charming presence Aframericans could be convinced that Ethiopians are not white or Mongolians, but authentic native Africans."[14] He was married to an African American woman, and "owing to the conspicuousness of his Ethiopian skin, he was unceremoniously shunted up to the inconvenience of Harlem" after first attempting to lodge downtown.[15] Lij Zaphiro, on the other hand, like Lij Alamaya, was light enough to pass and had been staying in white hotels in New York until convinced by Dr. P. H. M. Savory, owner of the *Amsterdam News*, to move to Harlem. Bayen was a family man and trained physician, while Zaphiro was young—perhaps not even twenty—and a bit of a dandy, attracting the attention of besotted would-be princesses. Zaphiro was seen wearing "a purple cape embroidered with gold" or "short black cloak, lined with red, the collar of which decorated [*sic*] with golden braid."[16]

The newspapers of *Amiable with Big Teeth* suggest the same of Alamaya, who is "depicted as a sybarite in his private life, enjoying a dandy's bohemian existence in a hotel downtown" (115). As with Alamaya, too, women ushered their marriageable daughters in Zaphiro's direction, and "he was besieged on all hands by autograph seekers and others whose greatest aim was to shake his hand." Although some dismissed the English-accented youth as "an Anglicized fop, carried on the crest of a wave of sentimental attachment for Ethiopia and meeting situations as they came," most came away thoroughly impressed by him.[17] He caused such a sensation during his visit to Chicago that the back page of an issue of the *Chicago Defender* was covered with photographs of him, accompanied by the following caption: "From the time he stepped from the train at 8:30 a.m. Sunday until his departure Monday night at 11:40 o'clock, not a single move was made that was not duly recorded for The Chicago Defender's discriminating reading public."[18]

Lij Zaphiro identified himself as "a private secretary to the Ethiopian minister in London" who had "arrived in New York to raise funds for his government and to coordinate the activities of the pro-Ethiopian societies operating in this country."[19] He began a speaking tour of the United States at the Abyssinian Baptist Church, as McKay's Alamaya would. He was apparently a public enough figure to be included in an early draft of Arthur Arent's play for the Federal Theater project, *Ethiopia*, discussed in the fifth chapter of this book, in which he asserted a fraternal connection between Ethiopians and African Americans.[20] And, like Alamaya, Zaphiro welcomed collaboration with communists, as he did when he appeared before the National Negro Congress alongside James W. Ford. He conducted this work despite carrying "no papers, no letters of introduction nor anything to officially stand him in good stead when called upon to prove his status"; he was trusted implicitly.[21]

After a speaking engagement in Chicago, however, the committee hosting Zaphiro "began wondering whether he was indeed an accredited Ethiopian representative."[22] The *Chicago Defender* claimed that "in the minds of some policemen lurked deep suspicions brought on by long schooling in the ways of expert confidence men."[23] After only a few months of fundraising, Zaphiro disappeared, and his sudden departure from the United States was the subject of further controversy in various newspapers. The *Pittsburgh Courier* speculated that his departure was in fact a punitive ejection from the country, signaling that John H. Shaw, the Ethiopian consul, was "certainly the official and only representative in this country authorized by the Ethiopian government."[24] Shaw himself, however, denied that Zaphiro's return to London was a surprise. "I know nothing of published reports of a three-way feud among various Ethiopian aid groups," he said, adding that "it was not Zaphiro's business to be associated with any particular group. He simply had a working agreement to appear before different groups and talk to them." In defense of Zaphiro's authenticity, Shaw criticized demands that he "show credentials," noting that he was an employee of the Ethiopian embassy in London but insisting at the same time that "he was not accredited as a deplomatic [*sic*] representative by Ethiopia either in England or in America."[25]

Incidentally, McKay had encountered his own issues with credentials a few years earlier: as Michael North writes, his "credentials were challenged by the American delegation" while visiting the Soviet Union in 1922 for a labor conference. North even argues that "this might be considered the quintessential experience of McKay's life, for his credentials were always being questioned," so perhaps he was sympathetic to Zaphiro's situation.[26] In any case, clearly there was confusion about Zaphiro's role, confusion that he may have encouraged. In addition to this misrepresentation, he may have even embezzled funds raised from his tour.[27]

Most damning of all, however, were the challenges to Zaphiro's Ethiopianness itself—much like those confronted by McKay's Alamaya, whose overshadowing by Koazhy at the start of the novel leaves him to prove his authenticity. Curiously, a bit of digging into Zaphiro's personal history prior to his U.S. trip reveals a name change similar to Koazhy's. As an example of the generosity of Ethiopian ambassador Hakim Wärqenäh (also known as Charles Martin—a reverse Koazhy, known by a Western name), Peter Garretson cites the employment of one "Reginald (or Reggie) Zaphiro who was also known in Ethiopia as Täsfay." (Needless to say, Reggie Zaphiro is not a typical Ethiopian name.) He was apparently hired as a favor to his mother after the death of his father, a Greek translator for the British embassy in Addis Ababa.[28] McKay borrows the detail of Zaphiro's heritage in the suspicion surrounding Alamaya, who is hounded by newspaper gossip "that he was fair of countenance because his father was a Levantine (some said a Greek) who had married an Ethiopian woman" (115). Zaphiro does not appear to have been very effective in his job; in *Reminiscences of My Life*, Emmanuel Abraham, another Ethiopian delegate in London, writes,

> Aware that the work was becoming too much for one person and that it was necessary to get someone to help, the Minister employed Tesfaye (Reginald) Zaphiro . . . to help me. He was a little younger than myself.

> Although he was useful in answering telephone calls and receiving visitors, he had no experience in office work and was not hard-working. That meant that my burden was not much lighter. A little later on he was sent to New York because American blacks who were so sympathetic to the Ethiopian cause had requested the Minister to send them someone to speak on Ethiopia at their meetings.

Upon Zaphiro's return to London, according to Abraham, he was unable to "settle down to do office work" and subsequently left his post.[29] Furthermore, as late as 25 October 1935—only weeks before Zaphiro's trip to the United States—the *Ottawa Citizen* published a photograph of him under the title "The Youngest Diplomat in Action" that claimed in its caption that the nineteen-year-old had been "an agricultural student working on a farm in Cambridgeshire, England" a few weeks earlier.[30] All evidence suggests that Zaphiro, if not a sham, was at least ill prepared for his campaign overseas.

A year later, in September 1936, "by which time most of the fund-raising frenzy had plummeted," Selassie sent Bayen, a Howard University alumnus with unimpeachable connections to the emperor, back to the United States.[31] The *Pittsburgh Courier* distinguished him from Zaphiro in pointing out that, although their missions are "somewhat similar," "Dr. Bayen comes as the Emperor's special envoy, with full authority."[32] He arrived in the United States with a letter bearing Selassie's signature, the seal of Ethiopia, and a message from Selassie authorizing Bayen to accept donations.[33] In addition, unlike Zaphiro, who had accepted communist assistance, Bayen was "fearful . . . of growing communist infiltration" of the United Aid for Ethiopia, the group with which he was affiliated, deciding to disband it and start anew with a group called the Ethiopian World Federation.[34]

Bayen shared this suspicion of the Communists with McKay, whom, as Cloutier points out, he considered a friend. Completely disenchanted with communism by the late 1930s, McKay writes in *Harlem: Negro Metropolis*:

> The Communist zealots adopted ridiculous subterfuges to obtain their ends. They sent up white artists from downtown to reside in Harlem and qualify as members. Events came about which unfortunately are not suitable for these pages, because they would appear better in the form of fiction than of fact.[35]

Apparently inspired by his own suggestion, his novelization of the recent history of Harlem's engagement with the Ethiopian crisis depicts tensions resulting from the participation of Communists active in the cause. The chairman of the novel's Hands to Ethiopia group headquartered in Harlem, Pablo Peixota, believes his group should be all-black; the black communist Newton Castle instead argues the perspective that efforts at exclusion would give ammunition to those who would advocate for segregating all-white organizations. Prudhomme Bishop, a black member of the White Friends of Ethiopia and president of the Equal Rights Action (an NAACP-type organization), encourages Peixota to admit into his group "as many whites as possible to illuminate it" (61). The racial and political tensions among these feuding factions—none of which are depicted entirely favorably—drive the action of McKay's novel.

"A Fantastic Imposture"

In an attempt to harness the power of the public's appetite for Ethiopianist romance and win the battle among these factions, Alamaya and his secret communist colleague Maxim Tasan, working for the White Friends of Ethiopia, craft an elaborate ruse to raise funds by "inventing" an Ethiopian princess. In this scheme, McKay plays upon the phenomenon of Ethiopian royal imposters characterized by Robert A. Hill as the "now largely vanished order . . . of *Æthiopis vagantes*"; Harlem, he writes, "was infested with . . . [i]ndividuals who indulged the vicarious pretence of being African princes and princesses" (209).[36] One of these was Princess Tamanya, who emerged in 1933 as a "Falasha Songstress" from Abyssinia, promoted by her agent, Chappie Gardner. After granting interviews to newspapers on the looming Italo-Abyssinian conflict in 1935, boasting that Italy would be defeated, she drew the attention of the Ethiopian government and was subsequently exposed as a hoax. Readers identifying themselves as "Ethiopian sympathizers" also recognized that something was amiss, telephoning the *New York Times* to "poin[t] out that no member of the ruling family of Ethiopia would be permitted to tour a foreign country—or even her own country—on a singing tour."[37] Residents of Harlem, too, exposed her: "A gayly costumed belle has presented herself to Lenox avenue as Rassari Heshla Tamanya, Falasha Princess of Ethiopia, but Lenox avenue said it knew her as Mrs. Iselyn Smith Harvey, housemaid at times."[38] After this exposé, Gardner was credited with "execut[ing] the slickest publicity stunt of the age" and compared to P. T. Barnum, whose successful promotion of the Swedish Nightingale, Jenny Lind, resulted in a blockbuster tour.[39] The unmasked Princess Tamanya, however, maintained that she was Ethiopian royalty and dismissed the Ethiopian government's denials. The *New York*

Amsterdam News claimed that "her biggest scoffs she saved for Lij Tasfaye Zaphiro . . . the man whom thousands of Harlemites cheered wildly on his first appearance here," calling him "merely a secretary attached to the London legation."[40] Ironically, Princess Tamanya joined an Italian touring company in the 1940s.

Like Garvey, who warned his audiences to "keep a close eye on African princes, African chiefs, princesses and all such fake personalities," McKay mocks the public's gullible acceptance of hoaxes such as these.[41] Alamaya, however, justifies his actions as something other than a hoax. While costuming a local Harlem woman, he tells her, "Ethiopian is a generic word and you are entitled to be called Ethiopian exactly as you are called colored or Aframerican." Moving toward a more synthetic view of Ethiopianness, he presents her to the public in the guise of a princess and in essence transforms her into a princess, mirroring Koazhy's self-inventive transformation into a prince. Alamaya has no reservations about calling Gloria "as genuine an article as myself as a Lij" (247). The term "lij," incidentally, operates as a perfect illustration of what Brent Hayes Edwards calls *décalage* in the context of diasporic difference: "the kernel of precisely that which cannot be transferred or exchanged, the received biases that refuse to pass over when one crosses the water."[42] Throughout the novel, Alamaya's friends in Harlem translate "lij" as "prince," despite his constant insistence that they refrain from doing so. (Again, McKay appears to have borrowed this detail from the real-life examples of Lij Zaphiro, who "at first vigorously denied" the title "His Highness," "but in vain," and Malaku Bayen, who "denied that he had authorized his friends here to affix this title [of prince] to his name.")[43] The literal translation of "lij" in Amharic is "child," applicable to sons of noblemen, and it is an aristocratic title for which there is no exact translation in English. The confusion surrounding the term in fact appears to have facilitated Lij Zaphiro's real-life alleged imposture as a prince during his U.S. lectures. So, when Alamaya calls Gloria as "genuine an article as myself as Lij," he is not saying much, especially since he has spent the novel attempting (in his modesty) to downplay the title.

The news of the princess's arrival is accompanied in the local papers by a photograph depicting "an arresting marvel of jet radiance whose lovely features were heightened by a gorgeously filigreed gown and antique jewels ornamenting her neck and arms" (177). Interestingly, Gloria, as Princess Benebe Zarihana, is advertised as an "amateur pantomimist" and actress, displaying herself as a performing spectacle—precisely the aspect of Princess Tamanya's appearances that attracted the skepticism of those familiar with the customs of Ethiopian royals. Her act must be understood in the context of the subgenre of the "Ethiopia" pageant—for instance, W. E. B. Du Bois's "The Star of Ethiopia"—in which a beautiful young woman becomes an abstract symbol of the race. She performs her pantomime for crowds that have traveled down from Harlem, because it was believed "more appropriate to the dignity of Ethiopia as a nation that the princess should be launched from downtown[,] . . . the seat of wealth and power," in contrast to "the fiasco of Lij Alamaya's spectacular debut" uptown (177–78). In an attempt to correct their previous mistakes, they manufacture the perfect Ethiopian royal diversion to captivate the public, having also learned from Koazhy's studied approach to costume and showmanship in order to appeal to the masses effectively.

In addition to her warm reception by the masses, the princess is "just as fortunate in the impression she registered among the representatives of the Fourth Estate" (179). Recalling Henry Higgins's deception in presenting Eliza Doolittle to society in George Bernard Shaw's *Pygmalion*, Alamaya's and Tasan's hoax tricks the press into admiring the princess's "poise and aplomb, her gait and charm and composite magnetism[,] . . . the nobility inherent in her consummate African dignity, the indefinable artistry manifested in every shade of her movement" (179). Not surprisingly, because the scheme is Tasan's, the most extensive coverage appears in the *Labor Herald*, exhibiting a thrill that echoes the language McKay uses to describe Koazhy, as if inspired to ecstatic performance themselves: "The deftly arranged poses of Princess Benebe in her gilded costumes and golden slippers and jeweled tiara whipped the eye to dance with delight" (179).

The *Labor Herald* is, ironically, the same "Sovietist" newspaper that covered Alamaya's first public appearance with dignity and moderation, in contrast to the sensationalistic coverage in other papers. In attempting to convince Peixota that Hands to Ethiopia needs the help of the communists, Castle shows him the article in which "there was no photograph of Professor Koazhy and no mention of his speech." Unlike other newspapers, the *Labor Herald* emphasizes Alamaya's role and, more important, "in the center the people were pictured massed before the church" (33). As Castle says, "What capitalist newspaper would have played up our demonstration like that?" When Peixota complains about the paper's circulation, Castle counters with the claim that "the circulation doesn't matter. It's getting into print that counts" (34).

And yet, as the various newspaper accounts of this event illustrate, one cannot always trust what gets into print. With the aim of lifting the spirits of readers invested in the outcome of the doomed Italo-Ethiopian War, some African American newspapers in the novel present an intensely propagandistic picture that could be considered a form of imposture. In reproducing photographs of the Ethiopian army, "they doctored them so that readers could not detect the unshod feet under the trim uniforms"; in the same vein, Selassie "was pictured in his most martial pomp and shown at the front operating an anti-airplane gun" (176). What was seen as charmingly backward during the parade that opens the novel needs to be airbrushed into modernity by the end of a war that, it has become abundantly clear, Ethiopia appears to be losing. The antique Orientalist spectacle of royalty represented by Koazhy and his sword has succumbed to the equally embellished vision of Selassie's contemporary war machine. In response to a published remark allegedly by Selassie denying that Ethiopians were black (a historically accurate element in McKay's novel), many black newspapers—aside from the conservative ones that had never supported the cause—revealed their pro-Ethiopian bias and "cautioned against blandly accepting without question all statements which appeared in the 'white' press concerning their African brothers" (135). Eventually, however, the illusion becomes too difficult to sustain. The newspapers abandon the "embarrassing subject" of Ethiopia, and "like a fall of late hoar upon the verdant earth quickly dissipated by the rising sun, Ethiopia had suddenly evaporated from the headlines and disappeared from the front page and the sidewalk forums of conversation" (246, 249). With this natural metaphor, McKay points to the caprices of the press, who will devote columns to a topic only if they can marshal their readers' enthusiasm. In the wake of this disillusioning thaw, Alamaya now laments his role in the Princess Benebe hoax as a "cheap masquerade to ridicule Ethiopia and Aframericans" (253), an inauthentic display.

When Pedro Peixota's daughter Seraphine realizes the hoax, she wonders why "Alamaya, who was an authentic Ethiopian and a patriot, [would] become an accomplice to such a fantastic imposture" (209). But, again, this raises the question of whether he is in fact an "authentic Ethiopian." As Cloutier writes, "The evidentiary challenges surrounding authentication become a prime concern of the narrative," and "most major plot points in *Amiable* hinge on testing the authenticity of documents and people, on questioning and qualifying declarations of fact."[44] For instance, the minor character of Delta Buckton is introduced as the holder of an authenticating artifact that opens the door of Harlem's elite society to her: she "retained in her possession the cameo brooch that was presented by Queen Victoria to her grand-aunt, the celebrated mocking-bird of the Jubilee Singers" (86). This object stamps her as "'in' in the right way, and not even her straitened circumstances could keep her out" (86). The most significant of the novel's authenticating objects, however—one also mentioned by Cloutier—is the document allegedly verifying Alamaya as the Ethiopian envoy. Recalling the real-life example of Lij Zaphiro and McKay's own experiences, Alamaya admits cagily that a signed letter from the emperor establishing his bona fides "was authentic, but . . . not genuine," being a letter written in Amharic by the Ethiopian government for a member of an entirely different diplomatic mission years earlier, and that he himself "was not as genuine a diplomat as [he] pretended to be" (251, 250). Earlier in the novel, Alamaya had been "trounced as a fake representative, a swindler and parasite upon gullible colored people who were enamored of tinsel and title"—presumably the same masses who were entranced by Koazhy's appearance at the parade—and accusations flew that "he was not an authentic Ethiopian" (130). The fact that the textual proof that would authenticate him is not itself authentic would seem to give credence to this earlier public discrediting. Even before the authenticity of this letter is questioned, the issue of textual qualification arises when the letter goes missing at a party. Scolding himself for carelessly displaying it for the partygoers, Alamaya says, "When a man loses a letter like that, he disqualifies himself" (46). In other words, he inauthenticates himself.

Alamaya's false document, incidentally, may not verify his role as a representative of imperial Ethiopia but it is one that authenticates him as pan-African. As he tells Peixota, the letter was originally written years earlier for a "mission to the Aframericans" initiated by "some prominent Africans, Haitians, Cubans, Aframericans and others who were identified with the Pan-African movement of that period" (251). According to Alamaya, "The plan was abandoned just before it was put into execution, because powerful states of the League of Nations disapproved of it" (251). At the time of McKay's writing of *Amiable with Big Teeth*, the failure of the League of Nations to protect its member nations adds bite to Alamaya's remark. The League's treachery in respect to Ethiopia throws doubt upon its principles and its commitment to rectitude but, in impeding the development of pan-African connections years earlier, Alamaya suggests, the institution had already confirmed its white supremacist biases. Now exposed as a pan-Africanist, Alamaya is finally freed from the strictures of Ethiopian imperial culture. Alamaya's process of Americanization begins when his "earlier attitude of cavalier curiosity in the Aframericans had changed to active sympathy," reciprocating the sympathy of Harlemites for the Ethiopian cause (134). His final break from imperial culture comes when he seeks a job from Peixota as "an ordinary refugee" (252).

By the end of the novel, embracing the inauthenticity of the constructed Princess Benebe as he embraces his own inauthenticity, Alamaya approaches a "high-powered salesman of modern amusement" in hopes of securing a position for Princess Benebe in his act. As Peixota had instructed him soon after meeting him, "in this country our group is identified with entertainment" (32). With a metaphor that gestures toward the construction of the Ethiopian cause in the press, the impresario dismisses the idea by calling Ethiopia "an unimportant and worthless 'back number'" (247). He tells Alamaya that, precisely because "colored people are all natural-born actors," he would suggest instead that Haile Selassie "consent to appear in a dervish dance on the American stage," which would allow him to earn back everything lost in the war (248). Outraged and disgusted, Alamaya storms out. However, as the Western aspects of Selassie's imperial culture suggest, even the "authenticity" of Selassie himself is called into question. Wilfred Thesiger, a guest at Selassie's coronation in 1930, lamented that the "age-old splendour of Abyssinia" had been "slightly tarnished round the edges by innovations copied from the West: the bodyguard now wore khaki, some of the palace secretaries were in tailcoats and top hats."[45] Ethiopian pageantry had, in his view, been encroached upon by the European style.

Although Selassie never appears on the impresario's stage, McKay's novel ends with a final—and disturbing—staged performance of Africanness in its place. The villainous Tasan decides that, "as Aframericans were obsessed with synthetic ideas of Africa, . . . he would treat them to something genuine" (261). The disparaging reference to synthesis points a finger squarely at Koazhy, the target of Tasan's disdain. Tasan stages what he calls "a glorified modernized version of an authentic African pastime," a performance of the Society of African Leopard Men that would culminate in a ceremonial killing (261). The victim he chooses is Koazhy, whom he derides as a "fakir pretending to know all the mysteries of ancient Africa"; it would therefore be "appropriate if he were destroyed by real African magic" (266). In executing his plan, he consults Diup Wuluff, a West African man who "had made several attempts to create an African theatre in Harlem" (261).

Tasan's plan, unsurprisingly, backfires, resulting instead in his own murder as a sort of karmic retribution. Koazhy and Wuluff, it turns out, are in cahoots, as Tasan discovers when he hears them speaking phrases that are "unintelligible" to him, revealing to him that "the pledge of a Senegambian is more sacred than the oath of a member of the Society of

Leopard Men" (268–69). The Senegambians, a group founded by Koazhy and his students, choose their name in order to express a felt genealogy with Africa. In other words, allegiance to the Senegambian pledge over that of the Leopard Men is a triumph of the synthetic over the authentic—or, rather, the authentic is subsumed by the synthetic in the service of a viable pan-Africanism. Perhaps Tasan might have been tipped off by the fact that Wuluff calls "all the available African natives in New York, whether they came from the West or the North or the South or the East," to participate in the Leopard Dance, and the Africans are then "supplemented by Aframericans" (262).

Wuluff originally tells Tasan that the sacrificial murder "must be done by a special person"; only one man in New York is qualified for the role that "in Africa . . . is the privilege of certain families" (265). When this leopard man—the "authentic one" (268)—approaches Tasan, he never suspects that this man is only the escort who will take him to the roof of the building to meet the true threat: the authentically synthetic Koazhy, who reverses the sacrifice Tasan expects. It is not the "authentic," well-born man who is in charge but Koazhy, who commands the other Leopard Men to capture Tasan. Wuluff then commands Tasan to "do to yourself what you told us to do to Professor Koazhy," and he is forced to jump off the building to his death (269).

I end with the grisly suggestion that we consider Koazhy's ritualistic murder of Tasan an enactment of his "aristocracy of service." The phrase recalls a statement made by Garvey in "Africa for the Africans": "Africa shall develop an aristocracy of its own, but it shall be based upon service and loyalty to race."[46] McKay uses the phrase in the novel in his description of a white character. Mrs. Hobison "lived an aristocratic life, but . . . believed in the aristocracy of service" and, as a result, starts an international and interracial publication titled *The Interlink*, which "disseminat[ed] . . . valuable and authentic information concerning the way of life and the thought of different groups of people" (169, 168). Similarly, Koazhy is the novel's true Ethiopian "prince" not because of birthright—not because he is the "authentic one"—but because of a commitment to serve those he leads, as is illustrated in the novel's opening scene of the Harlem parade. His symbolic murder of Tasan eliminates the novel's only obstacle to reviving the pan-African sentiment that thrived during the war. Again, Koazhy is not mocked by the novel. It seems, in fact, the novel argues that the only way forward for an authentic pan-Africanism grounded in imperial culture is paradoxically an inauthentic one that shifts from an aristocracy of birth to an "aristocracy of service." This shift would sound the death knell for imperial Ethiopianism.

Conclusion

LANGSTON HUGHES'S BUSINESS SUIT

The prince desired a little kingdom, in which he might administer justice in his own person, and see all the parts of government with his own eyes; but he could never fix the limits of his dominion, and was always adding to the number of his subjects.

—SAMUEL JOHNSON, *THE HISTORY OF RASSELAS, PRINCE OF ABYSSINIA*

The coronation festivities were thus the final move in a long and well-planned strategy. . . . [Tafari] wished to impress on his European visitors that Ethiopia was no mere agglomeration of barbarous tribes open to foreign exploitation, but a powerful, organised, modern State. . . . They saw just how far the emperor's word ran in the more distant parts of his dominions; they saw the frail lines of communication which bound the Government to its outposts; they saw something of the real character of the people, and realised how inadequate an introduction to the national life were the caviare and sweet champagne of Addis Ababa.

—EVELYN WAUGH, *REMOTE PEOPLE*

AFTER HAVING WRITTEN a number of poems about Ethiopia and about Haile Selassie in the 1930s, Langston Hughes wrote an occasional poem in 1966 to celebrate the emperor in honor of the twenty-fifth anniversary of the end of the Italian occupation and presented it in person. Later that year, he responded to a letter sent to him by Rita Pankhurst, Sylvia's daughter-in-law and librarian at the university in Addis Ababa, that he "remember[ed] with much pleasure my sojourn in Addis last spring."[1]

However, according to Arnold Rampersad, the truth is that his reception disillusioned him, as he was "made to wait in a depressingly long line of cowed supplicants," in a formal and ritualistic performance of submission that struck him as symptomatic of "African medievalism"; he "left the country hating Haile Selassie."[2] Or, to put it in terms that make it clear that Hughes objected not to the man but to the seat of the empire he represented, he claimed that, while he loved Ethiopia, he "'*LOATHED*' Addis Ababa."[3]

We learn a bit more about Hughes's reaction to his reception in George Houston Bass's 1982 article, "Five Stories about a Man Named Hughes: A Critical Reflection." Bass was executor of Hughes's estate and founder of the then newly established Hughes Society, and his article appeared as the lead essay in the premier issue of the *Langston Hughes Review*, which Bass also founded. In it, he recalls that Hughes, when asked about the Haile Selassie Medal of Honor on his mantel, recounted the story about his invitation to the palace. He was given two options: to arrive in the afternoon in a business suit or in the evening in "white tie and full formal dress." As someone who "did not wear neckties unless it was absolutely necessary," he chose the former, which required that he rush to prepare for his meeting.[4]

Upon arrival, Hughes joined the receiving line. Finally, Selassie shook his hand, said, "I have something for you," and presented him with the medal. Later, at home in Harlem, Hughes complained to his awed and impressed friends, "Who does he think he is, asking me to put on a white tie and tails to shake his hand?" His aunt Toy Harper challenged him: "I bet you wouldn't have a second thought about putting on white tie and tails to bow before her Highness Queen Elizabeth." Bass notes that Hughes "was neither smiling nor laughing" after Harper's remark, indicating that he was struck by the challenge and had taken it seriously. Eventually he said, "Haile Selassie wasn't born European."[5]

Despite Bass's predictable conclusion that Hughes was "ambivalent about the character of the pomp and regality about him," it is revealed to be specifically European regality that Hughes finds objectionable. We might have expected Hughes's response to also express a general disappointment with imperial culture itself, which exploits formality and sartorial excess in order to reinforce its own hierarchical structure. But had Hughes been asked to dress in formal, extravagant traditionally Ethiopian attire, he may not have noticed that Selassie, rather than serving as a bridge among black peoples, had become in his exceptionalism an unexpectedly disruptive figure. The poem Hughes had written for Selassie's 1966 Liberation Day ceremony, titled "Emperor Haile Selassie, on Liberation Day, May 5, 1966," was presented to the emperor with, one imagines, the same degree of ceremony with which Selassie presented the medal to Hughes. In fact, the semiotics of the "rolled hand-written scroll" demonstrates an even greater investment than Selassie's in the "African medievalism" to which Hughes ostensibly objected.

Considering Hughes's aversion to the archaic ritualism of his experience in Addis Ababa, his dedicatory poem's first lines suddenly fill with prescient irony: "That he is human . . . and living . . . / And of our time."[6] It appears that Hughes does not know with any certainty *when* Selassie belongs. The poem expresses not only an awestruck veneration but the familiar bafflement regarding the seeming dissonance between modernity and antiquity, between the modern business suit and the archaic scroll. Imperial events such as this one only serve to exaggerate the apparent disjuncture between the modern and the ancient, as Addison E. Southard said of the coronation decades earlier. Representatives gathered from all corners of the country for the occasion, resulting in the spectacle of "modern civilization cheek by jowl with medievalism."[7]

This impression was so pervasive that it was used to market, for example, *John Hoy of Ethiopia*, by Canadian journalist Robinson MacLean. Coincidentally, Selassie's relationship to the business suit features prominently on the book's cover, which includes the following blurb below the author's name: "There's a little brown man in lion skins and whiskers who sits on the Imperial bed-throne of Ethiopia and wishes he could wear a blue serge suit and learn boxing." Elaborating upon this strange biographical approach, MacLean shares an anecdote about the day when Selassie dressed in one of his five English blue-serge suits and walked around the palace grounds. He waved to a chamberlain who, "with his nose in the air, busy with his own dignity," ignored his emperor. This reaction made him realize, according to MacLean, that the people of Ethiopia "were not yet ready for blue serge." The emperor returned to the palace and "slowly, tenderly, stripped off the modern raiment and resumed his white jodhpurs and black cape," vowing never again "to lead his people at too stiff a sartorial pace."[8] Without the royal garments, he is an ordinary man. Just like Sam, Ted, and Ray, he had to put on the iconic and easily recognizable imperial "costume" in order to become Selassie.

The allegorical significance of the business suit—in both MacLean's story and in Hughes's—illustrates imperial Ethiopia's impulse to Westernize in the late nineteenth and early twentieth centuries. One might even say that imperial Ethiopia's outreach to African America is an attempt to Westernize, to accept the representative "African medievalism" as a quaint relic made artifice when placed in the U.S. context. When Haile Selassie visited Harlem in 1954 after his restoration to the throne, he stopped at the Abyssinian Baptist Church, where, it is estimated, hundreds of thousands greeted him waving Ethiopian flags, some even carrying signs in Amharic, the language of Ethiopia. Unlike the fiasco of his visit to the set of *Desirée*, Selassie's arrival in Harlem was marked by pomp and ceremony. In a ritualistic and performative gesture, he presented Adam Clayton Powell Jr. with an enormous Ethiopian Orthodox cross for the church, signaling a shared "Abyssinian" spiritual heritage.

Selassie was hardly insensible to the symbolism behind the gifts he bestowed. In 1945, during a meeting with Franklin Delano Roosevelt on the Great Bitter Lake in Egypt, as Roosevelt was returning from the Yalta conference, Selassie gave Roosevelt the transparently symbolic gift of a small gold globe, one small enough to fit easily in one's hands as it passes from world leader to world leader. John H. Spencer, Selassie's American legal advisor, describes the gift as "a confection by a palace jeweler of a four-inch globe with the continents incised on it, along with the location of their meeting, fashioned out of the slightly reddish gold from the Adola mines," and adds that "apart from the large amount of 24-carat gold that went into the production, the result appeared to me to be rather crude," and so he expresses surprise "at the seemingly genuine enthusiastic response which Roosevelt reserved for this token of friendship."[9] In presenting Roosevelt with a so-called "token of friendship" that represents the world as the plaything of the gods, it appears that Selassie is asserting a position of parity for himself. In fact, that the location of their meeting is marked (reinforced also by the documentation of the exchange carved on the globe's stand: "To Franklin Delano Roosevelt President of the United States of" on one side, and "America from Haile Selassie, Emperor February 14, 1945") is itself an assertion of simultaneity. The continents are delineated—natural boundaries for the most part—but the nations are not. This decision reads as a deliberate choice for a leader whose continent had been "carved up" the century before, but lest it be misread as a sign of humility, disavowing sovereignty, it is worth noting that the gift resembles a secular version of the *globus cruciger* that Selassie himself received during his coronation. Images of the just-crowned Selassie show him carrying an orb crowned with a cross, an ancient symbol indicating that, though God is King, the emperor rules (in his place) all that he holds in his hand.[10] In this respect, the gift as a gesture both recognizes Roosevelt's role in the world and exalts him or anoints him as imperial, while asserting Selassie's own divine right to rule.

This doctrine—that Selassie's imperial claim was divine—contributed to the development of a new faith that would place the emperor at the center of its cosmology. Although it is beyond the scope of this book, it is worth noting that, like Hughes's trip to Ethiopia, Selassie's momentous visit to Jamaica also happened in the spring of 1966. At the Kingston airport, an elated crowd of RasTafari welcomed him; the day has since been celebrated as Grounation Day.[11] The development of the RasTafari religious tradition from the 1930s (beginning with Leonard Howell, the "first Rasta") to this landmark moment in 1966 is practically the inverse of the increasing disenchantment with Selassie felt by many African Americans during this period.

The sympathy felt by African America for Ethiopia from the late nineteenth century through the 1930s, channeled mainly through its emperors, demanded the acceptance of a paradox: the emperor is just like you, and yet the emperor is nothing like you. As MacLean writes, "It would take little imagination to see him, clean-shaven, rubbing his hands behind the counter of a second-hand store in the unofficial ghetto of some American city—if first you could rob him of the dignity that fits him as smoothly as a worn suit of clothes—the dignity that tiny men acquire so easily—the dignity that is in him enriched by noble birth, solidified by long, unceasing effort towards a high ambition."[12] This small jump, from salesman to emperor and back, requires even less imagination than MacLean supposes. Even the chamberlain of his anecdote cited above fails to recognize the "dignity" Selassie supposedly wears like a suit. Belief in an intimate bond to the emperor was crucial to the success of imperial Ethiopianism as a project. As mobilized by the black world in the late nineteenth- and early twentieth-century press, imperial Ethiopianism often pressed black people to imagine themselves as part of the empire Selassie held in his hand. The Ethiopian empire—sometimes geographically bound and sometimes seemingly infinitely expansive—threatens, with its amorphous and porous boundaries, to pull all of the black world into its orbit. It stands for a violent defiance that is both defensive and offensive, both imperialist and anti-imperialist. It, to paraphrase Whitman, contains multitudes.

What happens, however, when Ethiopianist connections are pursued *outside* of imperial culture? Although Hughes identifies Selassie as "a symbol / Of our Negritude" and "food / On which men who are neither / Kings of Kings nor Lions of Judah / Yet may feed their pride," he also predicts that his example will bring about a day "when . . . each is king in common / Of all his eyes survey"—with these lines, dethroning the emperor. Hughes's poem for Selassie was notably translated into Amharic, and this translation appeared in an Ethiopian newspaper and was given to Selassie during the presentation ceremony. In the margin of the copy held by the Beinecke Library at Yale University, Hughes asked his translator—noted Ethiopian poet and playwright Tsegaye Gabre-Medhin, himself a promoter of pan-Africanism and author of a poem that would be selected by the African Union in 2002 as its anthem—to sign the publication in both English and Amharic.[13] The accompanying note reads, "I am honored to autograph his own poem I translated into Amharic to my celebrated friend Langston Hughes." As opposed to the other fictive works addressed in this book, here we find a poem by an African American writer on the topic of Ethiopia circulating *within* Ethiopia. Furthermore, in contrast to Hughes's reception by Selassie, this bilingual piece of paper presents a viable alternative to the imperial model as a means of connecting the various black peoples of the world. The American soldier and the wounded Moor of Hughes's "Letter from Spain" can now grasp each other's hands across what would appear to divide them. Ironically, Hughes's poem honoring the emperor ultimately demonstrates how the obsolescence of imperial Ethiopianism can give way to a more productive and modern network of black internationalism. The weak bonds that had always characterized the relationships between imperial center and periphery were more visible than ever.

Embedded in imperial Ethiopianism is a modernizing force that marches apace, but still it cannot transcend the expectation that time stands still there. But then, as Southard asserts, "what matters time in a country which can reach with such apparent certainty directly back into the dim mists of the past!"[14] Even now, the misty and timeless vision of Ethiopia that once dominated the outside world's impression of the country has not completely lifted. Unlike time, space refuses to stand still, despite the nationalizing work done by the black press in the United States, which tended to insist upon the picture of a strong and coherent empire. Like the protagonists of Schuyler's and McKay's fiction, we are instructed to trust the black press on the subject of Ethiopia, even when its perspectives, shaped by imperial Ethiopianism, elide the violence of empire-building. The pageantry of Ethiopian imperial culture, fortified by its magnetic and dynamic leaders, made—for a time—for a compelling and seductive model of black empire.

NOTES

Introduction

1. Chicago Commission, *Negro in Chicago*, 59–60.

2. Ibid., 61.

3. Qtd. in ibid., 64.

4. "'Abyssinians' on Trial."

5. "Chicago 'Riot.'"

6. "Flag Burners Must Die."

7. "Chicago 'Riot.'"

8. Chicago Commission, *Negro in Chicago*, 60.

9. It is difficult to determine with certainty how successful this call was. According to Christopher Robert Reed, "Newspaper accounts report that nine men were arrested for their part in the 'Abyssinian incident' and no mention was made of anything other than small crowds of observers at their meetings" (*Rise of Chicago's Black Metropolis*, 246n121).

10. Qtd. in Chicago Commission, *Negro in Chicago*, 62.

11. Robinson, "African Diaspora and the Italo-Ethiopian Crisis," 60.

12. Qtd. in Chicago Commission, *Negro in Chicago*, 487–88.

13. Gebrekidan, "Ethiopia in Black Studies," 6.

14. Moses, *Golden Age of Black Nationalism*, 168–69.

15. Hassen Ali and Hameso, "Ethiopia," 736.

16. Zewde, *History of Modern Ethiopia*, 1.

17. Ibid., 111–14.

18. Alden, "John Bull in Abyssinia," 333.

19. Tibebu, *Making of Modern Ethiopia*, xv.

20. Qtd. in Shilliam, "Ethiopianism," 249.

21. Taketani, *Black Pacific Narrative*, 79.

22. "Red Agitator Is Sought."

23. The treaty had been ratified, however, in 1914.

24. Metaferia, *Ethiopia and the United States*, 25, 27.

25. Plessy was a mixed-race man who boarded a whites-only train car in Louisiana to protest against racial segregation laws and was arrested. An appeal to the Supreme Court proved unsuccessful, and the decision gave authority to Jim Crow laws throughout the United States.

26. Qtd. and trans. in Carey and Trakulhun, "Universalism, Diversity, and the Postcolonial Enlightenment," 262n56.

27. Auf der Maur, "*Ethiopia* and *Abyssinia* in English Writing up to 1790," 529.

28. Markakis, *Ethiopia*, 19–20.

29. Taketani, "Colored Empires in the 1930s," 123.

30. Although there has been considerable scholarship of late treating Ethiopia as an empire, there have been challenges to this view. Abbas H. Gnamo cites Mesfin

Wolde Mariam, "who firmly contests the validity of the imperial category in the Ethiopian case." Gnamo, *Conquest and Resistance in the Ethiopian Empire*, 106–7.

31. Markakis, *Ethiopia*, 3–4.
32. Woolbert, "Feudal Ethiopia and Her Army," 71.
33. Woolbert, "Peoples of Ethiopia," 344.
34. Kuru, "Conquest and Environmental Degradation of Oromia," 31–32.
35. Markakis, *Ethiopia*, 91.
36. Hassen, *Oromo of Ethiopia*, 1–2.
37. "Harlem Ponders Ethiopia's Fate."
38. Vivian, "A Capital That Moves," 612.
39. Zewde, *History of Modern Ethiopia*, 61.
40. "No Longer the Dark Continent."
41. Markakis, *Ethiopia*, 129.
42. Goyal, *Romance, Diaspora, and Black Atlantic Literature*, 2.
43. Garvey, "Haile Selassie Is Bad Historian," in *Marcus Garvey and Universal Negro Improvement Association Papers*, vol. 7, 720.
44. Anderson, *Imagined Communities*, 34.
45. Warren, "Appeals for (Mis)recognition," 394.
46. Gibbon, *History of the Decline and Fall of the Roman Empire*, 165.
47. Putnam, *Insistent Call*, 110, 114.
48. Dean, *Pedro Gorino*, 119.
49. McKay, *Amiable with Big Teeth*, 251.
50. Du Bois, *Writings*, 365.

Chapter One: Recognizing the Ethiopian Flag

1. "Charlton," "Magdala," in *Songs of the Year and Other Poems*, 28–33.
2. Zewde, *History of Modern Ethiopia*, 37.
3. Ibid., 40.
4. [Gage], "Late Sovereign of Abyssinia," 89.
5. Whitman, *Notebooks and Unpublished Prose Manuscripts*, 1972.
6. Whitman, "Salut au Monde!" in *Leaves of Grass*, 116.
7. Folsom, "Lucifer and Ethiopia," 53.
8. Wilson, "Looking with a Queer Smile," ix.
9. Hutchinson, "Whitman and the Black Poet," 46.
10. Whitman, "Ethiopia Saluting the Colors," in *Leaves of Grass*, 249.
11. Folsom, "Lucifer and Ethiopia," 53.
12. Erkkila, *Whitman the Political Poet*, 241.
13. Baker, "On Abyssinia, or Ethiopia," 404.
14. Ness, "'Bathed in War's Perfume,'" 262.
15. Ibid., 251.
16. Ibid.
17. Mancuso, *Strange Sad War Revolving*, 85; Folsom, "Lucifer and Ethiopia," 67. Even though Folsom emphasizes that the "blear" view of her is the soldier's own, he still attributes the passive-voiced representation of her speech to her, not the soldier's projection.

18. Mancuso, *Strange Sad War Revolving*, 85.
19. Ness, "'Bathed in War's Perfume,'" 252.
20. Smith, *Wonders of Nature and Art*, 49–50.
21. Qtd. in Chojnacki, "Some Notes," 60.
22. Chojnacki, "A Second Note," 140; Chojnacki, "Some Notes," 59.
23. Chojnacki, "Third Note," 37.
24. Wellby, *'Twixt Sirdar and Menelik*, 26–27.
25. Chojnacki, "Flags and Banners," 740.
26. Ibid., 739.
27. Winstanley, *Visit to Abyssinia*, 245.
28. Chojnacki, "Flags and Banners," 739–40.
29. Ness, "'Bathed in War's Perfume,'" 265.
30. Qtd. in Chojnacki, "Some Notes," 59–60.
31. Mancuso, *Strange Sad War Revolving*, 86.
32. Ness, "'Bathed in War's Perfume,'" 261.
33. Ibid.
34. According to the *OED*, an antiquated definition of "greet" is "To assail, attack." Given as an obsolete sense, it is followed by the note, "After 15th c. prob. only as a transferred or ironical use of sense 3," which is "To accost or address with the expressions of goodwill or courtesy usual on meeting." However, given Whitman's predilection for obsolete and unusual language usage elsewhere in the poem (and, in fact, throughout his corpus), it is not unreasonable to expect that he might use this obsolete sense of "greet." Consider this roughly contemporaneous example of usage from John O'Hagan's 1880 translation of the *Song of Roland* given by the *OED*: "I will him body to body greet, Give him the lie with my brand of steel."
35. Qtd. from *Whitman Archive*, www.whitmanarchive.org/manuscripts/figures/pml.00004.002.jpg.
36. Of course, then we must deal with "No further does she say," which indicates that she has spoken those italicized lines, but it is extremely unlikely that she would approach the soldier to say these words.
37. Ness, "'Bathed in War's Perfume,'" 261.
38. Folsom makes a similar point when he says that "'Ancient' offsets primitive, modulating the 'hardly human' so that it could suggest either 'subhuman' or 'superhuman,' primitive or mythical" ("Lucifer and Ethiopia," 82).
39. "How They Fight in Abyssinia," 731, 732.
40. "Inclosure 2 in No. 74," 88.
41. "'Alabama' Claims in Congress."
42. "Inclosure 2 in No. 74," 89, 91.
43. Ibid., 90, 92.
44. Ibid., 91.
45. "England and the United States," 128.
46. "British Neutrality Laws." The *Alabama* was permitted to port in Britain under the guise of a mercantile ship and, with a crew composed half of Englishmen, was responsible for attacking several Union ships. England eventually paid damages for these actions.

47. As reported by the *Brooklyn Daily Eagle*, "Quite a lively debate ensued, and although no action on the proposition was had it was evident that a majority of Senators did not agree with Chandler." "Topics of To-Day," *Brooklyn Daily Eagle*, 10 December 1867, 2.

48. "The Anglo-Abyssinian War: A Question for Congress"; "The Anglo-Abyssinian War."

49. "The Anglo-Abyssinian War: A Question for Congress."

50. Ibid.; "The Abyssinian War," *Wilkes's Spirit of the Times*, 21 December 1867, 324.

51. "The Abyssinian War," *Wilkes's Spirit of the Times*, 2 May 1868, 174.

52. "National Freedmen's Aid Union," 30.

53. "Quilibet," "Nation's Repentance and Faith," 785.

54. "The Abyssinian War," *Brooklyn Daily Eagle*, 27 April 1868, 2.

55. "Foreign Notes," 638–39.

56. "Rise of King Theodore," 573.

57. Burette, "Notes from King Theodore's Country," 289.

58. Reynolds, "Abyssinia and King Theodore," 705, 706.

59. Brown, *The Rising Son*, 100.

60. Hack, *Reaping Something New*, 2.

61. "The Anglo-Abyssinian War: A Question for Congress."

62. Kaplan, *Anarchy of Empire*, 26.

63. Pankhurst, introduction to *Diary of a Journey to Abyssinia*, 22; J. C., "Foreign Correspondence."

64. Hotten, preface to *Abyssinia and Its People; or, Life in the Land of Prester John*, 6.

65. "Nov. 19."

66. "Close of the Abyssinian War."

67. Schooling, "War Pictures in 'Punch,'" 326.

68. Bernstein, *Racial Innocence*, 196.

69. Spofford, "Boys," 836.

70. "Charlton," "Magdala," in *Songs of the Year and Other Poems*, 28–33.

71. Charlotte Pendleton to Daniel Coit Gilman, 12 May 1885, Daniel Coit Gilman Papers, https://jscholarship.library.jhu.edu/handle/1774.2/42864.

72. Davidson, "The Death of King Theodore," in *Death of King Theodore and Other Poems*, 1–4.

73. Dunbar, "Ode to Ethiopia," in *Lyrics of Lowly Life*, 30–32.

74. Dunbar, "The Colored Soldiers," in *Lyrics of Lowly Life*, 114–18.

75. Dunbar, "Frederick Douglass," in *Lyrics of Lowly Life*, 8–11; Paul Laurence Dunbar to Matilda Dunbar, in *Letters from Black America*, ed. Pamela Newkirk, 12.

76. Hawkins, "Negro's Triumph."

Chapter Two: Pauline E. Hopkins and the Shadow of Transcription

1. Thompson, *Black Fascisms*, 8.

2. Ibid.

3. Carby, introduction, xxxv.

4. Ammons, *Conflicting Stories*, 81.

5. Doreski, "Inherited Rhetoric and Authentic History," 72.

6. Later in the same issue, a brief article by Hopkins herself appeared, titled "Venus and the Apollo Modeled from Ethiopians."

7. Carby, introduction, xlvii.

8. Moses, *Wings of Ethiopia*, 113.

9. Gruesser, *Black on Black*, 24.

10. Ammons, *Conflicting Stories*, 84.

11. Hopkins, *Of One Blood*, 469. Subsequent quotations to *Of One Blood* will be cited parenthetically in the text.

12. Ong, *Orality and Literacy*, 93.

13. Garber, *Shakespeare's Ghost Writers*, 25.

14. McDowell, introduction, xviii.

15. Luciano, "Passing Shadows," 169; Harris, "Not Black and/or White," 388.

16. Garber, *Shakespeare's Ghost Writers*, 29.

17. Gleichen, *With the Mission to Menelik, 1897*, 230.

18. Richard Brodhead points out that "the virtually mandatory item" in the quality journals was "the short piece of touristic or vacationistic prose, the piece that undertakes to locate some little-known place far away and make it visitable in print" (*Culture of Letters*, 125). That place, in these periodicals, was likely to be in Europe and therefore a possible vacation destination for some; the far-off places profiled in the *Colored American Magazine*, on the other hand, were not literally accessible to its readers for the most part.

19. Hack, *Reaping Something New*, 137.

20. Sanborn, "Wind of Words," 74.

21. Hoskins, *Travels in Ethiopia*, 83.

22. Runciman, "King Plagiarism and His Court," 421.

23. Sanborn, "Wind of Words," 72.

24. Ibid.

25. Macfarlane, *Original Copy*, 8.

26. Qtd. in ibid., 76.

27. Matthews, *Pen and Ink*, 33–34.

28. Pavletich, "The Practice of Plagiarism in a Changing Context," e10.

29. Howells, "The Psychology of Plagiarism," 129.

30. Sanborn, "Wind of Words," 80.

31. Cramer, "Of Serpentina and Stenography," 135.

32. Ibid., 134.

33. Ibid., 136.

34. Daniels, "Fundamentals of Grammatology," 730.

35. Helms-Park et al., "From Proto-writing to Multimedia Literacy," 11.

36. Hopkins, *Primer of Facts*, 340.

37. Bennett, introduction, xxiii.

38. Piatt, "The Black Princess: A True Fable of My Old Kentucky Nurse," in *Palace-Burner*, 38–39.

39. Japtok, "Pauline Hopkins's *Of One Blood*, Africa, and the 'Darwinist Trap,'" 409.

40. Gleichen, *With the Mission to Menelik, 1897*, 153.

41. Gebrekidan, *Bond without Blood*, 19.
42. Delany, *Principia of Ethnology*, 52.
43. Millet, "The Meroitic Script," 85.
44. Delany, *Principia of Ethnology*, 52, 54.
45. Hoskins, *Travels in Ethiopia*, 7.
46. Ibid., 56.
47. Ibid., 21.
48. Dawson, *Modern Science in Bible Lands*, 291.
49. Upham, *Rameses*, 318n89.
50. Hamedoe, "Menelik, Emperor of Abyssinia," 149, 133.
51. Ibid., 153.
52. Ibid., 130.
53. Gleichen, *With the Mission to Menelik, 1897*, 146.
54. Hamedoe, "Menelik, Emperor of Abyssinia," 150.
55. Ibid., 149.
56. Gleichen, *With the Mission to Menelik, 1897*, 152.
57. Vanderheym, *Une expédition avec le négous Ménélik*, i–ii, my translation.
58. Gleichen, *With the Mission to Menelik, 1897*, 317.
59. Hamedoe, "Menelik, Emperor of Abyssinia," 151.
60. Hill, "King Menelik's Nephew," 28.
61. Hamedoe, "Menelik, Emperor of Abyssinia," 152.
62. Gleichen, *With the Mission to Menelik, 1897*, 226.
63. Ibid., 4.
64. Ibid., 234.
65. Ibid.
66. Ibid., 152.
67. Hopkins, "Dark Races of the Twentieth Century," in *Daughter of the Revolution*, 323.
68. Hopkins, *Primer of Facts*, 344.

Chapter Three: Fashioning the Imperial Self

1. Hughes, *Big Sea*, 8, 112; Warren, "Appeals for (Mis)recognition," 401.
2. McHenry, "Toward a History of Access," 391.
3. C. C., *Anecdotes of Alamayu*, 71.
4. Qtd. in Gullick, "Captain Speedy of Larut," 5.
5. Ibid., 60.
6. Qtd. in Pankhurst, "Captain Speedy's 'Entertainment,'" 434.
7. Speedy, "Abyssinia and Its People," 15.
8. Pankhurst, "Captain Speedy's 'Entertainment,'" 428.
9. Ibid., 429.
10. "Topics of To-Day," *Brooklyn Daily Eagle*, 15 July 1868, 2.
11. Ibid.; W. W., "Abyssinia," 278–79.
12. "Miscellaneous Items."
13. Simpson, *Autobiography*, 200–201.

14. Qtd. in Gullick, "Captain Speedy of Larut," 16.
15. Qtd. in Amulree, "Prince Alamayou of Ethiopia," 10–11.
16. Ibid., 14.
17. Qtd. in Rubenson, *Internal Rivalries and Foreign Threats*, 40.
18. "Young Abyssinian Prince."
19. Woolf, "Introduction," 92–93.
20. Koppen, *Virginia Woolf, Fashion, and Literary Modernity*, 24.
21. Woolf qtd. in Johnston, "Virginia Woolf's Talk," 14.
22. "Bogus Princes on the Dreadnought."
23. Woolf qtd. in Johnston, "Virginia Woolf's Talk," 18.
24. "Naval Hoax."
25. Ibid.
26. deCourcy, "Dreadnought Hoax Portrait," 413.
27. Woolf qtd. in Johnston, "Virginia Woolf's Talk," 15–16.
28. Ibid., 24–25.
29. deCourcy, "Dreadnought Hoax Portrait," 416.
30. Woolf, "*Dreadnought* Notes (1940)," 167.
31. Reid, "Virginia Woolf," 346, 348.
32. Hill, "King Menelik's Nephew," 16.
33. Ibid, 19n5.
34. Ibid., 19, 38.
35. Quoted in ibid., 36.
36. Ibid., 17.
37. Ibid., 42.
38. "Prince Tells of Struggles in Abyssinia."
39. "Proposed Japanese Bride for Abyssinian Royalty."
40. "Prince Tells of Struggles in Abyssinia."
41. Hickey and Wylie, *Enchanting Darkness*, 254; "Abyssinian Speaks before N.C. Students"; "Mount Hermon Federate School of Missions."
42. "Blayechettai's Answer."
43. Ibid.
44. "Prince Tells of Struggles in Abyssinia."
45. "Abyssinian Speaks before N.C. Students."
46. "Prince Blayechetta [*sic*] of Abyssinia Addresses A. and T. Student Body."
47. Blayechettai, *Pen of an African*, n.p.
48. Ibid., 12–13.
49. Hill, "King Menelik's Nephew," 36.
50. Qtd. in ibid., 27, 23, 18.
51. Qtd. in ibid., 18.
52. Qtd. in ibid., 38.
53. Ibid., 39.
54. Bloch, *Royal Touch*, 142.
55. Ibid., 146.
56. Tibebu, *Making of Modern Ethiopia*, 118.
57. C. C., *Anecdotes of Alamayu*, 43, 44.

Chapter Four: Imperial Embellishment

Note to epigraph: Untitled poem, Captain Harry Dean Papers, Box 1, Folder 1A, DuSable Museum of African American History, Chicago.

1. "Pays Tribute to African Explorer."

2. Dean, *Pedro Gorino*, 119. All subsequent quotations from *The Pedro Gorino* will be cited parenthetically in the text.

3. Dean, "Liberia Asks America to Develop Commerce." Gruesser cites "an anonymous essay in the New Bedford Public Library's Paul Cuffe Collection titled 'Uncle John's Burying Place' that probably dates from the 1970s [in which] Dean is described as 'a man who claims descent, and I think must have looked into the Cuffe papers and then let his truly inspired imagination flow freely'" (*Confluences*, 149n12).

4. Qtd. in Goyal, *Romance, Diaspora, and Black Atlantic Literature*, 3; Du Bois, review of *Pedro Gorino.*

5. "Trader Dean."

6. Finger, "Literature of Adventure," 777.

7. "Trader Dean."

8. Schomburg, review of *Pedro Gorino*, 224.

9. Shepperson, introduction, xviii.

10. Collis, "Anxious Records," 68.

11. "Editorial and Publishers' Announcements," 467.

12. Hopkins, "Letter to William Monroe Trotter, April 16, 1905," in 244.

13. According to another letter from Johnson, however, Dean apparently ran afoul of the company for spending funds he collected; Johnson warned Dean that he was "in a precarious predicament" and scolded, "Be cautious in dealing with your fellow men." Fenton Johnson to Harry Dean, 24 March 1920, Captain Harry Dean Papers, Box 3, Folder 76, DuSable Museum of African American History, Chicago.

14. "Negro Activities: Harry Dean, and 'Habasher's Promised Land,' Projected Negro Magazine," Captain Harry Dean Papers, Box 3, Folder 76, DuSable Museum of African American History, Chicago.

15. Bloch, *The Royal Touch*, 148.

16. "Pays Tribute to African Explorer."

17. Gruesser, *Black on Black*, 74.

18. "Famous African Explorer Will Lecture Here."

19. Gilroy, *Black Atlantic*, 12.

20. Stephens, *Black Empire*, 108.

21. Collis argues that "in Kid's uttering, the term evokes a shared experience of oppression. Despite his assertion that he is not of the same class as 'Cape Town nigguhs,' his difference is one of place; he comes from Texas, not Cape Town. They are all 'nigguhs,' what marks him out is that being from Texas he is unwilling to accept unfair treatment because of his racial identity" ("Anxious Records," 80).

22. Gruesser, *Black on Black*, 75.

23. Collis, "Anxious Records," 73–74.

24. Shepperson, introduction, xiii.

25. "Pays Tribute to African Explorer."
26. Borough, "Liberian Captain Arrives in U.S. to Purchase a Ship."
27. Shepperson, introduction, xii.
28. Edwards, "Much Interest in 'Pedro Gorino.'"
29. "Pays Tribute to African Explorer."
30. "African Explorer Presents His View on Dark Continent."
31. "Captain Dean's Manuscripts."
32. "Capt. Harry Dean, World Traveler, Dies."
33. "Harry Foster Dean."
34. "Captain Dean's Manuscripts."
35. Stephens, *Black Empire*, 108.
36. Ibid.
37. Tennyson, "Ulysses," in *Alfred Tennyson: The Major Works*, 80–81.
38. Qtd. in Pankhurst, "William H. Ellis," 90.
39. Shepperson, introduction, xv.
40. "Strange Career of the Big Cuban."
41. Buranelli, "Ellis, American Who Wanted to Be King."
42. Hill, "King Menelik's Nephew," 39.
43. Buranelli, "Ellis, American Who Wanted to Be King."
44. Ibid.
45. "William H. Ellis: Bearer of Treaty to King Menelik."
46. Buranelli, "Ellis, American Who Wanted to Be King."
47. "William H. Ellis: Bearer of Treaty to King Menelik."
48. "Race Gleanings"; Buranelli, "Ellis, American Who Wanted to Be King."
49. "More about the Career of Ellis."
50. Buranelli, "Ellis, American Who Wanted to Be King."
51. "Mr. Ellis Formerly of Texas."
52. Buranelli, "Ellis, American Who Wanted to Be King."
53. "Refused Ride in Elevator, Sues"; Jacoby, *Strange Career of William Ellis*, 18.
54. "Is a Lavish Spender."
55. "Great Ruler."
56. Walker, "Hawaiian Croesus Was Just Plain Sambo."
57. Adejumobi, *History of Ethiopia*, 69.
58. "Mr. Ellis Formerly of Texas."
59. Jacoby, *Strange Career of William Ellis*, xxi, xxvi–xxvii.
60. "American Promoter in Abyssinia," 100.
61. Sotiropoulos, *Staging Race*, 145.
62. "American Promoter in Abyssinia."
63. "Tells of King Menelik."
64. "Negro Haven."
65. "Back from Abyssinia."
66. "Mysterious Disappearance."
67. "Kent J. Loomis's Body Found?"
68. "Grewsome [*sic*] Suspicion Dissipated."
69. "Mysterious Disappearance."
70. "Secretary Loomis's Theory."

71. Crosby, "Personal Impressions of Menelik"; "Menelik! The Great African King."
72. "Tells of King Menelik."
73. Ibid.
74. Ibid.
75. W. H. Ellis to the Department of State, 6 August 1904, Theodore Roosevelt Papers, Library of Congress Manuscript Division, http://www.theodorerooseveltcenter.org/Research/Digital-Library/Record/?libID=o46241.
76. "Tells of King Menelik."
77. Buranelli, "Ellis, American Who Wanted to Be King."
78. Qtd. in Herrera, "Transnational Immigration Politics in Mexico," 73.
79. "Not Maltreated in Mexico."
80. Qtd. in Herrera, "Transnational Immigration Politics in Mexico," 66–67.
81. Ibid., 68.
82. Ibid., 76.
83. "To Found Modern Ethiopia."
84. Ibid.
85. "Tells of King Menelik"; qtd. in Pankhurst, "Ellis," 90.
86. "Tells of King Menelik."
87. "Menelik! The Great African King."
88. "Tells of King Menelik."
89. "An American Promoter in Abyssinia," 100.
90. "Two Lions for Roosevelt."
91. Shinn, introduction, [9].
92. Harlan and Smock, *Booker T. Washington Papers*, 31.
93. "Mysterious Disappearance."
94. "The Rise of a Victoria Negro."
95. W. H. Ellis to the Department of State, 6 August 1904, Theodore Roosevelt Papers, Library of Congress Manuscript Division, http://www.theodorerooseveltcenter.org/Research/Digital-Library/Record/?libID=o46241; "The Man Who Would Be King Passes Away in Mexico City."
96. "An American Promoter in Abyssinia," 100.
97. Qtd. in Pankhurst, "William H. Ellis," 95.
98. Ibid., 102, 103.
99. Buranelli, "Ellis, American Who Wanted to Be King"; "Strange Career of the Big Cuban."
100. "Strange Career of the Big Cuban."
101. Buranelli, "Ellis, American Who Wanted to Be King."
102. Qtd. in Pankhurst, "William H. Ellis," 102.
103. "Mysterious Disappearance."
104. Shinn, introduction, [7].
105. Sotiropoulos, *Staging Race*, 146.
106. "Rise of a Victoria Negro."
107. W. E. B. Du Bois to W. H. Ellis, 8 July 1919, W. E. B. Du Bois Papers, Special Collections and University Archives, University of Massachusetts–Amherst Libraries, http://credo.library.umass.edu/view/full/mums312-b014-i071.

Chapter Five: Empire on the World Stage

1. "Haile Selassie Brings Dance Feet to 'Scandals.'"
2. "New Plays in Manhattan."
3. "'Scandals' Star to Arizona."
4. "Trio Tip Top in Taps"; Collins, "New 'Scandals' Comely, Comic, and Bountiful"; Morris, "Great Dance Trio."
5. "The Emperor Trucks" [photo].
6. "George White's Scandals Here for Run."
7. "Calls 1936 'Scandals' Burlesque on Race."
8. "New Plays in Manhattan."
9. "3 'Scandals' Hoffers [*sic*] Good."
10. "New Plays in Manhattan."
11. "Ethiopia: Man of the Year," 17.
12. Ibid., 17.
13. Ibid., 16.
14. Ibid.
15. Siraganian, "Wallace Stevens's Fascist Dilemmas," 348.
16. Jonas, *Battle of Adwa*, 3.
17. "Tafari's Coronation to Take Place Nov. 2."
18. Pankhurst, "Economic Change," 216.
19. Schuyler, *Revolt in Ethiopia*, in *Ethiopian Stories*, 201.
20. Whitman, "Haile Selassie of Ethiopia Dies at 83," 40.
21. "Ethiopia Goes Modern," 57.
22. Zewde, *History of Modern Ethiopia*, 37.
23. Although Bentley just preceded the German Arnold Holtz in delivering an automobile to the emperor, Holtz's *Im Auto zu Kaiser Menelik* was published in 1908, a few years before *To Menelek in a Motor-Car* (1913).
24. Hallé, *To Menelek in a Motor-Car*, xii.
25. Ibid., 272.
26. Pankhurst, "Economic Change," 214.
27. "Race Gleanings."
28. "An American Promoter in Abyssinia," 100.
29. Hallé, *To Menelek in a Motor-Car*, 295.
30. Powell-Cotton, *Sporting Trip through Abyssinia*, 81–82.
31. Goedorp, "At the Court of the 'Lion of Judah,'" 511.
32. "Telephones in Abyssinia."
33. MacLean, *John Hoy of Ethiopia*, 2.
34. Hallé, *To Menelek in a Motor-Car*, 292.
35. "Menelik and Queen Victoria"; "Menelik's Phonograph."
36. Qtd. in Demoz, "Emperor Menelik's Phonograph Message to Queen Victoria."
37. The *Hawkes Bay Herald* argued that Menelik "was obviously flattered by the interest thus shown by the Queen, and as he had been somewhat perturbed by the Soudan advance, Her Majesty's expression of the hope that the friendship between the two Empires constantly increase came at an opportune moment to reassure Menelik" ("Menelik and Queen Victoria"). See also Demoz, "Emperor Menelik's Phonograph Message to Queen Victoria."

38. Moffett, "Menelik and His People," 609.
39. Garretson, "Ethiopia's Telephone and Telegraph System," 60.
40. Moffett, "Menelik and His People," 609.
41. Gitelman, *Scripts, Grooves, and Writing Machines*, 122.
42. Wellby, *'Twixt Sirdar and Menelik*, 76.
43. Garretson, "Ethiopia's Telephone and Telegraph System," 59.
44. Ibid., 64.
45. Ibid., 66–67.
46. Ibid., 63.
47. "Ethiopia: Man of the Year," 14.
48. Jonas, *Battle of Adwa*, 3.
49. Krasner, *Resistance, Parody, and Double Consciousness*, 100.
50. "Jesse A. Shipp as a Playwright."
51. Shipp, *Abyssinia*.
52. Ibid.; Hallé, *To Menelek in a Motor-Car*, 262.
53. Shipp, *Abyssinia*.
54. "The Abyssinian War," *Brooklyn Daily Eagle*, 27 April 1868, 2.
55. [Gage], "Late Sovereign of Abyssinia," 86.
56. Rosen, *Julia Margaret Cameron's "Fancy Subjects,"* 221.
57. "Williams and Walker in *Abyssinia*."
58. "Topics of To-Day," *Brooklyn Daily Eagle*, 26 June 1868, 2.
59. Carnochan, *Golden Legends*, 67.
60. Sitwell, *Great Morning*, 115.
61. Ibid.
62. "King's Banquet."
63. "Royalty in Abyssinia."
64. The characters of Mary Dutton's 1967 novel *Thorpe*, listening to the news on the radio, hear that "the Haile Selassie frock, introduced in Bermuda last month . . . has been an immediate success." It is described as "cool white, with a slit, [and] flowing skirt" (*Thorpe*, 205).
65. "Ethiopian Brown."
66. McKay, *Amiable with Big Teeth*, 248.
67. "Ethiopia: Man of the Year," 14.
68. Vestal, *Lion of Judah*, 6; S. M. T., "About Town."
69. Poston, "Robeson to Play King Christophe."
70. "Reel Emperor Meets Real Emperor."
71. Porter, *Brando Unzipped*, 363–64.
72. Isaac, introduction, 15.
73. Ibid.
74. Qtd. in ibid., 16.
75. Ibid.
76. Arent, "Technique of the Living Newspaper," 821.
77. Ibid., 821, 822.
78. Scott, *Sons of Sheba's Race*, 42.
79. Logan, "Abyssinia Breaks into the Movies," 339.
80. Isaac, introduction, 19.

81. Arent, "Technique of the Living Newspaper," 822.

82. Ibid.

83. Arent, "Ethiopia," 19.

84. Ibid., 20.

85. Ibid., 21.

86. Ibid., 23.

87. Ibid.

88. Ibid.

89. "Ethiopia Orders Full Mobilization."

90. Arent, "Ethiopia," 25.

91. Arent, "Technique of the Living Newspaper," 821.

92. Ibid.

93. Arent, "Technique of the Living Newspaper," 822.

94. Ibid., 825.

95. Isaac, introduction, 18.

96. Arent, "Ethiopia," 19.

97. "WPA Theatre Plan Turns to AAA Skit."

98. Atkinson, "The Play: 'Ethiopia.'"

99. "Rice Quits in Row over WPA Drama."

100. Qtd. in Quinn, *Furious Improvisation*, 67.

101. Atkinson, "The Play: 'Ethiopia.'"

102. Isaac, introduction, 17.

Chapter Six: Martial Ethiopianism in Verse

1. Moses, *Afrotopia*, 15.

2. Preece, "War and the Negro," 338.

3. Ibid.

4. As Robin D. G. Kelley points out in his introduction to *African Americans in the Spanish Civil War: "This Ain't Ethiopia, but It'll Do,"* the quotation comes from a story titled "700 Calendar Days" by Oscar Hunter.

5. Baxter, "To the Barefoot Lads," in *Sonnets for the Ethiopians*, 25.

6. [Huggins], *The Friends of Ethiopia in America*, 6.

7. Ibid., 4.

8. Ibid., 5.

9. Bayen, *The March of Black Men*, 6.

10. Bayen to Leora Hadley, undated, in Dorothy Hadley Bayen Papers, 1931–1947, Manuscripts and Archives, Yale University Library, New Haven, CT.

11. The book appears to have been self-published. The only books I have come across published by Magic City Press were ones authored by Baxter.

12. Baxter, *Sonnets for the Ethiopians*, xi, xii, xiii.

13. Baxter, "Well May I Sing of the Proud Ethiope," in *Sonnets for the Ethiopians*, 5.

14. Baxter, "Italy to Ethiopia," in *Sonnets for the Ethiopians*, 7.

15. Baxter, "Ethiopia to Italy," in *Sonnets for the Ethiopians*, 8.

16. Baxter, "Latin or Greek," in *Sonnets for the Ethiopians*, 21. A similar distinction features in a story told by William M. Steen, an African American newspaper editor

living in Ethiopia: "When I asked them if they were Negroes their answer was 'No, and neither are you. . . . If we call ourselves Negroes we have nothing to gain but your background of slavery; if you call yourselves Ethiopians, you gain not only a country, a language, and a flag, but more than 2,000 years of glorious history." Qtd. in Gebrekidan, "Ethiopia in Black Studies," 14.

17. Baxter, "King of Kings," in *Sonnets for the Ethiopians*, 22–24.

18. Baxter, "Haile Selassie," in *Sonnets for the Ethiopians*, 15.

19. Baxter, preface, "The World," and "To the League of Nations," in *Sonnets for the Ethiopians*, xiii, 3, 31.

20. Baxter, "The Emperor's Voice," in *Sonnets for the Ethiopians*, 10.

21. Gibson, "The Voice of Ethiopia."

22. Hill, "An Ethiope in Spain."

23. Gruesser, *Black on Black*, 95. A notable exception is Tolson's allusion to the Greek etymology of "Ethiopian," appearing in the poem twice as "burnt faces."

24. Nelson, Editorial Statement.

25. As Lorenzo Thomas writes, this is part of "Tolson's deliberate attempt to demonstrate parity between the wisdom and eloquence of the great texts of European literature and the proverbial wisdom of the African griots" (*Extraordinary Measures*, 111).

26. Tolson, "The Bard of Addis Ababa."

27. A *grazmatch* is a type of military leader; *hakim* means healer. Thank you to my father, Mohammed A. Nurhussein, for these translations from Amharic.

28. Thomas, *Extraordinary Measures*, 116.

29. As Hill writes, "Blaming Haile Selassie for a weak defense and a naïve faith in intervention by the League of Nations, Garvey was further incensed when the Ethiopian leader spurned a delegation of black Pan-Africanists (including Garvey) who had gathered to greet him upon his arrival in exile in England in 1936." *Marcus Garvey and Universal Negro Improvement Association Papers*, vol. 7, xlviii.

30. Garvey, "Ras Nasibu of Ogaden."

31. Garvey, "Failure of Haile Selassie as Emperor," in *Marcus Garvey and Universal Negro Improvement Association Papers*, vol. 7, 739.

32. Edwards, "Langston Hughes," 690.

33. Atzel, "Ras Nasibu."

34. Garvey, "Ras Desta."

35. Postcards and printed ephemera documenting the Italian occupation of Ethiopia (MS 1898), Manuscripts and Archives, Yale University Library, New Haven, CT.

36. Qtd. in Benjamin, *Illuminations*, 241–42.

37. Qtd. in Zewde, *History of Modern Ethiopia*, 159.

38. Baxter, "To the Askaris," in *Sonnets for the Ethiopians*, 13.

39. Garvey, "The Brutal Crime."

40. Edwards, *Practice of Diaspora*, 13.

41. Edwards, "Langston Hughes," 703.

42. Hughes, "Letter from Spain, Addressed to Alabama," in *Collected Poems of Langston Hughes*, 201–2.

43. Edwards, "Langston Hughes," 694.

44. Hughes, *I Wonder as I Wander*, 350.

45. Ibid., 349–50.

46. Ibid., 352.

47. Ibid., 350.

48. "To the Editor."

49. Ibid.

50. Pankhurst, "Sylvia," 158.

51. W. E. B. Du Bois to *New Times and Ethiopia News*, 16 January 1942, W. E. B. Du Bois Papers, Special Collections and University Archives, University of Massachusetts–Amherst Libraries, http://credo.library.umass.edu/view/full/mums312-b098-i262.

52. "To One and All."

53. Garvey, "The Failure of Haile Selassie as Emperor," in *Marcus Garvey and Universal Negro Improvement Association Papers*, vol. 4, 741; qtd. in Kelley, introduction, 20. Garvey's view of Selassie shifted as the war waged on. In a 1935 editorial in the *Black Man*, he writes, "The facts reveal Mussolini as a barbarian, compared to Selassie . . . one man is a tyrant, a bully, an irresponsible upstart, whilst the other is a sober, courteous and courageous gentleman," with clear parallels to the escalating Louis-Carnera rivalry. Huggins's view shifted as well. Gruesser, *Black on Black*, 99.

54. Kelley, introduction, 20.

55. Hughes, "Ballad of Ethiopia." Written early in the conflict, this poem displays an optimism obviously missing from later poems such as "Air Raid over Harlem" and "Broadcast on Ethiopia."

56. Taketani, "Colored Empires in the 1930s," 123.

57. Stephens, *Black Empire*, 2, 38.

58. Runstedtler, "In Sport the Best Man Wins," 56.

59. "Harlem Ponders Ethiopia's Fate."

60. McKay, *Long Way from Home*, 53.

Chapter Seven: George S. Schuyler and the Appeal of Imperial Ethiopia

1. "Ethiopia: Man of the Year," 13.

2. I am grateful to one of Princeton University Press's anonymous peer reviewers for the reference to this expression.

3. "Ethiopia: Man of the Year," 13.

4. Munro, "Ethiopia Stretches Forth," 46–47.

5. The *Courier* "vied with the *Chicago Defender* to be ranked as the nation's leading black newspaper." Its circulation was around 250,000 when Schuyler's *Ethiopian Stories* were published. Wintz and Finkelman, *Encyclopedia of the Harlem Renaissance*, 973–74.

6. Hill, introduction, 16. In a 11 February 1936 letter to Schuyler, Ira F. Lewis, manager of the *Pittsburgh Courier*, wrote that "surely no one is in a more authoritative position than Mr. Rogers to tell the yokels about the situation in Ethiopia." George S. Schuyler Papers, Special Collections Research Center, Syracuse University Libraries, Syracuse, NY.

7. Rogers, "J. A. Rogers Gets Exclusive Interview," 1.

8. Stephens, *Black Empire*, 81.

9. Hill, introduction, 14.

10. Taketani, "Colored Empires in the 1930s," 122.

11. Schuyler, *The Ethiopian Murder Mystery*, in *Ethiopian Stories*, 121. Subsequent quotations will be cited parenthetically in text, with the abbreviation *EMM*.

12. "Protect Us from Poison Gases!"

13. Rogers, "J. A. Rogers Gets Exclusive Interview," 1.

14. Schuyler, "Views and Reviews," 27 July 1935, 10.

15. Schuyler, *Revolt in Ethiopia: A Tale of Black Insurrection against Italian Imperialism*, in *Ethiopian Stories*, 215. Subsequent quotations will be cited parenthetically in text, with the abbreviation *RE*.

16. Benjamin, *Illuminations*, 241–42.

17. Thompson, *Black Fascisms*, 75.

18. Stephens, *Black Empire*, 13.

19. Bain, "*Shocks Americana*!" 940.

20. Schwarz, "Colonial Struggle on Manhattan Soil,'" 202, 206.

21. Thompson, *Black Fascisms*, 78.

22. Rogers, "Ring of Ethiopian Steel Surrounds Italian Army," 1.

23. Calvin, "Race Eager for Rogers' Ethiopian War News."

24. This letter writer, Edwin Horde, was a Jamaican man who "periodically wrote articles and letters to the editor of [the *Plain Talk*] on the topics of Ethiopianism and the crisis in Ethiopia." *Plain Talk* was a "radical pro-Ethiopian organ" published in Jamaica. *Marcus Garvey and Universal Negro Improvement Association Papers*, vol. 7, 739n1; vol. 1, 106n2.

25. Munro, "Ethiopia Stretches Forth," 47.

26. Thompson, *Black Fascisms*, 9.

27. Bain, "*Shocks Americana*!" 950.

28. Gilroy, *Black Atlantic*, 4.

29. Bayen, *March of Black Men*, 6.

30. Bain, "*Shocks Americana*!" 957.

31. Wilson, "'Are You Man Enough?'" 270.

32. Schuyler, *Revolt in Ethiopia*, 126, 176, 145; Mills, "Selassie Says Ethiopia Will Defeat Italy."

33. "Ethiopia: Man of the Year," 13; Gibbon, *History of the Decline and Fall of the Roman Empire*, 165.

34. "Ethiopia: Man of the Year," 13.

35. Zewde, *History of Modern Ethiopia*, 136.

36. Ibid., 159.

37. Schilz, "Air Age in the Ethiopian Empire," 177.

38. Gruesser, *Black on Black*, 114.

39. "Italian Case."

40. Rogers, "J. A. Rogers Gets Exclusive Interview," 2.

41. Schuyler, *Slaves Today*, 5.

42. Rogers, "J. A. Rogers Gets Exclusive Interview," 2.

43. Garvey to Una Brown, in *Marcus Garvey and Universal Negro Improvement Association Papers*, vol. 7, 701. Garvey wrote elsewhere, "We must admit that we

glorified Haile Selassie when the war started, fought his battles to win international support, but we ever felt deep down in our hearts that he was a slave master." Garvey, "Failure of Haile Selassie as Emperor," in *Marcus Garvey and Universal Negro Improvement Association Papers*, vol. 7, 741.

44. Crosby, review of *Sympathy in American Literature*, 379.

45. Paul, "Ethnicity and the New Constitutional Orders of Ethiopia and Eritrea," 176. Although Menelik is often credited with consolidating the lands that would form the modern Ethiopian empire, the work of empire-building can be said to have begun in earnest with Tewodros (1855–68), who "pacified much of the country north of the Rift Valley." But Tewodros "had sought a rather modest Nilitic empire, one in line with a previous medieval incarnation; whereas Menelik created the Ethiopia of today, one which straddles equally both sides of the Rift Valley." Allain, *Law and Slavery*, 126.

46. Robinson, "African Diaspora and the Italo-Ethiopian Crisis," 55.

47. Thompson, *Black Fascisms*, 72.

48. Taketani, "Colored Empires in the 1930s," 139–40.

49. "Ethiopia: Man of the Year," 13.

50. Henze, *Layers of Time*, 193. According to Henze, "Although Iyasu had a strong leaning toward Islam, there is no firm evidence that he actually converted" (195n20).

51. Zewde, *History of Modern Ethiopia*, 124.

52. "The Front: Gugsa Makes Good."

53. Edwards, *Practice of Diaspora*, 13.

54. Garvey, "Failure of Haile Selassie as Emperor," in *Marcus Garvey and Universal Negro Improvement Association Papers*, vol. 7, 741.

55. DeGabriele, "Sympathy for the Sovereign," 1–3.

56. Taketani, "Colored Empires in the 1930s," 121; Thompson, *Black Fascisms*, 73.

57. Stephens, *Black Empire*, 14–15, 13, 20.

58. "Ethiopia: Man of the Year," 15.

59. Garvey, "Failure of Haile Selassie as Emperor," in *Marcus Garvey and Universal Negro Improvement Association Papers*, vol. 7, 739.

60. Schuyler, "Views and Reviews," 23 November 1935, 10.

61. Edwards, *Practice of Diaspora*, 13.

62. Ibid., 109.

Chapter Eight: Claude McKay and the Display of Aristocracy

1. McKay, *Amiable with Big Teeth*, 249. Subsequent quotations to *Amiable with Big Teeth* will be cited parenthetically in the text.

2. MacLean, *John Hoy of Ethiopia*, 3.

3. Gilroy, "Black Fascism," 73.

4. Du Bois, "Marcus Garvey," 265.

5. McKay, *Harlem: Negro Metropolis*, 155.

6. Hill qtd. in Stephens, *Black Empire*, 76.

7. Du Bois, "Marcus Garvey," 272–73.

8. McKay, *Harlem: Negro Metropolis*, 210.

9. Raiford, "Marcus Garvey in Stereograph," 272.

10. Ibid., 270.
11. Du Bois, "Marcus Garvey," 265.
12. Cloutier, "*Amiable with Big Teeth*," 568.
13. Ibid.
14. McKay, *Harlem: Negro Metropolis*, 177.
15. Ibid.
16. Burley, "Romance Encircles"; Burley, "Ethiopian Envoy Insulted," 12.
17. Burley, "Romance Encircles."
18. "Scottsboro Sensation."
19. Scott, "Black Nationalism and the Italo-Ethiopian Conflict," 142.
20. See McCandless, "The Last Dress Rehearsal."
21. Burley, "Romance Encircles."
22. Ross, "Black Americans and Italo-Ethiopian Relief," 170.
23. Burley, "Romance Encircles."
24. "Report Zaphiro Was Sent out of Country."
25. "Speculations on Zaphiro's Recall Called Just Bosh."
26. North, *Reading 1922*, 12.
27. Gebrekidan, *Bond without Blood*, 55.
28. This genealogy is hardly unique to Zaphiro; there has been a Greek presence in Ethiopia for centuries, and in particular "the early years of the century . . . witness the migration to Addis Ababa of several hundreds of Greeks, Armenians, Indians and Arabs." Pankhurst, "Economic Change," 212.
29. Abraham, *Reminiscences of My Life*, 27.
30. "Youngest Diplomat in Action."
31. Gebrekidan, *Bond without Blood*, 55.
32. "Haile Selassie's Nephew Is Snubbed."
33. Ibid.
34. Scott, "Black Nationalism and the Italo-Ethiopian Conflict," 144.
35. McKay, *Harlem: Negro Metropolis*, 250.
36. Hill, "King Menelik's Nephew," 16.
37. "Denies Relationship to Haile Sellassie."
38. "Harlem: Housemaid in Purple."
39. "Ethiopian 'Princess,' Who Duped Nation's Press"; Ottley, "Hectic Harlem."
40. "Extra! Chappy's Princess Is in Again," 1.
41. Qtd. in Hill, "King Menelik's Nephew," 40.
42. Edwards, *Practice of Diaspora*, 14.
43. Burley, "Romance Encircles"; "Haile Selassie's Nephew Is Snubbed."
44. Cloutier, "*Amiable with Big Teeth*," 565.
45. Thesiger, *Life of My Choice*, 91.
46. Garvey, "Africa for the Africans," in *Marcus Garvey and Universal Negro Improvement Association Papers*, vol. 4, 612.

Conclusion: Langston Hughes's Business Suit

1. Hughes to Rita Pankhurst, Langston Hughes Papers, James Weldon Johnson Collection in the Yale Collection of American Literature (JWJ MSS 26), Beinecke Rare Book and Manuscript Library, Yale University, New Haven, CT.

2. Rampersad, *Life of Langston Hughes*, 405.

3. Hughes to Raoul Abdul, Langston Hughes Papers, James Weldon Johnson Collection in the Yale Collection of American Literature (JWJ MSS 26), Beinecke Rare Book and Manuscript Library, Yale University, New Haven, CT.

4. Bass, "Five Stories about a Man Named Hughes," 4–5.

5. Ibid., 5.

6. "Emperor Haile Selassie, on Liberation Day."

7. Southard, "Modern Ethiopia," 679.

8. MacLean, *John Hoy of Ethiopia*, 184–85.

9. Spencer, *Ethiopia at Bay*, 160.

10. Angelova, *Sacred Founders*, 189.

11. Vestal, *Lion of Judah*, 154–55.

12. MacLean, *John Hoy of Ethiopia*, 109.

13. McKinley, "Tsegaye Gabre-Medhin, Ethiopian Poet Laureate, Dies at 69."

14. Southard, "Modern Ethiopia," 683.

BIBLIOGRAPHY

Abraham, Emmanuel. *Reminiscences of My Life*. Oslo: Lunde forlag, 1995.

"The Abyssinian Gammon in the Senate." *New York Times*, 11 December 1867, 4.

"Abyssinian Speaks before N.C. Students." *Indianapolis Recorder*, 10 November 1928, 3.

"The Abyssinian War." *Brooklyn Daily Eagle*, 27 April 1868, 2.

"The Abyssinian War." *Wilkes's Spirit of the Times*, 21 December 1867, 324.

"The Abyssinian War." *Wilkes's Spirit of the Times*, 2 May 1868, 174.

"'Abyssinians' on Trial for Riot Last Summer." *Savannah Tribune*, 15 January 1921, 8.

Adejumobi, Saheed A. *The History of Ethiopia*. Westport, CT: Greenwood Press, 2007.

"African Explorer Presents His View on Dark Continent." *Arizona Republican*, 7 October 1920, 7.

"The 'Alabama' Claims in Congress." *Public Opinion*, 28 December 1867, 692.

Alden, H. M. "John Bull in Abyssinia." *Harper's*, 1 August 1868, 333–48.

Allain, Jean. *The Law and Slavery: Prohibiting Human Exploitation*. Leiden: Brill Nijhoff, 2015.

"An American Promoter in Abyssinia." *World's Work* (June 1904): 99–100.

Ammons, Elizabeth. *Conflicting Stories: American Women Writers at the Turn into the Twentieth Century*. New York: Oxford University Press, 1992.

Amulree, Lord. "Prince Alamayou of Ethiopia." *Ethiopia Observer* (1970): 8–15.

Anderson, Benedict. *Imagined Communities*. 1983. London: Verso, 2006.

Angelova, Diliana N. *Sacred Founders: Women, Men, and Gods in the Discourse of Imperial Founding, Rome through Early Byzantium*. Oakland: University of California Press, 2015.

"The Anglo-Abyssinian War." *Wilkes's Spirit of the Times*, 7 December 1867, 292.

"The Anglo-Abyssinian War: A Question for Congress." *Wilkes's Spirit of the Times*, 23 November 1868, 260.

Arent, Arthur. "Ethiopia: The First 'Living Newspaper.'" *Educational Theatre Journal* 10, no. 1 (March 1968): 15–31.

———. "The Technique of the Living Newspaper." *Theatre Arts Monthly* (November 1938): 820–25.

Atkinson, Brooks. "The Play: 'Ethiopia,' the First Issue of the Living Newspaper, Which the Federal Theatre Cannot Publish." *New York Times*, 25 January 1936, 18.

Atzel, Baroness Maria. "Ras Nasibu." *New Times and Ethiopia News*, 11 December 1937, 3.

Auf der Maur, Lorenz. "*Ethiopia* and *Abyssinia* in English Writing up to 1790." In *Proceedings of the XVth International Conference of Ethiopian Studies, Hamburg July 20–25, 2003*, ed. Siegbert Uhlig, 523–31. Wiesbaden: Harrassowitz Verlag, 2006.

"Back from Abyssinia: W. H. Ellis Silent Regarding Death of His Traveling Companion, F. Kent Loomis, Near Portsmouth, Eng." *Boston Daily Globe*, 30 October 1904, 27.

Bain, Alexander M. "*Shocks Americana*!: George Schuyler Serializes Black Internationalism." *American Literary History* 19, no. 4 (2007): 937–63.

Baker, Sir Samuel White. "On Abyssinia, or Ethiopia." In *Notices of the Proceedings at the Meetings of the Members of the Royal Institution of Great Britain, with Abstracts of the Discourses Delivered at the Evening Meetings, Vol. V.: 1866–1869*, 404–18. London: William Clowes and Sons, 1869.

Bass, George Houston. "Five Stories about a Man Named Hughes: A Critical Reflection." *Langston Hughes Review* 1 (Spring 1982): 1–12.

Baxter, J. Harvey L. *Sonnets for the Ethiopians*. Roanoke, VA: Magic City Press, 1936.

Bayen, Dorothy Hadley. Papers, 1931–1947 (MS 1570). Manuscripts and Archives, Yale University Library, New Haven, CT.

Bayen, Malaku. *The March of Black Men—Ethiopia Leads*. New York: Voice of Ethiopia Press, 1939.

Benjamin, Walter. *Illuminations*, ed. Hannah Arendt. New York: Schocken Books, 2007.

Bennett, Paula Bernat. Introduction to *Palace-Burner: The Selected Poetry of Sarah Piatt*, ed. Paula Bernat Bennett, xxiii–lviii. Champaign: University of Illinois Press, 2001.

Bernstein, Robin. *Racial Innocence: Performing American Childhood from Slavery to Civil Rights*. New York: New York University Press, 2011.

Blayechettai, Dr. J. E. *The Pen of an African*. N.p., 1922.

"Blayechettai's Answer." *California Eagle*, 14 August 1925, 1.

Bloch, Marc. *The Royal Touch: Sacred Monarchy and Scrofula in England and France*. Trans. J. E. Anderson. 1973. Oxon: Routledge, 2015.

"Bogus Princes on the Dreadnought: Amazing Hoax." *Aberdeen Journal*, 15 February 1910, 6.

Borough, R. W. "Liberian Captain Arrives in U.S. to Purchase a Ship; Would Raise Funds among Colored Folk to Finance His Scheme; Africa Needs Machinery; Country Has Plenty of Land and Foodstuff, but Cannot Use It All." *Baltimore Afro-American*, 16 March 1923, 11.

"The British Neutrality Laws." *New York Times*, 8 July 1868, 4.

Brodhead, Richard. *Culture of Letters: Scenes of Reading and Writing in Nineteenth-Century America*. Chicago: University of Chicago Press, 1993.

Brown, William Wells. *The Rising Son; or, The Antecedents and Advancement of the Colored Race*. 1873. Boston: A. G. Brown & Co, 1882.

Buranelli, Prosper. "Ellis, American Who Wanted to Be King, Goes on His Last Adventure. Death Cuts Short Career of Reckless Soldier of Fortune Who During His Strange Life Won and Lost Millions and Was the Center of International Scandals and the Bold Manipulator of Dubious Central American Intrigues." *Milwaukee Sentinel Sunday Magazine*, 9 December 1923, 4.

Burette, H. A. "Notes from King Theodore's Country." *London Society* (April 1868): 289–99.

Burley, Dan. "Ethiopian Envoy Insulted by Two Chicago Hotels; Barred; Lij Zaphiro Turned out into the Cold; Hotel Suit Planned; Youthful Diplomat Captures Heart of Chicago; $1500 Raised to Aid Ethiopia." *Chicago Defender*, 1 February 1936, 1, 12.

———. "Romance Encircles Shy Lij Tasfaye Zaphiro." *Chicago Defender*, 9 January 1937, 14.

C. C. *Anecdotes of Alamayu: The Late King Theodore's Son*. London: William Hunt and Company, [1869].

"Calls 1936 'Scandals' Burlesque on Race; George White's Latest Is Worst Ever on Broadway." *Chicago Defender*, 11 January 1936, 9.

Calvin, Floyd J. "Race Eager for Rogers' Ethiopian War News; Hundreds Awaiting Truthful Reports." *Pittsburgh Courier*, 30 November 1935, 2.

"Capt. Harry Dean, World Traveler, Dies; Noted Author Had Been Ill Seven Years." *Chicago Defender*, 27 July 1935, 1.

"Captain Dean's Manuscripts May Be Printed." *Kansas City Plaindealer*, 4 October 1935, 3.

Carby, Hazel V. Introduction to *The Magazine Novels of Pauline Hopkins*, xxix–l. New York: Oxford University Press, 1988.

Carey, Daniel, and Sven Trakulhun. "Universalism, Diversity, and the Postcolonial Enlightenment." In *Postcolonial Enlightenment: Eighteenth-Century Colonialism and Postcolonial Theory*, ed. Daniel Carey and Lynn Festa, 240–80. New York: Oxford University Press, 2009.

Carnochan, W. B. *Golden Legends: Images of Abyssinia, Samuel Johnson to Bob Marley*. Stanford: Stanford University Press, 2008.

"Charlton." *Songs of the Year and Other Poems*. Cincinnati: Robert Clarke & Co., 1875.

Chicago Commission on Race Relations. *The Negro in Chicago: A Study of Race Relations and a Race Riot*. Chicago: University of Chicago Press, 1922.

"Chicago 'Riot.'" *Kansas City Sun*, 26 June 1920, 1.

Chojnacki, Stanislaw. "Flags and Banners." *Encyclopaedia Aethiopica Vol. 4: O–X*, ed. Siegbert Uhlig, 739–41. Wiesbaden: Harrassowitz, 2010.

———. "A Second Note on the Ethiopian National Flag, with Comments on Its Historical and Sociological Sources." In *Proceedings of the Third International Conference of Ethiopian Studies*, 137–53. Addis Ababa: Institute of Ethiopian Studies, Haile Selassie I University, 1969.

———. "Some Notes on the History of the Ethiopian National Flag." *Journal of Ethiopian Studies* 1, no. 2 (1963): 49–63.

———. "Third Note on the History of the Ethiopian National Flag: The Discovery of Its First Exemplar and the New Documents on the Early Attempts by Emperor Menilek to Introduce the Flag." *Rassegna di Studi Etiopici* 28 (1980–81): 23–41.

"Close of the Abyssinian War." *Illustrated London News*, 2 May 1868, 422.

Cloutier, Jean-Christophe. "*Amiable with Big Teeth*: The Case of Claude McKay's Last Novel." *Modernism/Modernity* 20, no. 3 (September 2013): 557–76.

Collins, Charles. "New 'Scandals' Comely, Comic, and Bountiful." *Chicago Daily Tribune*, 29 June 1936, 13.

Collis, Victoria J. "Anxious Records: Race, Imperial Belonging, and the Black Literary Imagination, 1900–1946." PhD diss., Columbia University, 2013.

Cramer, Alfred W. "Of Serpentina and Stenography: Shapes of Handwriting in Romantic Melody." *19th-Century Music* 30, no. 2 (Fall 2006): 133–65.

Crosby, Oscar T. "Personal Impressions of Menelik." *Century* (April 1902): 875–84.

Crosby, Sara. Review of *Sympathy in American Literature: American Sentiments from Jefferson to the Jameses* by Kristin Boudreau, *Early American Literature* 41, no. 2 (2006): 379–82.

Daniels, Peter T. "Fundamentals of Grammatology." *Journal of American Oriental Society* 110, no. 4 (October–December 1990): 727–31.

Davidson, E. *The Death of King Theodore and Other Poems*. Newton-on-the Moor: A. Davidson, 1874.

Dawson, Sir J. W. *Modern Science in Bible Lands*. New York: Harper and Brothers, 1889.

Dean, Captain Harry. "Liberia Asks America to Develop Commerce." *San Francisco Chronicle*, 8 July 1923, 5.

———. Papers. DuSable Museum of African American History, Chicago.

———. *The Pedro Gorino: The Adventures of a Negro Sea-Captain in Africa and on the Seven Seas in His Attempts to Found an Ethiopian Empire: An Autobiographical Narrative*. 1929. Yardley, PA: Westholme, 2011.

deCourcy, Elisa. "The Dreadnought Hoax Portrait as an Affront to the Edwardian Age." *Early Popular Visual Culture* 15, no. 4 (2017): 405–24.

DeGabriele, Peter. "Sympathy for the Sovereign: Sovereignty, Sympathy, and the Colonial Relation in Edward Gibbon's *The Decline and Fall of the Roman Empire*." *Eighteenth Century* 53 (2012): 1–22.

Delany, Martin. *Principia of Ethnology: The Origin of Races and Color, with an Archeological Compendium of Ethiopian and Egyptian Civilization from Years of Careful Examination and Enquiry*. 1879. Baltimore: Black Classic Press, 1991.

Demoz, Abraham. "Emperor Menelik's Phonograph Message to Queen Victoria." *Bulletin of the School of Oriental and African Studies* 32, no. 2 (1969): 251–56.

"Denies Relationship to Haile Sellassie: But 'Princess' Who Talked on War in Ethiopia Insists She Is Kin of Ex-Emperor." *New York Times*, 18 July 1935, 4.

Doreski, C. K. "Inherited Rhetoric and Authentic History: Pauline Hopkins at the *Colored American Magazine*." In *The Unruly Voice: Rediscovering Pauline Elizabeth Hopkins*, ed. John Cullen Gruesser, 71–97. Champaign: University of Illinois Press, 1996.

Du Bois, W. E. B. "Marcus Garvey." In *The Oxford W. E. B. Du Bois Reader*, ed. Eric J. Sundquist, 265–76. New York: Oxford University Press, 1996.

———. Papers. Special Collections and University Archives, University of Massachusetts–Amherst Libraries. http://credo.library.umass.edu/view/full/mums312-b014-i071.

———. Review of *The Pedro Gorino*. *Crisis* (November 1929): 376.

———. *The Souls of Black Folk*, ed. Henry Louis Gates Jr. and Terri Hume Oliver. New York: Norton, 1999.

———. *Writings: The Suppression of the African Slave-Trade, The Souls of Black Folk, Dusk of Dawn, Essays*. New York: Library of America, 1986.

Dunbar, Paul Laurence. *Lyrics of Lowly Life*. 1896. New York: Citadel, 1984.

Dutton, Mary. *Thorpe*. Cleveland: World Publishing Company, 1967.

"Editorial and Publishers' Announcements." *Colored American Magazine* (May–June 1903): 466–67.

Edwards, Brent Hayes. "Langston Hughes and the Futures of Diaspora." *American Literary History* 19, no. 3 (2007): 689–711.

———. *The Practice of Diaspora: Literature, Translation and the Rise of Black Internationalism*. Cambridge, MA: Harvard University Press, 2003.

Edwards, Thyra J. "Much Interest in 'Pedro Gorino.'" *Philadelphia Tribune*, 1 August 1929, 6.

"The Emperor Trucks." *Pittsburgh Courier*, 5 September 1936, 2:7.

"England and the United States." *Saturday Review*, 1 February 1868, 128–29.

Erkkila, Betsy. *Whitman the Political Poet*. New York: Oxford University Press, 1989.

"Ethiopia Goes Modern: Since Returning to Power Haile Selassie Has Introduced Western Ways in His Ancient Land." *Life*, 10 November 1947, 57–60.

"Ethiopia: Man of the Year." *Time*, 6 January 1936, 13–17.

"Ethiopia Orders Full Mobilization." *New York Times*, 4 October 1935, 2.

"Ethiopian Brown Newest Color to Dominate the Styles of London." *Baltimore Afro-American*, 18 January 1936, 17.

"Ethiopian 'Princess,' Who Duped Nation's Press, Turns Out to Be a Harlem Relief Client; N.Y. Press Agent Turned Housemaid into Princess." *Baltimore Afro American*, 27 July 1935, 8.

"Extra! Chappy's Princess Is in Again—Now She's Scoffing at Ethiopian Envoy." *New York Amsterdam News*, 25 January 1936, 1, 5.

"Famous African Explorer Will Lecture Here; Harry Dean, 'Abona' of Liberia, Trying to Establish Commercial Relations." *Prescott Evening Courier*, 25 September 1920, 1.

Finger, Charles J. "The Literature of Adventure." *English Journal* 19 (December 1930): 771–81.

"Flag Burners Must Die." *St. Louis Clarion*, 2 April 1921, 1.

Folsom, Ed. "Lucifer and Ethiopia: Whitman, Race, and Poetics Before the Civil War and After." In *A Historical Guide to Walt Whitman*, ed. David S. Reynolds, 45–95. New York: Oxford University Press, 2000.

"Foreign Notes." *Every Saturday*, 16 November 1867, 638–40.

"The Front: Gugsa Makes Good." *Time*, 18 November 1935, 20.

[Gage, W. L.] "The Late Sovereign of Abyssinia." *Putnam's* (July 1868): 85–89.

Garber, Marjorie. *Shakespeare's Ghost Writers: Literature as Uncanny Causality*. 1987. New York: Methuen, 2010.

Garretson, Peter. "Ethiopia's Telephone and Telegraph System, 1897–1933." *North-East African Studies*, 2, no. 1 (1980): 59–71.

Garvey, Marcus. "The Brutal Crime." *Black Man* (December 1935): 4.

——. *The Marcus Garvey and Universal Negro Improvement Association Papers*. Vols. 1, 4, 7, ed. Robert A. Hill. Berkeley: University of California Press, 1983–91.

——. "Ras Desta." *Black Man* (March–April 1937): 7.

——. "Ras Nasibu of Ogaden." *Black Man* (January 1937): 11.

Gebrekidan, Fikru Negash. *Bond without Blood: A History of Ethiopian and New World Black Relations, 1896–1991*. Trenton: Africa World Press, 2005.

——. "Ethiopia in Black Studies from W. E. B. Du Bois to Henry Louis Gates, Jr." *Northeast African Studies* 15, no. 1 (2015): 1–34.

"George White's Scandals Here for Run; George Dewey Washington and Four Others in Cast." *Chicago Defender*, 4 July 1936, 11.

Gibbon, Edward. *The History of the Decline and Fall of the Roman Empire*, vol. 5. 1788. London: Methuen, 1901.

Gibson, Rufus. "The Voice of Ethiopia." *Crisis* (January 1936): 13.

Gillman, Susan. *Blood Talk: American Race Melodrama and the Culture of the Occult*. Chicago: University of Chicago Press, 2003.

Gilman, Daniel Coit. Papers. Johns Hopkins University Libraries Archives. https://jscholarship.library.jhu.edu/handle/1774.2/42864.

Gilroy, Paul. *The Black Atlantic: Modernity and Double Consciousness*. Cambridge, MA: Harvard University Press, 1993.

———. "Black Fascism." *Transition* 81–82 (2000): 70–91.

Gitelman, Lisa. *Scripts, Grooves, and Writing Machines: Representing Technology in the Edison Era*. Stanford: Stanford University Press, 1999.

Gleichen, Count Edward. *With the Mission to Menelik, 1897*. London: Edward Arnold, 1898.

Gnamo, Abbas H. *Conquest and Resistance in the Ethiopian Empire, 1880–1974: The Case of the Arsi Oromo*. Leiden: Brill, 2014.

Goedorp, Victor. "At the Court of the 'Lion of Judah.'" *Wide World Magazine* (January 1900): 507–18.

Goyal, Yogita. *Romance, Diaspora, and Black Atlantic Literature*. Cambridge: Cambridge University Press, 2010.

"A Great Ruler." *Topeka Plaindealer*, 13 November 1903, 1.

"A Grewsome [*sic*] Suspicion Dissipated." *Christian Advocate*, 8 December 1904, 6–7.

Gruesser, John Cullen. *Black on Black: Twentieth-Century African American Writing about Africa*. Lexington: University Press of Kentucky, 2000.

———. *Confluences: Postcolonialism, African American Literary Studies and the Black Atlantic*. Athens: University of Georgia Press, 2005.

Gullick, John M. "Captain Speedy of Larut." *Journal of the Malayan Branch of the Royal Asiatic Society* 26, no. 3 (November 1953): 3–103.

Hack, Daniel. *Reaping Something New: African American Transformations of Victorian Literature*. Princeton: Princeton University Press, 2017.

"Haile Selassie Brings Dance Feet to 'Scandals.'" *New York Herald–Tribune*, 19 January 1936, n.p. Houghton Library, Harvard University, Cambridge, MA.

"Haile Selassie's Nephew Is Snubbed by N.Y. Hotel; Ethiopian Monarch's Kin and Personal M.D., Here to Seek Aid for His Nation, Discriminated Against in Gotham Hotel." *Pittsburgh Courier*, 3 October 1936, 1:4.

Hallé, Clifford. *To Menelek in a Motor-Car*. London: Hurst and Blackett, 1913.

Hamedoe, S. E. F. C. C. "Menelik, Emperor of Abyssinia." *Colored American Magazine* (December 1900): 130, 133, 149–53.

Harlan, Louis R., and Raymond W. Smock, eds. *The Booker T. Washington Papers, Vol. 12: 1912–14*. Urbana: University of Illinois Press, 1982.

"Harlem: Housemaid in Purple." *Washington Post*, 20 July 1935, 1.

"Harlem Ponders Ethiopia's Fate, Negroes Stirred by Speakers Who Make Common Cause with Haile Selassie." *New York Times*, 14 July 1935, E10.

Harris, Marla. "Not Black and/or White: Reading Racial Difference in Heliodorus's *Ethiopica* and Pauline Hopkins's *Of One Blood*." *African American Review* 35 (2001): 375–90.

"Harry Foster Dean, African Explorer and Lecturer." *Indianapolis Freeman*, 10 February 1912, 8.

Hassen, Mohammed. *The Oromo of Ethiopia: A History, 1570–1860*. Cambridge: Cambridge University Press, 1990.

Hassen Ali, Mohammed, and Seyoum Hameso. "Ethiopia." In *Nations and Nationalism: A Global Historical Overview, Vol. 1: 1770–1880*, ed. Guntram H. Herb and David H. Kaplan, 736–46. Santa Barbara, CA: ABC-Clio, 2008.

Hawkins, Stella. "The Negro's Triumph Over Obstacles Under Which Nations Go Down—Unequal in the Start, He Outdistances Other Enslaved Nations—His Chart for Guidance." *The Freeman*, 13 May 1893, 2.

Helms-Park, Rena, et al. "From Proto-writing to Multimedia Literacy: Scripts and Orthographies through the Ages." In *Reading in a Second Language: Cognitive and Psycholinguistic Issues*, ed. Xi Chen et al., 1–31. London: Routledge, 2016.

Henze, Paul B. *Layers of Time: A History of Ethiopia*. New York: Palgrave, 2000.

Herrera, Ricardo. "Transnational Immigration Politics in Mexico, 1850–1920." PhD diss., University of Arizona, 2013.

Hickey, Dennis, and Kenneth C. Wylie. *An Enchanting Darkness: The American Vision of Africa in the Twentieth Century*. East Lansing: Michigan State University Press, 1993.

Hill, Jay N. "An Ethiope in Spain." *Crisis* (July 1937): 202.

Hill, Robert A. Introduction to *Ethiopian Stories* by George S. Schuyler, 1–50. Boston: Northeastern University Press, 1994.

———. "King Menelik's Nephew: Prince Thomas Mackarooroo, aka Prince Ludwig Menelek of Abyssinia." *Small Axe* 26 (June 2008): 15–44.

Hopkins, Pauline E. "The Dark Races of the Twentieth Century." In *Daughter of the Revolution: The Major Nonfiction Works of Pauline E. Hopkins*, ed. Ira Dworkin, 305–31. New Brunswick, NJ: Rutgers University Press, 2007.

———. "Letter to William Monroe Trotter, April 16, 1905." In *Daughter of the Revolution: The Major Nonfiction Works of Pauline E. Hopkins*, ed. Ira Dworkin, 238–48. New Brunswick, NJ: Rutgers University Press, 2007.

———. *Of One Blood; or, The Hidden Self*. In *The Magazine Novels of Pauline Hopkins*, 439–621. New York: Oxford University Press, 1988.

———. *Primer of Facts Pertaining to the Early Greatness of the African Race and the Possibility of Restoration by its Descendants—with Epilogue*. In *Daughter of the Revolution: The Major Nonfiction Works of Pauline E. Hopkins*, ed. Ira Dworkin, 335–52. New Brunswick, NJ: Rutgers University Press, 2007.

Horne, Gerald. "Tokyo Bound: African Americans and Japan Confront White Supremacy." *Souls: A Critical Journal of Black Politics, Culture and Society* 3, no. 3 (Summer 2001): 16–28.

Hoskins, G. A. *Travels in Ethiopia, above the second cataract of the Nile; exhibiting the state of that country, and its various inhabitants, under the dominion of Mohammed Ali; and illustrating the antiquities, arts, and history of the ancient kingdom of Meroe*. London: Longman, 1835.

Hotten, John Camden. *Abyssinia and Its People; or, Life in the Land of Prester John*. London: John Camden Hotten, 1868.

"How They Fight in Abyssinia." *Chambers's Journal of Popular Literature, Science, and Art*, 16 November 1867, 731–34.

Howe, Stephen. *Afrocentrism: Mythical Pasts and Imagined Homes*. London: Verso, 1998.

Howells, W. D. "The Psychology of Plagiarism." *Literature: An International Gazette of Criticism*, 18 August 1899, 129–30.

[Huggins, Willis N.]. *The Friends of Ethiopia in America*. New York: N.p., [1935].

Hughes, Langston. "Ballad of Ethiopia." *Baltimore Afro-American*, 28 September 1935, 3.

——. *The Big Sea: An Autobiography*. 1940. New York: Hill and Wang, 1993.

——. *The Collected Poems of Langston Hughes*, ed. Arnold Rampersad. New York: Vintage, 1995.

——. "Emperor Haile Selassie, on Liberation Day, May 5, 1966." *Negro Digest*, November 1966, 48.

——. *I Wonder as I Wander*. 1956. New York: Hill and Wang, 1993.

——. Papers. James Weldon Johnson Collection in the Yale Collection of American Literature (JWJ MSS 26). Beinecke Rare Book and Manuscript Library, Yale University, New Haven, CT.

Hutchinson, George B. "Whitman and the Black Poet: Kelly Miller's Speech to the Walt Whitman Fellowship." *American Literature* 61, no. 1 (March 1989): 46–58.

"Inclosure 2 in No. 74. Extract from the 'Globe.' Relations with Great Britain." In *Correspondence Respecting the Negotiations with the United States' Government on the Questions of the "Alabama" and British Claims, Naturalization, and San Juan Water Boundary, 1868–69*, 83–94. Printed for the Use of the Foreign Office.

"Is a Lavish Spender: W. H. Ellis, of Hawaii, Going on Hunt to Africa with Twenty-Five Friends and Guests." *Washington Bee*, 18 June 1904, 8.

Isaac, Dan. Introduction to "Ethiopia: The First 'Living Newspaper'" by Arthur Arent. *Educational Theatre Journal* 10, no. 1 (March 1968): 15–19.

"The Italian Case. Charges against Abyssinia. Memorandum to League." *The Times*, 6 September 1935, 7.

J. C. "Foreign Correspondence. Affairs in England. The Abyssinian Expedition—A Vexatious War—A Great Point Gained in Church Matters—Report of the Royal Commission—Collapse of English Railway Property." *New York Times*, 13 September 1867, 2.

Jacoby, Karl. *The Strange Career of William Ellis, the Texas Slave Who Became a Mexican Millionaire*. New York: Norton, 2016.

Japtok, Martin. "Pauline Hopkins's *Of One Blood*, Africa, and the 'Darwinist Trap.'" *African American Review* 36 (2002): 403–15.

"Jesse A. Shipp as a Playwright." *Indianapolis Freeman*, 19 May 1906, 5.

Johnson, Samuel. *The History of Rasselas, Prince of Abyssinia*. 1759. Gloucestershire: Nonsuch, 2007.

Johnston, Georgia. "Virginia Woolf's Talk on the Dreadnought Hoax." *Woolf Studies Annual* 15 (2009): 1–45.

Jonas, Raymond. *The Battle of Adwa: African Victory in the Age of Empire*. Cambridge, MA: Harvard University Press, 2011.

Kaplan, Amy. *The Anarchy of Empire in the Making of U.S. Culture*. Cambridge, MA: Harvard University Press, 2002.

Kelley, Robin D. G. Introduction to *African Americans in the Spanish Civil War: "This Ain't Ethiopia, but It'll Do,"* ed. Danny Duncan Collum and Victor A. Berch, 5–57. New York: G. K. Hall, 1992.

"Kent J. Loomis's Body Found? Reported Washed Ashore at Cherbourg—Brother Has No News." *New York Times*, 28 June 1903, 1.

"King's Banquet. Edward and Alexandra Dined 70 Royal Personages. Czarewitch of Russia Headed the Imposing Array." *Boston Globe*, 24 June 1902, 4.

Koppen, R. S. *Virginia Woolf, Fashion, and Literary Modernity*. Edinburgh: Edinburgh University Press, 2009.

Krasner, David. *Resistance, Parody, and Double Consciousness in African American Theatre, 1895–1910*. New York: St. Martin's Press, 1997.

Kuru, Assefu. "The Conquest and Environmental Degradation of Oromia." *Journal of Oromo Studies* 2, no. 1–2 (Winter–Summer 1995): 30–50.

Logan, Rayford W. "Abyssinia Breaks into the Movies." *Southern Workman* (August 1929): 339–44.

Luciano, Dana. "Passing Shadows: Melancholic Nationality and Black Critical Publicity in Pauline E. Hopkins's *Of One Blood*." In *Loss: The Politics of Mourning*, ed. David L. Eng and David Kazanjian, 148–87. Berkeley: University of California Press, 2003.

Macfarlane, Robert. *Original Copy: Plagiarism and Originality in Nineteenth-Century Literature*. Oxford: Oxford University Press, 2007.

MacLean, Robinson. *John Hoy of Ethiopia*. New York: Farrar & Rinehart, [c. 1936].

Mancuso, Luke. *The Strange Sad War Revolving: Walt Whitman, Reconstruction, and the Emergence of Black Citizenship, 1865–1876*. Columbia, SC: Camden House, 1997.

"The Man Who Would Be King Passes Away in Mexico City: Successful Promoter and Speculator Failed in Attempt to Gain the Abyssinian Crown." *Boston Globe*, 30 September 1923, 18.

Markakis, John. *Ethiopia: The Last Two Frontiers*. Woodbridge, UK: James Currey, 2011.

Matthews, Brander. *Pen and Ink: Papers on Subjects of More or Less Importance*. New York: Longmans, Green, and Co., 1888.

Matthews, Ralph. "Manhattan Merry-Go-Round: Harlem and Ethiopia." *Baltimore Afro-American*, 16 May 1936, 4.

McCandless, Michael J. "The Last Dress Rehearsal: A Critical Study of the Production and Censorship of the Federal Theatre Project's *Ethiopia* (1936)." MA thesis, University of Nebraska–Omaha, 1993.

McDowell, Deborah E. Introduction to *Of One Blood; or, The Hidden Self*, v–xx. New York: Simon and Schuster, 2004.

McHenry, Elizabeth. "Toward a History of Access: The Case of Mary Church Terrell." *American Literary History* 19, no. 2 (July 2007): 381–401.

McKay, Claude. *Amiable with Big Teeth: A Novel of the Love Affair between the Communists and the Poor Black Sheep of Harlem*. New York: Penguin, 2017.

———. *Harlem: Negro Metropolis*. 1940. New York: Harcourt Brace Jovanovich, 1968.

———. *A Long Way from Home*, ed. Gene Andrew Jarrett. 1937. New Brunswick, NJ: Rutgers University Press, 2007.

McKinley, Jesse. "Tsegaye Gabre-Medhin, Ethiopian Poet Laureate, Dies at 69." *New York Times*, 9 March 2006, C18.

"Menelik and Queen Victoria: The Message by Phonograph." *Hawkes Bay (NZ) Herald*, 31 March 1899, 4.

"Menelik! The Great African King and His Country Extend the 'Glad Hand' to America." *Cleveland Gazette*, 9 January 1904, 1.

"Menelik's Phonograph." *Victoria [TX] Advocate*, 15 July 1899, [7].

Metaferia, Getachew. *Ethiopia and the United States: History, Diplomacy, and Analysis*. New York: Algora Publishing, 2009.

Millet, N. B. "The Meroitic Script." In *The World's Writing Systems*, ed. Peter T. Daniels and William Bright, 84–87. New York: Oxford University Press, 1996.

Mills, James A. "Selassie Says Ethiopia Will Defeat Italy." *Evening Independent*, 22 August 1935, 1.

"Miscellaneous Items." *Brooklyn Daily Eagle*, 28 October 1869, 1.

"A Model Monarch." *Judy; or, The London Serio-Comic Journal*, 28 August 1867, 225.

Moffett, Cleveland. "Menelik and His People." *Windsor Magazine* 10 (1899): 603–10.

"More about the Career of Ellis," *Victoria Advocate*, 9 April 1910, 13.

Morris, Earl J. "Great Dance Trio, Says George White of Sam, Ted and Ray: Lads Now Appearing with 'Scandals' Are Show-Stoppers—George Dewey Washington and Helen Morgan Shine." *Pittsburgh Courier*, 5 September 1936, 2:7.

Moses, Wilson Jeremiah. *Afrotopia: The Roots of African American Popular History*. Cambridge: Cambridge University Press, 1998.

———. *The Golden Age of Black Nationalism*. New York: Oxford University Press, 1988.

———. *The Wings of Ethiopia: Studies in African-American Life and Letters*. Ames: Iowa State University Press, 1990.

"Mount Hermon Federate School of Missions." *Woman's Home Missions of the Methodist Episcopal Church* 41–42 (1924): 22.

"Mr. Ellis Formerly of Texas." *Appeal (MN)*, 5 November 1904, 4.

Munro, John. "Ethiopia Stretches Forth across the Atlantic: African American Anticolonialism during the Interwar Period." *Left History* 13, no. 2 (2008): 37–63.

"A Mysterious Disappearance." *The Week's Progress*, 9 July 1904, 24.

"National Freedmen's Aid Union: Farewell Meeting with William Forster Mitchell." *British Friend* 26, no. 2 (1867): 29–31.

"Naval Hoax. Sham Princes Visit the Dreadnought. A Bogus Telegram. An Amazing Story. Merriment at Weymouth." *Western Gazette (Yeovil, England)*, 18 February 1910, 2.

"Negro Haven; Gotham Millionaire to Provide Place in Abyssinia." *Milwaukee Journal*, 7 September 1903, 10.

Nelson, Raymond. Editorial Statement to *"Harlem Gallery" and Other Poems of Melvin B. Tolson*, xxvii–xxviii. Charlottesville: University of Virginia Press, 1999.

Ness, William B. "'Bathed in War's Perfume': Whitman and the Flag." *Prospects* 27 (2002): 247–70.

"New Plays in Manhattan." *Time*, 6 January 1936, 24.

Newkirk, Pamela, ed. *Letters from Black America*. New York: Farrar, Straus, and Giroux, 2009.

"No Longer the Dark Continent . . . Except in Spots." *"So You're Going" News* (October 1935): 8–9.

North, Michael. *Reading 1922: A Return to the Scene of the Modern*. Oxford: Oxford University Press, 1999.

"Not Maltreated in Mexico. Story of Cruelty to Negro Colonists Denied by the Consul. Some Left the Colony, but Nearly All Returned of Their Own Accord. None Shot or Wounded." *Morning Times (Washington, DC)*, 8 July 1895, 8.

"Nov. 19." In *Mr. Punch's Victorian Era, Vol. 2*, 160. London: Bradbury, Agnew, & Co., 1888.

Ong, Walter J. *Orality and Literacy: The Technologizing of the Word*. London: Routledge, 1982.

Ottley, Roi. "Hectic Harlem." *New York Amsterdam News*, 27 July 1935, 11.

Pankhurst, Richard. "Captain Speedy's 'Entertainment': The Reminiscences of a Nineteenth Century British Traveller to Ethiopia." *Africa: Rivista trimestrale di studi e documentazione dell'Istituto italiano per l'Africa e l'Oriente* 38, no. 3 (September 1983): 428–48.

———, ed. *Diary of a Journey to Abyssinia, 1868: With the Expedition under Sir Robert Napier, K.C.S.I.: The Diary and Observations of William Simpson of the* Illustrated London News. Hollywood, CA: Tsehai Publishers, 2002.

———. "Economic Change in Late Nineteenth and Early Twentieth Century Ethiopia: A Period of Accelerated Innovation." *Annales d'Ethiopie* 20, no. 1 (2004): 195–219.

———. "Sylvia and *New Times and Ethiopia News*." In *Sylvia Pankhurst, From Artist to Anti-Fascist*, ed. Ian Bullock and Richard Pankhurst, 149–91. Houndmills: Macmillan, 1992.

———. "William H. Ellis—Guillaume Enriques Ellesio: The First Black American Ethiopianist?" *Ethiopia Observer* 15 (1972): 89–121.

Paul, James C. N. "Ethnicity and the New Constitutional Orders of Ethiopia and Eritrea." In *Autonomy and Ethnicity: Negotiating Competing Claims in Multi-Ethnic States*, ed. Yash Ghai, 173–96. Cambridge: Cambridge University Press, 2000.

Pavletich, JoAnn. "The Practice of Plagiarism in a Changing Context." *American Literary History* 30, no. 4 (2018): e9–e13.

"Pays Tribute to African Explorer, Says Harry Dean's Spirit Will Lead Ethiopia; Sterling North, Author and Literary Editor of Chicago Daily, Pays Tribute at Passing of 72-Year-Old Patriarch." *Pittsburgh Courier*, 3 August 1935, 5.

Piatt, Sarah. *Palace-Burner: The Selected Poetry of Sarah Piatt*, ed. Paula Bernat Bennett. Champaign: University of Illinois Press, 2001.

Porter, Darwin. *Brando Unzipped: Bad Boy, Megastar, Sexual Outlaw*. New York: Blood Moon Productions, 2006.

Poston, T. R. "Robeson to Play King Christophe in British Production, He Reveals. Actor, Here, Answers Critics of 'Sanders of the River.'" *New York Amsterdam News*, 5 October 1935, 1–2.

Powell-Cotton, P. H. G. *A Sporting Trip through Abyssinia: A Narrative of a Nine Months' Journey from the Plains of the Hawash to the Snows of the Simien, with a Description of the Game, from Elephant to Ibex, and Notes on the Manners and Customs of the Natives*. London: Rowland Ward, 1902.

Preece, Harold. "War and the Negro." *Crisis* (November 1935): 329, 338.

"Prince Blayechetta [*sic*] of Abyssinia Addresses A. and T. Student Body." *California Eagle*, 9 November 1928, 1.

"Prince Tells of Struggles in Abyssinia: Now Making Speeches throughout South." *Chicago Defender*, 20 September 1924, 1.

"Proposed Japanese Bride for Abyssinian Royalty Recalls L.A. Wedding of Prince Blayechettai." *California Eagle*, 9 February 1934, 3.

"Protect Us from Poison Gases! Beseeches Ethiopian Princess." *Pittsburgh Courier*, 11 April 1936, 4.

Putnam, Aric. *The Insistent Call: Rhetorical Moments in Black Anticolonialism, 1929–1937*. Amherst: University of Massachusetts Press, 2012.

"Quilibet, Philip." "A Nation's Repentance and Faith." *Galaxy* (June 1868): 784–86.

Quinn, Susan. *Furious Improvisation: How the WPA and a Cast of Thousands Made High Art out of Desperate Times*. New York: Walker and Company, 2008.

"Race Gleanings." *Indianapolis Freeman*, 26 November 1904, 7.

Raiford, Leigh. "Marcus Garvey in Stereograph." *Small Axe* 17, no. 1 (March 2013): 263–80.

Rampersad, Arnold. *The Life of Langston Hughes, Vol. II: 1914–1967, I Dream a World*. Oxford: Oxford University Press, 2002.

"Red Agitator Is Sought for Part in Chicago Riot. Burning of Flag in Black Belt Starts Race War—Two White Men Killed, Several Negroes Hurt." *News Scimitar*, 21 June 1920, 1.

Reed, Christopher Robert. *The Rise of Chicago's Black Metropolis, 1920–1929*. Urbana: University of Illinois Press, 2011.

"Reel Emperor Meets Real Emperor." *Jet*, 1 July 1954, 60.

"Refused Ride in Elevator, Sues. Harry F. Dean, Colored, Says He Sustained Injury to His Rights." *Oakland Tribune*, 10 October 1911, 7.

Reid, Panthea. "Virginia Woolf, Leslie Stephen, Julia Margaret Cameron, and the Prince of Abyssinia: An Inquiry into Certain Colonialist Representations." *Biography* 22, no. 3 (Summer 1999): 323–55.

"Report Zaphiro Was Sent out of Country." *Pittsburgh Courier*, 18 April 1936, 2:9.

Reynolds, G. "Abyssinia and King Theodore." *Atlantic Monthly* (June 1868): 701–17.

"Rice Quits in Row over WPA Drama." *New York Times*, 24 January 1936, L15.

"The Rise of a Victoria Negro." *Victoria Advocate*, 9 April 1910, 2.

"The Rise of King Theodore." *Every Saturday*, 2 November 1867, 573–75.

Robinson, Cedric J. "The African Diaspora and the Italo-Ethiopian Crisis." *Race & Class* 27, no. 2 (1985): 51–65.

Rogers, J. A. "J. A. Rogers Gets Exclusive Interview with Emperor: 'When the Last Italian Is Off Ethiopian Soil, Then and Not Until Then Can We Talk of Peace,' Haile Selassie Tells J. A. Rogers." *Pittsburgh Courier*, 7 March 1936, 1–2.

———. "Ring of Ethiopian Steel Surrounds Italian Army. 7,000 Ethiopian Soldiers Ready for Giant Offensive. Ethiopians Press Push on Makale." *Pittsburgh Courier*, 4 January 1936, 1, 4.

Roosevelt, Theodore. Papers. Library of Congress Manuscript Division. http://www.theodorerooseveltcenter.org/Research/Digital-Library/Record/?libID=o46241.

Rosen, Jeff. *Julia Margaret Cameron's "Fancy Subjects": Photographic Allegories of Victorian Identity and Empire*. Manchester: Manchester University Press, 2016.

Ross, Red. "Black Americans and Italo-Ethiopian Relief, 1935–1936." In *Race and U.S. Foreign Policy from the Colonial Period to the Present: A Collection of Essays; Vol. 3: Race and U.S. Foreign Policy from 1900 through World War II*, ed. Michael L. Krenn, 164–73. New York: Garland, 1998.

"Royalty in Abyssinia: Bizarre Costume King Menelik Wears on Christmas Day." *Boston Daily Globe*, 5 December 1902, 6.

Rubenson, Sven, ed. *Internal Rivalries and Foreign Threats, 1869–1879: Acta Aethiopica, vol. III*. Addis Ababa: Addis Ababa University Press, 2000.

Runciman, James. "King Plagiarism and His Court." *Fortnightly Review* 53, no. 47 (March 1890): 421–39.

Runstedtler, Theresa E. "In Sport the Best Man Wins: How Joe Louis Whupped Jim Crow." In *In the Game: Race, Identity and Sports in the Twentieth Century*, ed. Amy Bass, 47–92. New York: Palgrave Macmillan, 2005.

S. M. T. "About Town. Second Balcony. George White's Scandals. New Amsterdam Theatre." *Barnard Bulletin*, 3 March 1936, 2.

Sanborn, Geoffrey. "The Wind of Words: Plagiarism and Intertextuality in *Of One Blood*." *J19* 3, no. 1 (Spring 2015): 67–87.

"'Scandals' Star to Arizona." *Indianapolis Recorder*, 14 November 1936, 13.

Schilz, Gordon B. "The Air Age in the Ethiopian Empire, 1955–56." *Proceedings of the Oklahoma Academy of Science for 1958* 39 (1958): 177–78.

Schomburg, Arthur A. Review of *The Pedro Gorino*. *Opportunity* (July 1929): 223–24.

Schooling, J. Holt. "War Pictures in '*Punch*,' 1841–1899." *Strand Magazine* 19 (March 1900): 321–31.

Schuyler, George S. *Ethiopian Stories*, ed. Robert A. Hill. Boston: Northeastern University Press, 1994.

———. Papers. Special Collections Research Center, Syracuse University Libraries, Syracuse, NY.

———. *Slaves Today: A Story of Liberia*. 1931. New York: AMS Press, 1969.

———. "Views and Reviews." *Pittsburgh Courier*, 27 July 1935, 10.

———. "Views and Reviews." *Pittsburgh Courier*, 23 November 1935, 10.

Schwarz, A. B. Christa. "Colonial Struggle on Manhattan Soil: George Schuyler's 'The Ethiopian Murder Mystery.'" In *Postcolonial Postmortems: Crime Fiction from a Transcultural Perspective*, ed. Christine Matzke and Susanne Mühleisen, 201–27. Amsterdam: Rodopi, 2006.

Scott, William R. "Black Nationalism and the Italo-Ethiopian Conflict, 1934–1936." In *Race and U.S. Foreign Policy from the Colonial Period to the Present: A Collection of Essays; Vol. 3: Race and U.S. Foreign Policy from 1900 through World War II*, ed. Michael L. Krenn, 134–50. New York: Garland, 1998.

———. *The Sons of Sheba's Race: African Americans and the Italo-Ethiopian War, 1935–1941*. Hollywood, CA: Tsehai Publishers, 2006.

"Scottsboro Sensation and Chicago Visit of Ethiopian Envoy in Pictures." *Chicago Defender*, 1 February 1936, 24.

"Secretary Loomis's Theory: He Believes His Brother Accidentally Fell Overboard." *New York Times*, 17 July 1904, 1.

Shepperson, George. Introduction to *Umbala: The Adventures of a Negro-sea-captain in Africa and on the Seven Seas in His Attempts to Found an Ethiopian Empire*, by Harry Dean, vii–xxiii. London: Pluto Press, 1989.

Shilliam, Robbie. "Ethiopianism, Englishness, Britishness: Struggles over Imperial Belonging." *Citizenship Studies* 20, no. 2 (2016): 243–59.

Shinn, Ambassador David H. Introduction to *The 1903 Skinner Mission to Ethiopia & A Century of American-Ethiopian Relations*, by Robert P. Skinner, [3]–[78]. Hollywood, CA: Tsehai Publishers, 2003.

Shipp, Jesse A. *Abyssinia* [electronic edition], in *Black Drama, Second Edition: African, African American, and Diaspora 1850 to Present*. Alexander Street Press. http://solomon.bld2.alexanderstreet.com/.

Simpson, William. *The Autobiography of William Simpson R. I. (Crimean Simpson)*, ed. George Eyre-Todd. London: T. Fisher Unwin, 1903.

Siraganian, Lisa. "Wallace Stevens's Fascist Dilemmas and Free Market Resolutions." *American Literary History* 23, no. 2 (2011): 337–61.

Sitwell, Osbert. *Great Morning: Being the Third Volume of Left Hand, Right Hand! An Autobiography by Osbert Sitwell*. London: Macmillan & Co., 1957.

Smith, Rev. Thomas. *The Wonders of Nature and Art; or, A Concise Account of Whatever is Most Curious and Remarkable in the World; Whether relating to its Animal, Vegetable, and Mineral Productions, or to the Manufactures, Buildings, and Inventions of its Inhabitants, Compiled from Historical and Geographical Works of established Celebrity, and illustrated with the Discoveries of modern Travellers*. Vol. 8. London: J. Walker, 1804.

Sotiropoulos, Karen. *Staging Race: Black Performers in Turn of the Century America*. Cambridge, MA: Harvard University Press, 2006.

Southard, Addison E. "Modern Ethiopia: Haile Selassie the First, Formerly Ras Tafari, Succeeds to the World's Oldest Continuously Sovereign Throne." *National Geographic* (June 1931): 679–738.

"Speculations on Zaphiro's Recall Called Just Bosh." *Baltimore Afro-American*, 4 April 1936, 12.

Speedy, Captain T. C. S. "Abyssinia and Its People." *The Independent*, 5 May 1898, 14–15.

Spencer, John H. *Ethiopia at Bay: A Personal Account of the Haile Selassie Years*. Hollywood, CA: Tsehai Publishers, 2006.

Spofford, Harriet Prescott. "Boys." *Galaxy* (December 1868): 835–40.

Stephens, Michelle Ann. *Black Empire: The Masculine Global Imaginary of Caribbean Intellectuals in the United States, 1914–1962*. Durham: Duke University Press, 2005.

"Strange Career of the Big Cuban Who Accompanied Missing Kent J. Loomis." *Pittsburgh Press*, 11 July 1904, 6.

"Tafari's Coronation to Take Place Nov. 2. Representatives of World Powers on Way to See Ethiopian King of Kings Crowned." *New York Times*, 19 October 1930, E3.

Taketani, Etsuko. *The Black Pacific Narrative: Geographic Imaginings of Race and Empire between the World Wars*. Hanover, NH: Dartmouth College Press, 2014.

———. "Colored Empires in the 1930s: Black Internationalism, the U.S. Black Press, and George Samuel Schuyler." *American Literature* 82, no. 1 (March 2010): 121–49.

Talbot, David A. "Emperor Haile Selassie Moves Ahead." *The African* 3 (April 1945): 8–9, 15.

"Telephones in Abyssinia: Ants, Monkeys and Elephants among the Foes of the Wires." *Boston Daily Globe*, 9 October 1904, 55.

"Tells of King Menelik. W. H. Ellis Gives Description of Visit to Abyssinia's King. African Monarch Prepared to Welcome Consul Skinner and Americans Generally." *New York Times*, 1 January 1904, 9.

Tennyson, Alfred. *Alfred Tennyson: The Major Works*, ed. Adam Roberts. Oxford: Oxford University Press, 2000.

Thesiger, Wilfred. *The Life of My Choice*. New York: W. W. Norton, 1988.

Thomas, Lorenzo. *Extraordinary Measures: Afrocentric Modernism and Twentieth-Century American Poetry*. Tuscaloosa: University of Alabama Press, 2000.

Thompson, Mark Christian. *Black Fascisms: African American Literature and Culture between the Wars*. Charlottesville: University of Virginia Press, 2007.

"3 'Scandals' Hoffers [*sic*] Good." *Deseret News*, 1 October 1936, 9.

Tibebu, Teshale. *The Making of Modern Ethiopia, 1896–1974*. Lawrenceville, NJ: Red Sea Press, 1995.

"To Found Modern Ethiopia. New York Broker Starts to Make Abyssinia a Nation for Negroes." *Highland (VA) Recorder*, 11 September 1903, 1.

"To One and All." *New Times and Ethiopia News*, 16 July 1938, 8.

"To the Editor." *New Times and Ethiopia News*, 16 July 1938, 2.

Tolson, Melvin. "The Bard of Addis Ababa." In *Rendezvous with America*, 83–87. New York: Dodd, Mead & Company, 1944.

"Topics of To-Day." *Brooklyn Daily Eagle*, 10 December 1867, 2.

"Topics of To-Day." *Brooklyn Daily Eagle*, 26 June 1868, 2.

"Topics of To-Day." *Brooklyn Daily Eagle*, 15 July 1868, 2.

"Trader Dean." *Time*, 10 June 1929, 51.

"Trio Tip Top in Taps." *Chicago Defender*, 23 January 1937, 10.

"Two Lions for Roosevelt. From Menelik, Who Will Exhibit at the Fair. He Also Signs a Commercial Treaty Between This Country and Ethiopia—Elephant Tusks for President Roosevelt and Decorations for Mr. Skinner's Party." *New York Sun*, 1 January 1904, 7.

Upham, Edward. *Rameses; An Egyptian Tale: With Historical Notes of the Era of the Pharaohs*, vol. 2. London: G. B. Whittaker, 1824.

Vanderheym, J.-G. *Une expédition avec le négous Ménélik: Vingt mois en Abyssinie*. Paris: Librairie Hachette et Co., 1896.

Vestal, Theodore M. *The Lion of Judah in the New World: Emperor Haile Selassie of Ethiopia and the Shaping of Americans' Attitudes toward Africa*. Santa Barbara, CA: Praeger, 2011.

Vivian, Herbert. "A Capital That Moves." *Pearson's Magazine* (November 1900): 612–15.

"WPA Theatre Plan Turns to AAA Skit." *New York Times*, 14 February 1936, L22.

W. W. "Abyssinia." *Anti-Slavery Reporter* (December 1879): 278–90.

Walker, Ernest G. "The Hawaiian Croesus Was Just Plain Sambo; W. H. Ellis Who Claimed to Be a Rich Islander Got Accommodations in Hotels Which Do Not Receive Negroes." *Pacific Commercial Advertiser (Honolulu)*, 15 July 1904, 6.

Warren, Kenneth W. "Appeals for (Mis)recognition: Theorizing the Diaspora." In *Cultures of United States Imperialism*, ed. Amy Kaplan and Donald E. Pease, 392–406. Durham: Duke University Press, 1993.

Waugh, Evelyn. *Remote People*. London: Duckworth, 1931.

Wellby, M. S. *'Twixt Sirdar and Menelik: An Account of a Year's Expedition from Zeila to Cairo through Unknown Abyssinia*. London: Harper and Brothers, 1901.

White, P. J. "Vestis Virumque Cano: A Sonnet on American Officials Greeting an Ethiopian Potentate." *Opportunity* (January 1936): 10.

Whitman, Alden. "Haile Selassie of Ethiopia Dies at 83. Deposed Emperor Ruled Ancient Land 50 Years in Medieval Style." *New York Times*, 28 August 1975, 1, 40.

Whitman, Walt. *Leaves of Grass*, ed. Jerome Loving. Oxford: Oxford University Press, 1990.

———. *Notebooks and Unpublished Prose Manuscripts, Vol. 5: Notes*, ed. Edward F. Grier. New York: New York University Press, 1984.

"William H. Ellis: Bearer of Treaty to King Menelik—Suspected in Connection with Disappearance of His Colleague Loomis." *Appeal (MN)*, 23 July 1904, 2.

"Williams and Walker in *Abyssinia*." *Indianapolis Freeman*, 20 October 1906, 5.

Wilson, Ivy G. "'Are You Man Enough?': Imagining Ethiopia and Transnational Black Masculinity." *Callaloo* 33, no. 1 (2010): 265–77.

———. "Looking with a Queer Smile: Walt Whitman's Gaze and Black America." In *Whitman Noir: Black America and the Good Gray Poet*, ed. Ivy G. Wilson, vii–xix. Iowa City: University of Iowa Press, 2014.

Winstanley, W. *A Visit to Abyssinia: An Account of Travel in Modern Ethiopia*, vol. 2. London: Hurst and Blackett, 1881.

Wintz, Cary D., and Paul Finkelman, eds. *Encyclopedia of the Harlem Renaissance*, vol. 2. New York: Routledge, 2004.

Woolbert, Robert Gale. "Feudal Ethiopia and Her Army." *Foreign Affairs* 14, no. 1 (October 1935): 71–81.

———. "The Peoples of Ethiopia." *Foreign Affairs* 14, no. 2 (January 1936): 340–44.

Woolf, Virginia. "*Dreadnought* Notes (1940)." In *The Platform of Time: Memoirs of Family and Friends*, ed. S. P. Rosenbaum, 165–67. London: Hesperus, 2008.

———. "Introduction (1926)." In *The Platform of Time: Memoirs of Family and Friends*, ed. S. P. Rosenbaum, 85–95. London: Hesperus, 2008.

Wright, Arthur N. "Ethiopia's Blacks." *Baltimore Afro-American*, 3 August 1935, 6.

"The Young Abyssinian Prince." *New York Evangelist*, 8 October 1868, 1.

"The Youngest Diplomat in Action." *Ottawa Citizen*, 25 October 1935, 13.

Zewde, Bahru. *A History of Modern Ethiopia, 1855–1991*. Oxford: Oxford University Press, 2001.

INDEX

Page numbers in *italics* refer to illustrations.

A NOTE ON THE TYPE

THIS BOOK has been composed in Miller, a Scotch Roman typeface designed by Matthew Carter and first released by Font Bureau in 1997. It resembles Monticello, the typeface developed for The Papers of Thomas Jefferson in the 1940s by C. H. Griffith and P. J. Conkwright and reinterpreted in digital form by Carter in 2003.

Pleasant Jefferson ("P. J.") Conkwright (1905–1986) was Typographer at Princeton University Press from 1939 to 1970. He was an acclaimed book designer and AIGA Medalist.

The ornament used throughout this book was designed by Pierre Simon Fournier (1712–1768) and was a favorite of Conkwright's, used in his design of the *Princeton University Library Chronicle.*

CPSIA information can be obtained
at www.ICGtesting.com
Printed in the USA
JSHW031036300422
25375JS00005B/5

9 780691 234625